MODERN HUMANITIES RESEARCH ASSOCIATION
BIBLIOGRAPHIES
VOLUME 3

Editor
DAVID GILLESPIE
(Slavonic)

UNIVERSITY THESES IN RUSSIAN, SOVIET AND EAST EUROPEAN STUDIES, 1907-2006

A CENTENNIAL BIBLIOGRAPHY OF RESEARCH IN THE BRITISH ISLES

UNIVERSITY THESES IN RUSSIAN, SOVIET AND EAST EUROPEAN STUDIES, 1907-2006

A CENTENNIAL BIBLIOGRAPHY OF RESEARCH IN THE BRITISH ISLES

Compiled and edited by
GREGORY WALKER and J. S. G. SIMMONS

MODERN HUMANITIES RESEARCH ASSOCIATION

2008

Published by
The Modern Humanities Research Association
1 Carlton House Terrace
London SW1Y 5AF

First published 2008
ISBN 978-0-947623-80-7

Copies may be ordered from www.bibliographies.mhra.org.uk

CONTENTS

PREFACE

When the late John S.G. Simmons published his original list of British higher-degree theses in Slavonic studies in *Oxford Slavonic Papers* in 1967, he noted in his introduction that '...British theses in Slavonic studies have not so far attracted the attention of the bibliographer'. It was characteristic of him to identify an unmet bibliographical need, in this case for access to postgraduate research on Russia, the USSR and Eastern Europe: research that was difficult to trace through general and subject-based bibliographies because of its multidisciplinary nature. Equally typical was his decision to meet that need himself by compiling the first list, covering theses approved from 1907 to 1966, drawing not only on existing published sources but also on reports from university departments. He followed it with three five-yearly supplements before convincing me to carry on the undertaking. Four further quinquennial supplements have since appeared, taking coverage up to 2001*. It was the long-standing intention of both of us that a cumulated and further updated bibliography should be published in due course, and John took an active interest in its preparation until his death in 2005.

The present bibliography of 3,317 entries includes 1,067 theses not recorded in the previously published lists. Most are from the period 2002-2006, but the figure includes 229 theses from earlier years which have been added after a further extensive search of sources. On the other hand, 546 MA and other one-year masters' dissertations which appeared in previous lists have not been included here. On the rationale for this, see 'Criteria for Inclusion'. Fourteen further entries in the previous lists have been omitted because re-checking showed them to be duplications, two more because they proved to be collections of published works, and two because they were judged to be out of scope. Substantive corrections or additions have been made to 167 previously published entries

---

* 'Theses in Slavonic studies approved for higher degrees ...
... by British universities, 1907-1966', by J.S.G. Simmons, *Oxford Slavonic Papers*, xiii (1967), pp. 133-159 [entries 1-313];
... by British universities, 1967-1971', by J.S.G. Simmons, *Oxford Slavonic Papers*, n.s. vi (1973), pp. 133-147 [entries 314-474];
... by British universities, 1972-1976', by J.S.G. Simmons, *Oxford Slavonic Papers*, n.s. x (1977), pp. 120-138 [entries 475-712];
... by British universities, 1977-1981', by J.S.G. Simmons, *Oxford Slavonic Papers*, n.s. xv (1982), pp. 140-167 [entries 713-935];
... by British universities, 1981-1986', by Gregory Walker, *Oxford Slavonic Papers*, n.s. xx (1987), pp. 140-161 [entries 936-1202];
... by British universities, 1986-1991', by Gregory Walker, *Oxford Slavonic Papers*, n.s. xxvii (1994), pp. 144-173 [entries 1203-1532];
... by British universities, 1992-1996', by Gregory Walker, *Oxford Slavonic Papers*, n.s. xxxi (1998), pp. 104-152 [entries 1533-2146];
... by universities in the British Isles, 1997-2001', by Gregory Walker, *The Slavonic and East European Review*, 82(1), January 2004, pp. 132-198 [entries 2147-2814].

(see 'Sources'). Entries have been rearranged into a single sequence under an expanded set of subject and country/language headings, and two completely new Indexes have been compiled.

Despite our best efforts, and even within its carefully-defined scope and criteria for inclusion, the bibliography does not claim to be truly complete. Universities' procedures for the recording, deposit, cataloguing and reporting of their own theses have not always been – nor are they always now – either prompt or rigorous. However, the database from which the bibliography has been derived will remain in being, in the expectation that it will be made available online to students and researchers in due course. This will offer greatly enhanced search facilities, as well as the opportunity for regular updating, and for the inclusion of a wider range of masters' dissertations if support for that expansion of coverage is found. Corrections and additions are welcome, and should be sent to me care of the publishers (mail@mhra.org.uk).

The earliest thesis listed here was written for an Oxford B.Litt in 1907 (see entry 3004), which has happily allowed this compilation to be presented as a centennial bibliography of British and Irish postgraduate research in Russian, Soviet, Slavonic and East European studies broadly defined. So far as I can establish, it is – chronologically speaking – the longest thesis bibliography produced for any sector of area studies. While its principal purpose is to guide the academics and students of today to the extraordinary range and depth of their predecessors' work, I hope it will also allow a fuller perception of the distinguished history of this field of scholarship in the British Isles – a history to which John Simmons was himself a notable contributor.

GREGORY WALKER
Wheatley, Oxford
December 2007

ACKNOWLEDGEMENTS

I am particularly grateful to Mr Godfrey B. Simmons for permission to make use of his late brother's thesis lists. The School of Slavonic and East European Studies, University College London, has kindly given permission to use the 1997-2001 quinquennial list published in *The Slavonic and East European Review*. The present bibliography is indebted, like all the earlier lists, to the catalogues of many university libraries and to the *Index to Theses* (formerly *Aslib Index to Theses*), and this is again appreciatively acknowledged.

Many individuals and university departments have also contributed to my compilation of quinquennial lists since 1987 and to the present bibliography, but I should mention especially Marea Arries, Graham Dix and Nigel Hardware (Birmingham); Damien McManus (Bristol); Ray Scrivens (Cambridge); Tania Konn-Roberts (Glasgow); Joginder Khambay (Open University); Dr Barbara Wyllie (UCL-SSEES); Mark Ashworth (Surrey); and Isolde Harpur (Trinity College Dublin). Dr Jenny Brine (Lancaster), Jill Russell and Tracy Kent (Birmingham), and Rob Wilkes (Bodleian Library) have kindly advised on access to theses.

Special thanks are due to the Modern Humanities Research Association, particularly its Honorary Secretary, Professor David Gillespie, for supporting the bibliography's publication; and to Gerard Lowe, the MHRA's Publications Manager, for invaluable technical and editorial expertise.

GW

INTRODUCTION

SCOPE OF THE BIBLIOGRAPHY

The bibliography records:

- doctoral and selected masters' theses (see 'Criteria for Inclusion') which
- have been accepted by any British or Irish degree-awarding body; which
- are dated up to and including 2006; and which
- deal wholly or in significant part with any subject in the broad field of Slavonic and East European studies, including the social sciences as well as the humanities.
- Geographically the bibliography covers Russia, the whole area of the former USSR and that of the formerly communist states of Eastern Europe except the GDR.

CRITERIA FOR INCLUSION

The bibliography includes all doctoral theses that have been identified as falling within the scope described above, but not doctorates awarded on the basis of published work. Theses (sometimes called dissertations) for the award of two-year masters' degrees have also been included, but not those for MAs and other one-year masters' degrees. The lack of uniformity among universities in attaching degree titles to periods of study has sometimes made this criterion difficult to apply, since some M.Litts (in Scotland) and many M.Phils are awarded after one year. The principle has been followed as the least inconsistent means of recording substantial non-doctoral research while remaining within reasonable space limits. B.Litts and B.Phils have been included where these degrees were later made convertible to M.Litts and M.Phils.

SOURCES

The preferred source for the bibliographical details of each thesis (author, title, awarding body, degree and date) is the awarding institution's own library catalogue record for a deposited copy. Most academic libraries now include theses in their online public access catalogues (OPACs), but in a few cases their card files or other manual catalogues have had to be consulted. If no such record has been found in the institution's own library, the data has been drawn where possible from the catalogues of the British Library, the Senate House Library (for London University institutions), the National Library of Wales (for University of Wales colleges), or from the COPAC online union catalogue.

All entries from the original 1907–1966 list and its seven quinquennial supplements (see the Preface) have been re-checked against libraries' own catalogue data where this is now available. As a result, 167 of the 2,250 entries appearing in the previously published lists and included in the present bibliography have been significantly amended. This has usually been done because the title of the thesis as catalogued differs — sometimes by a few words, sometimes entirely — from that originally listed. These discrepancies appear to stem largely from institutions' failure to record changes made by authors to their thesis titles after first registration, so perpetuating the superseded titles in their own records.

A small minority of theses listed here have not been found in library catalogues but have been recorded elsewhere. At the time of closing for press (October 2007), no library catalogue record of any kind had been traced for 69 theses (2 % of the total). Some of these (especially the most recent) will still be awaiting cataloguing, while others (especially the earliest) may never have been deposited. Particulars for such theses have been compiled from one or more other sources, among them the *Index to Theses*, other published thesis lists, university and departmental websites, and lists supplied by institutions. In these cases the entry has been annotated [NCR]. I am grateful to the many library and academic staff who have dealt with queries arising from conflicting and/or defective sources.

ARRANGEMENT

The bibliography is arranged under thirty-two subject headings, as listed in the Contents. Entries under each subject heading are sub-arranged by country/nation or language. Below that, entries are arranged in date order, then alphabetically by author within each year.

It has often been difficult to choose the most appropriate heading under which to place a thesis in which two or more disciplines come together, or which deals with more than one country or language. Alternative points of entry are provided by the indexing (see 'Indexes').

CONTENT OF ENTRIES

AUTHOR'S NAME. The spelling of the author's name normally follows that of the preferred source (see 'Sources'). Diacritics in the name are shown where they appear in that source or if their use elsewhere by the author has been established, but not otherwise. If the author has been found to be also catalogued or published under any name different from that recorded as appearing on the thesis, a cross-reference is given in the Author Index.

TITLE AND SUBTITLE. Titles and subtitles are normally given in full as they appear in the preferred source, but some very long subtitles have been abbreviated, indicated by [...]. Punctuation has been standardised by using a colon to separate title from subtitle. Diacritics have been added to non-English words (notably place and personal names) wherever they are standard in the original language. Transliterations from Cyrillic have not been standardised, but are shown as they appear in the preferred source. Minor misspellings and typos have been corrected without indication. Where titles are uninformative, an expansion or brief explanatory note has been added where possible.

AWARDING BODY. The name of the awarding body is given in the form – sometimes abbreviated – current at the date of the thesis. In the case of federal universities (London, Wales, National University of Ireland) and the former Council for National Academic Awards (CNAA), the name of the sponsoring college or other institution is also given where known. It should be noted that the awarding body for theses from the School of Slavonic and East European Studies in the University of London is shown as 'London

(SSEES)' up to 1999, and as 'London (UCL)' after that date, since the School became a constituent of University College London in 2000.

DEGREE. The title of the degree awarded is given after the name of the awarding body by one or more letters (see 'Abbreviations' below). The form is that current at the date of the thesis, even if the title was subsequently made convertible to another, e.g. a B.Litt to an M.Litt.

DATE. The date given is that appearing on the thesis itself, where this can be established from the preferred source. Where the catalogue record, or other available source, gives only the date of submission, approval or conferment, this has been used.

INDEXES

The Author Index contains entries for all authors' names, including changes of name.

The Subject Index contains entries for:

- Personal and institutional names appearing in titles, subtitles or title notes.
- A standard set of subject headings (see 'Arrangement' above).
- Countries and other major areas.
- Specific topics appearing in titles, subtitles or title notes.

ACCESS TO BRITISH AND IRISH THESES

Academic libraries will usually make the theses of their own institution available to bona fide researchers, either on a personal visit or by inter-library loan, although certain restrictions may apply (see below). In most cases, doctoral theses from UK universities must be requested on loan through the British Thesis Service, operated by the British Library (www.bl.uk/britishthesis). This gives access to the full text of over 170,000 British doctoral theses, mainly from the 1970s onwards. Most, though not all, UK universities now supply the BL with copies of their theses on request. The BL then sells paper copies or microfilms of the thesis. Microfilms are also available for loan to registered customers, which include most large libraries across the world. Many universities show the BL shelfmark (D-reference number) for theses listed in their own catalogues. The BTS website gives details of prices and a list of participating universities. A limited thesis search service is also available for titles from 1980 onwards. Applications for the loan of masters' dissertations, and of doctoral theses not available from the BL, are normally made direct to the library of the awarding institution.

At the time of writing (December 2007), theses are not yet available in any electronic format from the British Thesis Service. However, the British Library, in collaboration with UK higher education institutions, is developing EThOS (www.ethos.ac.uk) as a user-led service for providing direct links to the full electronic text of theses from summer 2008. The intention is to digitise theses requested through the BTS and make them available free at the point of use. Many universities have indicated their intention to participate. EThOS will also link to other hosts, such as Google Scholar and the online research repositories now being developed by individual universities. In some cases thesis texts are available directly from authors' own websites.

Reasonable quotation from theses is usually allowed if proper acknowledgement is given, but more extensive copying is not permitted without the consent of the copyright holder (usually the author). In some cases authors or institutions may place restrictions on the consultation of a specific thesis. Access may be embargoed for a stated number of years after acceptance. More commonly, a Thesis Declaration Form may have to be completed. This stipulates that the thesis is for the use of the named borrower only, and that no part of the text, nor any information derived from the thesis, may be quoted or published without the prior consent of the author or institution.

For a wider search of universities' thesis output, the principal general record of British and Irish theses is the *Index to Theses* (formerly *Aslib Index to Theses*), published by Expert Information. It is available online and in printed form, and most academic libraries in the British Isles subscribe to it. A subset of Irish theses is accessible separately. It offers bibliographical data for theses from 1716 onwards. Abstracts are provided for some theses from 1970, and for nearly all doctoral theses after 1985. Entries from 1716 to 1950 are reproduced from R.R. Bilboul and F.L. Kent, eds, *Retrospective Index to Theses of Great Britain and Ireland 1716–1950* (Santa Barbara, ABC Clio, 1975. 5 vols.) After that date the *Index* has depended on information supplied by the awarding institutions.

ABBREVIATIONS

In title

[NCR]   No catalogue record found (see 'Sources' above)

For Institutions

CNAA   Council for National Academic Awards
KCL   Kings College London
LBS   London Business School
LSE   London School of Economics
LSHTM London School of Hygiene and Tropical Medicine
NUI   National University of Ireland
QM   Queen Mary, University of London
SOAS   School of Oriental and African Studies
SSEES School of Slavonic and East European Studies
TC   Trinity College
UCL   University College London

For Degrees Awarded

BL   B.Litt.
BP   B.Phil.
D   Ph.D. or (Oxford and Sussex) D.Phil.
ML   M.Litt.
MP   M.Phil.

1. AGRICULTURE, PEASANTRY

Baltic States (see also under individual countries)

1. **BRUNS, M. M.** The Baltic provinces and the Russian empire: provincial privilege and Imperial prerogative in the process of agrarian reform in Livland, Estland and Kurland 1765–1849. *GLASGOW D 1994.*

Bulgaria

2. **BISHOP, S. C.** Farm organisational adjustment in a former centrally planned economy: the case of Bulgaria. *EXETER D 1997.*
3. **GEROVA, V.** The impact of macro-policy on agriculture in a country in transition: the case of Bulgaria. *LONDON (WYE) MP 2002.*
4. **VASSILEV, I. I.** Postsocialist bricoleurs: markets and trust in the restructuring of Bulgarian agriculture. *LANCASTER D 2004.*

Central and Eastern Europe (see also under individual countries)

5. **BARRETT, W. M.** Recent and prospective forest sector developments in Central Europe [Poland, Czech Republic and Hungary]. *ABERDEEN D 1999.*
6. **HUGHES, G. C.** Agricultural decollectivisation in Central Europe and the productivity of emergent farm structures. *LONDON (WYE) D 2000.*
7. **TALKS, P.** Agriculture in the Czech Republic, Hungary and Poland: from the transition towards EU accession. *NOTTINGHAM D 2000.*
8. **VAN STOLK, C. C.** Europeanization of regional and agricultural policy in the Czech Republic and Poland. *LONDON (LSE) D 2005.*

Central Asia (see also under individual countries)

9. **JULUM, J. D.** The consequences of Moscow's cotton policy on Central Asia. *OXFORD MP 1987.*

Estonia

10. **DEMBOVSKI, I.** Institutional evolution of agricultural extension in European countries — a conceptual framework and implications for Estonia. *EDINBURGH D 1993.*
11. **JOHNSON, S. P.** Rural Estonia a decade after re-independence: post-Soviet transformations and the non-agricultural sector. *LONDON (R HOLLOWAY) D 2004.*

Georgia

12. **OSEPASHVILI, I.** Towards sustainable forestry in Georgia: insights from transition and market economies. *EAST ANGLIA D 2003.*

Hungary

13. **SZABÓ, B. J.** The evolution of agricultural policies in Hungary, 1919–1956: a study in collectivisation. GLASGOW D 1988.
14. **FERTŐ, I.** Agri-food trade between Hungary and the European Union. NEWCASTLE D 2004.

Kazakhstan

15. **ROBINSON, S.** Pastoralism and land degradation in Kazakhstan. WARWICK D 2000.
16. **LING, S. D.** Spatial bioeconomics of subsistence hunting [with case study of hunting in N. Tien Shan along Kazakh-Kyrgyz border]. LONDON (IMPERIAL) D 2004.

Lithuania

17. **CATTOI, T.** The experience of Lithuanian agricultural transition in 1990–2000: an assessment. LONDON (UCL) D 2002.

Moldova

18. **JACOBS, E. M.** Post-war collectivization of agriculture in the Soviet Union: a case-study of the process in Right-Bank Moldavia (Bessarabia). LONDON (LSE) D 1979.
19. **ALEXANDROVICH, M.** Enterprise restructuring in Moldova: the case of agriculture. OXFORD MP 2001.

Poland

20. **LEWIS, P. G.** The politics of the Polish peasantry: the socialisation of political party organisations in the Polish countryside, 1956–70. BIRMINGHAM D 1974.
21. **SAFIN, M. B.** Direct and indirect impacts on the Polish livestock sector and the perspective of the accession to the European Union. [The role of exchange rate policy]. LONDON (WYE) D 1995.
22. **O'HAGAN, P.** EU agricultural policy making towards Poland, 1989–1995, and its implications for policy network theory. OXFORD D 1996.
23. **SCREENE, M. D.** An economic analysis of the response of Polish agriculture to Poland's economic transition to a free market economy. NOTTINGHAM TRENT D 1997.
24. **MECH, D. M.** The survival of peasant agriculture in Poland. LONDON (WYE) D 2000.
25. **LISZTWAN, I.** Regional dimensions in rural development policies? The case of Poland in the EU. NEWCASTLE D 2003.

Romania

26. **MITRANY, D.** The rural revolution in Rumania and in South Eastern Europe. LONDON (LSE) D 1929.

27. MITRANY, D. The land and the peasant in Rumania. *LONDON (LSE) DS 1931.*

28. ROBERTS, H. L. Politics and the agrarian problem in Rumania, 1922–1945. *OXFORD D 1948.*

29. WOOD, P. G. The agrarian problem in Wallachia, 1870–1907. *LONDON (UCL) D 1984.*

30. CARTWRIGHT, A. L. Implementing land reform in post-communist Romania. *WARWICK D 1999.*

31. ROMINGER, O. E. The potential role of the consumer in the revitalisation of the Romanian apple industry. *BOURNEMOUTH D 2001.*

32. COULOMB, C. A. Agricultural credit in Romania during the period of transition: farmers' access to credit. *LONDON (EXTERNAL) D 2002.*

33. CRISTOIU, A. Technical efficiency in transition economies: the case of Romanian crop production. *LONDON (IMPERIAL) D 2003.*

34. FIRICI, M. C. Distributional impacts of Common Agricultural Policy adoption by Romania. *ABERDEEN D 2003.*

35. POSEY, S. M. Masquerade and the meaning of work in rural Romania. *LONDON (UCL) D 2005.*

Russia (see also USSR)

36. PAVLOVSKY, G. A. The economics of Russian farming, with particular reference to the years 1900–1916. *LONDON (LSE) D 1929.*

37. OWEN, L. A. The Russian peasant movement, 1906–17. *LONDON (SSEES) D 1935.*

38. ELLISON, H. J. Peasant colonization of Siberia: a study of the growth of Russian rural society in Siberia with particular emphasis on the years 1890 to 1918. *LONDON (SSEES) D 1955.*

39. BONINE, R. P. The Russian peasant and the failure of rural government, March-October 1917. *LONDON (SSEES) D 1960.*

40. SHANIN, T. The socio-economic mobility of the Russian peasantry, 1910–1925, and the political sociology of rural society. *BIRMINGHAM D 1969.*

41. DIMOND, J. M. The peasantry in the Russian revolution of 1905–1906, with special reference to the All-Russian Peasant Union. *LONDON (LSE) MP 1971.*

42. DAS GUPTA, K. K. N. G. Chernyshevskii's economic views, with particular reference to the agrarian situation in mid-nineteenth-century Russia. *KEELE D 1972.*

43. MUNTING, R. Improvement in the peasant farm economy in early twentieth century Russia: Tula guberniya. *BIRMINGHAM D 1974.*

44. GILL, G. J. The role of the peasants in revolution in European Russia between March and November 1917. *LONDON (LSE) D 1975.*

45. SHIPLEY, S. M. The sociology of the peasantry, populism and the Russian peasant commune. *LANCASTER ML 1979.*

46. WHEATCROFT, S. G. Grain production and utilization in Russia and the USSR before collectivisation. *BIRMINGHAM D 1980.*

47. MOON, D. The Russian seigniorial peasantry and Tsarist legislation: aspects of the 'Peasant Movement', 1825–1855. *BIRMINGHAM D 1987.*

48. **ECHLIN, M. R.** The statistics of the Russian peasantry in the nineteenth century: a history. *OXFORD D 1990.*

49. **KLEBNIKOV, P. G.** Agricultural development in Russia, 1906–1917: land reform, social agronomy and cooperation. *LONDON (LSE) D 1991.*

50. **WILLIAMS, G.** Agrarian reform in Russia and the Nizhny Novgorod land privatisation project, 1990–1994. *OXFORD MP 1994.*

51. **BIRCHER, R.** Peasant resistance and the defence of servitude rights in Russia's South West, 1890–1914. *OXFORD D 1996.*

52. **HIVON, M.** Ploughing through the reforms: the domestic economy of rural households in post-Soviet Russia. *CAMBRIDGE D 1996.*

53. **BROOKS, E. T.** The heart of the *muzhik*: a study of the nineteenth-century Russian peasant with special reference to Tolstoy. *KEELE MP 1999.*

54. **DAVYDOVA, I.** Moral traditions of rural communities: a study of Russian collectivism. *MANCHESTER D 1999.*

55. **HABECK, J. E. O.** What it means to be a herdsman: the practice and image of reindeer husbandry among the Komi of Northern Russia. *CAMBRIDGE D 2003.*

56. **DENNISON, T. K.** Economy and society in rural Russia: the serf estate of Voshchazhnikovo, 1750–1860. *CAMBRIDGE D 2004.*

Serbia

57. **PALAIRET, M. R.** The influence of commerce on the changing structure of Serbia's peasant economy, 1860–1912. *EDINBURGH D 1976.*

Slovakia

58. **MORRISON, J. A.** Resource use efficiency in an economy in transition: an investigation into the persistence of the co-operative in Slovakian agriculture. *LONDON (WYE) D 2000.*

Slovenia

59. **FRELICH LARSEN, A.** Mountain farms in Slovenia: negotiating agri-environment production options. *OXFORD D 2005.*

Ukraine

60. **TAN, G. K. L.** Village social organisation and peasant action: right-bank Ukraine during the Revolution, 1917–1923. *LONDON (SSEES) D 1999.*

USSR *(see also Russia)*

61. **McCAULEY, C. M. A.** Khrushchev and Soviet agriculture, 1953–1964: some economic and political aspects. *LONDON (SSEES) D 1973.*

62. **HARRISON, R. M.** Theories of peasant economy: critique of the works of the 'organization of production' school of agricultural economy, with particular reference to A.V. Chayanov. *OXFORD D 1974.*

63. **CHANNON, J.** Peasant revolution and land reform: land redistribution in European Russia, October 1917–1920. *BIRMINGHAM D 1983.*

64. **FIGES, O. G.** The political transformation of peasant Russia: peasant Soviets in the Middle Volga, 1917–1920. *CAMBRIDGE D 1987.*

65. **HUGHES, J. R.** Bolsheviks and peasants in Siberia and the end of NEP: a study of the grain crisis of 1927–28. *LONDON (LSE) D 1987.*

66. **SLATTER, J. D.** The Commune state and the Communists: village soviets in the USSR, 1921–30. *LONDON (BIRKBECK) D 1987.*

67. **MORRISON, D. J.** Real expenditure on manufactured goods and processed agricultural products by the Soviet peasantry in retail socialised trade 1928, 1934–37. *GLASGOW D 1989.*

68. **MELVIN, N. J.** The politics of Soviet rural settlement policy 1953–1982. *OXFORD D 1992.*

2. ARCHAEOLOGY

Albania

69. **BESCOBY, D.** Roman Butrint: an enhanced geophysical representation using artificial neural networks. *EAST ANGLIA D 2003.*

Baltic States

70. **ZVELEBIL, M.** Prehistoric subsistence and settlement patterns in the north-east Baltic. *CAMBRIDGE D 1981.*

Bulgaria

71. **BAILEY, D. W.** The social reality of figurines from the Chalcolithic of northern Bulgaria: the example of Ovcharovo. *CAMBRIDGE D 1991.*

72. **PRICE, R. P. S.** Burial practice and aspects of social structure in the late Chalcolithic of North-East Bulgaria. *OXFORD D 1997.*

Central and Eastern Europe (see also under individual countries)

73. **CUMBERPATCH, C. G.** The production and circulation of Late Iron Age slip decorated pottery in Central Europe [Czechoslovakia, Transdanubian Hungary and Poland]. *SHEFFIELD D 1992.*

74. **PYDYN, A.** The social and cultural impact of exchange, trade and interregional contacts in the transition from the late Bronze Age to the early Iron Age in Central Europe. *OXFORD D 1997.*

Croatia

75. **EVANS, H. M. A.** The early mediaeval archaeology of Croatia, *c.* AD 600–900. *NEWCASTLE D 1988.*

76. **Gaffney, V.** Aspects of the archaeology of Hvar. *READING* D *1992*.
77. **Eaves, F. G.** Annulling a myth: a reassessment of the earlier phases of the Eufrasian basilica at Poreč and of the evidence for *domus ecclesiae*. *NOTTINGHAM* D *1993*.
78. **Bass, B.** An archeological assessment of the prehistoric and protohistoric evidence from the island of Korčula, Croatia. *EDINBURGH* D *1997*.

Czech Republic

79. **Lukes, A.** The constitution of the Czech LBK culture: a social perspective. *SHEFFIELD* D *2006*.

Georgia

80. **Tsetskhladze, G. R.** Cultural history of Colchis (6th–1st centuries BC). *OXFORD* D *1998*.

Hungary

81. **Krudy, K. M.** Settlement ecology of the Körös and linear pottery cultures in Hungary. *LONDON (INST ARCHAEOL)* D *1977*.
82. **Smith, P. L.** The exploitation of wild animals by early farmers: a case study from Hungary. *SHEFFIELD* MP *1994*.

Romania

83. **Bergquist, A. K.** The emergence of a pre-Roman state in Dacia: the archaeological and historical sources for Transylvania, 800 BC–AD 106. *CAMBRIDGE* D *1990*.
84. **Trick, S. G.** A GIS-based study of the visual contexts of early agricultural tells in southern Romania. *WALES (CARDIFF)* D *2002*.
85. **Oltean, I. A.** Later prehistoric and Roman rural settlement and land-use in western Transylvania. *GLASGOW* D *2004*.

Russia

86. **Minns, Ellis H.** Scythians and Greeks: a survey of ancient history and archaeology [NCR]. *CAMBRIDGE* DL *1920*.
87. **Comey, M. G.** Medieval stave-built wooden vessels in Ireland and Russia. *LONDON (UCL)* D *2003*.
88. **Meyer, H. -C.** The discovery, collection and scholarship of Classical Greek and Greco-Scythian antiquities in Imperial Russia. *OXFORD* D *2006*.

Slovakia

89. **Shennan, S. E.** Social organisation in the earliest Bronze Age in Czechoslovakia: a study based on the cemeteries of the Nitra Group. *CAMBRIDGE* D *1978*.

South Eastern Europe *(see also under individual countries)*

90. **YOUNG, B.** The metalwork of the Lower Danube, 5th century BC–4th century AD. EDINBURGH D 1981.

91. **DUNCAN, G. L.** The monetary system of the later Roman Empire, with special reference to coin circulation in the Danubian and Balkan provinces, 294–578 AD. LONDON (INST ARCHAEOL) D 1985.

92. **MULVIN, L.** Late Roman villas in the Danube-Balkan region. TC DUBLIN D 1999.

93. **KARAVAS, J.** The evolution of the Roman frontier defence systems and fortifications in the lower Danube provinces in the first and second centuries AD. DURHAM D 2002.

94. **PANAYOTOV, A.** The Jews in the Balkan provinces of the Roman Empire: an epigraphic and archaeological study. ST ANDREWS D 2004.

3. ART, ARCHITECTURE, DESIGN

Baltic States *(see also under individual countries)*

95. **RANDLA, A.** The architecture of the mendicant orders in Northern Europe: a comparative study of Scotland, the Northern Netherlands and Livonia. CAMBRIDGE D 1999.

Bulgaria

96. **Moss, L. M.** The art of Preslav: its sources of inspiration and influence. CAMBRIDGE D 1977.

Byzantium

97. **ANTONOVA, C.** Form, time and real presence in Eastern Orthodox art. OXFORD D 2005.

Central and Eastern Europe *(see also under individual countries)*

98. **KOLCZYNSKA, P.** Art promotion in new Europe: towards cultural integration. The case of Poland and the Czech Republic. ST ANDREWS MP 1995.

99. **FOWKES, R.** Monumental sculpture in post-war Eastern Europe, 1945–1960. ESSEX D 2002.

Croatia

100. **MOXLEY, M.** The analysis of the fortified hill town Kastav in the Rijeka area to establish its potential for design and renewal. CNAA (BRIGHTON POLY) D 1982.

Czech Republic

101. SIMPSON, A.   The connections between English and Bohemian painting during the second half of the fourteenth century. LONDON (COURTAULD) D 1978.

102. WALKER, F. A.   Architecture in the Czech Lands: a study in stylistic development, with special reference to the years c.1830–1930. STRATHCLYDE D 1979.

103. STONE-RICHARDS, M.   The conception of embodiment in French surrealist art, with reference also to Czech surrealism 1919–1939. LONDON (COURTAULD) D 1993.

104. ORMROD, L.   The Wenceslas Chapel in St Vitus' Cathedral, Prague: the marriage of imperial iconography and Bohemian kingship. LONDON (COURTAULD) D 1997.

105. BOWLING, H.   An investigation into Czech illustration. ROYAL COLLEGE OF ART MP 1999.

106. ROBERTS, D.   Beyond surrealism: the Grand Jeu, Josef Šima and the quest for unity. ESSEX D 2003.

Estonia

107. KERMIK, J.   The design and production of furniture with limited resources, with particular reference to Estonia. ROYAL COLLEGE OF ART D 1994.

108. KIVIMAA, K.   Feminist and gendered practices in Estonian art of the 1990s. OPEN MP 1999.

109. KIVIMAA, K.   Nationalism, gender and cultural identities: the case of Estonian art from the impact of modernity to the post-Soviet era 1850–2000. LEEDS D 2003.

Hungary

110. JULIER, G.   Design and transition in Spain and Hungary. LEEDS METROPOLITAN D 2000.

Macedonia

111. SUMANOV, L.   Conservation and seismic strengthening of architectural heritage: Byzantine churches of the ninth till the fourteenth centuries in Macedonia. YORK D 1999.

Poland

112. CROSSLEY, B. P.   The architecture of Kasimir the Great: a study in the architecture of Lesser Poland, 1320–1370. CAMBRIDGE D 1974.

113. PATRICK, M.   Im/possibilities: the development of conceptual and intermedial art in Poland. KENT D 1999.

114. TYSZCZUK, R.   In spem melioris aevi: the architecture and writings of Stanisław Leszczyński, roi bienfaisant, 1737–1766. CAMBRIDGE D 1999.

115. WALCZAK, B. M.   British experience in the conversion and rehabilitation of textile mills and the lessons for comparable work in Łódź, Poland. STRATHCLYDE D 2002.

116. **KĘPCZYŃSKA-WALCZAK, A.** A model proposal for digitisation and recording data on architectural heritage in Poland based on European guidelines and best practices. *STRATHCLYDE D 2004.*

117. **KIERKUC-BIELINSKI, J. J.** Confinement and illusions of freedom: the dialogue between Polish and American conceptual art 1970–1981. *LONDON (COURTAULD) D 2005.*

118. **LABNO, J. J.** The monumental body and the Renaissance child: funeral monuments in Poland and their European context (1500–1650). *SUSSEX D 2005.*

119. **KOUTNY-JONES, A.** Death personified in the Baroque art of the Kingdom of Poland. *CAMBRIDGE D 2006.*

Romania

120. **MILLER, S. M.** Constantin Brâncuşi (1876–1957). *LONDON (COURTAULD) D 1990.*

121. **PARIGORIS, A.** Constantin Brâncuşi, a peasant in Paris: a study of the persona and work of Constantin Brâncuşi from a post-Symbolist perspective. *LONDON (COURTAULD) D 1997.*

122. **WOOD, J. M.** The materials and metaphors of the sculptor's studio: Brâncuşi, Picasso and Giacometti in the 1920s and 1930s. *LONDON (COURTAULD) D 1999.*

123. **LOWE, S.** Eclectic and neo-national aspects of Romanian art and design, 1878–1930. *ST ANDREWS D 2001.*

124. **BROSCATAN, M. S.** 19th century furniture of Southern Transylvania: a survey and analysis of the vernacular tradition. *BRUNEL D 2002.*

125. **DRAGHICI-VASILESCU, N.** Changes in the phenomenon of icon-painting in Romania from the second half of the nineteenth century to the present day. *OXFORD D 2004.*

Russia (see also USSR)

126. **BOWLT, J. E.** The 'Blue Rose' Movement and Russian Symbolist painting. *ST ANDREWS D 1972.*

127. **HUGHES, L. A. J.** Moscow Baroque architecture: a study of one aspect of Westernisation in late seventeenth century Russia. *CAMBRIDGE D 1977.*

128. **MILNER, J.** Russian constructivism: the first phase: Rodchenko and Tatlin. *LONDON (COURTAULD) D 1979.*

129. **PARTON, A.** Mikhail Fedorovich Larionov (1881–1964): a study of the chronology and sources of his art. *NEWCASTLE D 1985.*

130. **FER, B.** Russian art and theory in France, 1918–25: a comparative study of artistic avant-gardes. *ESSEX D 1987.*

131. **ARCHER, K.** 'An absolutely violent feast for the eyes': the creation and reconstruction of Nicholas Roerich's costumes and décors for *Le Sacre du printemps. ESSEX D 1988.*

132. **FRANGOPOULOS, M.** A double language: formal and ideological aspects of Russian Constructivism, 1917–1923. *ESSEX MP 1988.*

133. **HUMPHREYS, C. M.** Cubo-Futurism in Russia, 1912–1922. The transformation of a painterly style. *ST ANDREWS D 1989.*

134. **BEHR, S.** Wassily Kandinsky as playwright: the stage-compositions 1909–1914. *ESSEX D 1991.*

135. **HOWARD, J. C.** Nikolai Kul´bin and the Union of Youth, 1908–1914. *ST ANDREWS D 1991.*

136. **JACKSON, D.** Ilya Repin: ideology and aesthetics in Russian art. *EDINBURGH D 1991.*

137. **McKAY, C. M.** Kandinsky: the sciences of man and the science of art. *CAMBRIDGE D 1992.*

138. **CHARLEY, J.** The dialectic of the built environment: a study in the historical transformation of labour and space [with special reference to Russia and Moscow, late 18th cent. to early 1990s]. *STRATHCLYDE D 1994.*

139. **GILCHRIST, M. M.** Images of the Petrine era in Russian history painting. *ST ANDREWS D 1994.*

140. **KOSTOTCHKINA, N.** The Baroque in seventeenth century Russian art. *LONDON (SSEES) MP 1994.*

141. **WINSKELL, S. K.** Dada, Russia and modernity. *LONDON (COURTAULD) D 1995.*

142. **GRAY, R.** Western influence on Russian genre painting 1820–1870. *OXFORD D 1997.*

143. **MAKHROV, A. V.** The architecture of Nikolai L´vov: a study of the architectural relationships between Britain and Russia at the end of the eighteenth century. *ST ANDREWS D 1998.*

144. **JONES, P.** Iconoclasm, restoration and the creation of new symbols in Russian visual culture, 1991–97 [NCR]. *OXFORD MP 2000.*

145. **KRAMER, C. A.** Natalia Goncharova and Mikhail Larionov's neo-primitivist depictions of social outcasts in their thematic series of 1907–14. *ST ANDREWS D 2000.*

146. **KIRKMAN, V.** The presentation of Russian constructivism in Britain. *LIVERPOOL MP 2001.*

147. **CAUDANO, A.-L. D. J.** 'Let there be lights in the firmament of the heaven': cosmological depictions in early Rus (tenth to thirteenth century). *CAMBRIDGE D 2004.*

148. **NOVIKOVA, E.** Towards the restored innocence of the creative impulse: anti-aestheticism in Larionov and Khlebnikov. *TC DUBLIN ML 2004.*

149. **MINNS, EMMA H.** 'A person does not always look like himself': the visual representation of Russian writers 1860–1899. *LONDON (UCL) D 2006.*

Slovenia

150. **MONROE, A.** Culture instead of a state, culture as a state: art, regime and transcendence in the works of Laibach and Neue Slowenische Kunst. *KENT D 2000.*

Ukraine

151. **DAREWYCH, D.** Soviet Ukrainian painting c. 1955–c. 1979: new currents and under-currents. *LONDON (UCL) D 1992.*

USSR *(see also Russia)*

152. **LODDER, C. A.** Constructivism: from fine art into design, Russia, 1913–1933. *SUSSEX D 1980.*

153. **Williams, F. E. K.** From Cubo-Futurism to the Left Front: Mayakovskii and Left art, 1917–21. *ST ANDREWS MP 1981.*

154. **Compton, S. P.** Kazimir Malevich: a study of the paintings, 1910–1935. *LONDON (COURTAULD) D 1983.*

155. **Riley, R. M.** Alexander Deineka: the artist and the state in Soviet Russia, 1920–1939. *LONDON (COURTAULD) MP 1983.*

156. **Gilhespy, T.** A theoretical appraisal and artistic response to Soviet monumental sculpture. *CENTRAL ENGLAND D 1993.*

157. **Buchli, V. A.** The Narkomfin Communal House, Moscow: the material culture of accommodation and resistance (1930–1991). *CAMBRIDGE D 1996.*

158. **O'Mahony, M. J.** Representing *fizkultura*: sport and Soviet culture from the first Five Year Plan to the Great Patriotic War. *LONDON (COURTAULD) D 1998.*

159. **Gérin, A.** Stories from Mayakovskaya Metro station: the production / consumption of Stalinist monumental space. *LEEDS D 2000.*

160. **Byers, M. H.** The rise of Socialist Realism in the exhibitions of the State Tret´iakov Gallery 1924–1934. *GLASGOW D 2004.*

4. CRIME, PRISONS, HOLOCAUST

Bosnia-Herzegovina

161. **Bassett, G. D.** A discourse analysis of rape in war: case studies from Bosnia, Burma and Rwanda. *BRISTOL D 2005.*

Central and Eastern Europe (see also under individual countries)

162. **Keep, J. L.** The impact of the fragmentation of the former USSR and of former communist Eastern Europe on heroin trafficking. *LEICESTER MP 2002.*

163. **Ridley, N.** Money laundering and financial crime in selected EU accession countries in Central and South East Europe during the transition from pre- to post-communist era and the role of the central bank [...]. *SOUTHAMPTON D 2004.*

Hungary

164. **Hignett, K.** The development of, and fight against organised crime in Hungary. *KEELE MP 2001.*

165. **Schulzke, S.** Corruption in Hungary: Problem or pretext? [NCR]. *OXFORD MP 2002.*

Jews

166. **Cole, T. J.** The ghettoization of the 'Jewish' community in Budapest during the Second World War. *CAMBRIDGE D 1997.*

167. **Paulsson, G. S.** Hiding in Warsaw: the Jews on the 'Aryan side' in the Polish capital, 1940–1945. *OXFORD D 1998.*

168. **SISSON, C.** Ignorance or apathy? Britain's Holocaust-related intelligence and information gathering during World War II and its impact upon related policy-making. LEICESTER MP 1998.

169. **HALL, J. D. R.** Towards a postmodern ethics: representation, memory, responsibility, with particular reference to literature of the Holocaust, communist Czechoslovakia and apartheid of South Africa. GLASGOW D 1999.

170. **LEWINSOHN, E.** Aspects of Jewish leadership in Terezín. LEICESTER MP 2001.

171. **WAXMAN, Z.** The Holocaust and the entwinement of identity, testimony and representation. OXFORD D 2001.

172. **KAVANAUGH, S.** The Jewish leadership of the Theresienstadt Ghetto: culture, identity and politics. SOUTHAMPTON D 2003.

173. **MARLOW, M.** Place, identity and memory: a study of American ante-bellum autobiographical slave narratives, and Holocaust survivor accounts by Jews living in Białystok, Poland, after 1918 and up to 1943. SOUTHAMPTON D 2006.

Poland

174. **GARLIŃSKI, J.** The underground movement in the Auschwitz concentration camp. LONDON (LSE) D 1973.

Romania

175. **GILES, G. W.** In the light of a vision: the development of delinquency and criminal justice in Eastern Europe before and since the collapse of communism, with special reference to Romania. EXETER MP 1996.

Russia (see also USSR)

176. **VARESE, F.** The emergence of the Russian mafia: dispute settlement and protection in a new market economy. OXFORD D 1996.

177. **LAUCHLAN, I. G.** The Tsarist secret police in St Petersburg, 1906–14. LEEDS D 1998.

178. **RAWLINSON, M. P.** Hunting the chameleon: the problems of identifying Russian organized crime. LONDON (LSE) D 1998.

179. **ALVEY, R.** Russian involvement in cybercrimes. KEELE MP 2001.

180. **PIACENTINI, L. F.** Work to live: the function of prison labour in the Russian prison system. WALES (BANGOR) D 2002.

181. **TURNER, G.** Contemporary Russian organised crime: the Solntsevo example. KEELE MP 2002.

Ukraine

182. **PANASYUK, M. B.** The concept of social tolerance and social policy: a case study of crime and penal practices in the transitional period in Ukraine. LONDON (LSE) D 2000.

183. **MARKOVSKA, A.** Economic crime and its impact on the development of financial markets: the case study of Ukraine. CITY D 2004.

USSR *(see also Russia)*

184. **Spier, H.** Felix Dzerzhinsky, founder of the Soviet secret police: a biography. MANCHESTER D 1973.

185. **Dobbs, L. P.** Juvenile justice in the Soviet Union. LONDON (LSE) D 1980.

186. **Bacon, E. T.** The Gulag at war: Stalin's forced labour system in the light of the archives. [With two articles:] 'Glasnost' and the Gulag' and 'Soviet Military Losses in World War Two'. BIRMINGHAM D 1997.

187. **Stevens, H.** Space and power in the Soviet forced labour camps. OXFORD MP 2000.

188. **Joyce, C. S.** The Gulag 1930–1960: Karelia and the Soviet system of forced labour. BIRMINGHAM D 2001.

189. **Knightley, J. F. S.** Party and NKVD in the Great Terror, 1935–1939. OXFORD MP 2003.

190. **Barksby, K.** The brotherhood of thieves: how the culture of the *vory v zakone* changed from the 1920s to the 1950s. KEELE MP 2004.

Yugoslavia *(see also under former republics)*

191. **Clark, J. N.** Slobodan Milošević: a case-study of the criminal leader. NOTTINGHAM D 2005.

5. ECONOMICS

Albania

192. **Schnytzer, A.** Economic planning and industrial policy in the People's Republic of Albania. OXFORD D 1977.

193. **Lati, L.** The causes and consequences of corporate restructuring in Albania. STAFFORDSHIRE D 2001.

Austria-Hungary

194. **Morys, I. M.** The classical gold standard in the European periphery: a case-study of Austria-Hungary and Italy, 1870–1913. LONDON (LSE) D 2006.

Baltic States *(see also under individual countries)*

195. **Shortland, A. K.** The role of institutional arrangements in the timing of currency crises [with special reference to the Baltic States]. LONDON (LSE) D 2002.

Bulgaria

196. **Davis, J. R.** Economic transition and food consumption in Bulgaria. LONDON (WYE) D 1994.

197. **WALLEY, S.** Monetary crises in Bulgaria: an empirical analysis. *TC DUBLIN ML 2003.*

Central and Eastern Europe (see also under individual countries)

198. **BATT, J.** Economic reform and political change in Eastern Europe: a comparison of the Czechoslovak and Hungarian experiences. *BIRMINGHAM D 1986.*

199. **LINOTTE, D.** Payments and adjustment problems of Eastern Europe and the USSR. *OXFORD D 1989.*

200. **SHARP, S.** State-owned enterprises in the transition from a command to a market economy: Poland, Hungary and Czechoslovakia. *OXFORD MP 1993.*

201. **HALLIGAN, L.** Social safety nets in transition economies. *OXFORD MP 1994.*

202. **BUCHANAN, P. A.** Central and Eastern Europe in transition: prospects for sustainable development. *ST ANDREWS MP 1995.*

203. **PUTHENKALAM, J. J.** Modelling a new economic growth thought for developing economies with particular reference to economies in transition [i.e. in Eastern Europe]. *GLASGOW D 1996.*

204. **WARMEDINGER, T.** Using a large scale macroeconomic model for the analysis of economic shocks — the case of an Eastern enlargement to the EU. *STRATHCLYDE D 1997.*

205. **DE BOER-ASHWORTH, E.** The global political economy and post-1989 change: the place of the Central European transition [Poland, Czech Republic, Hungary]. *LIMERICK D 1999.*

206. **MACHOLD, S.** Local-level policies for small firm sector development in Russia and Hungary: a comparative analysis. *WOLVERHAMPTON D 1999.*

207. **EBURNE, P. H.** Privatization, property rights and technical efficiency in Eastern Europe. *LEICESTER D 2000.*

208. **TSENOVA, T. S.** Macrotheoretic models of an economy in transition. *YORK D 2000.*

209. **WALKER, R.** Aggregate measures of output in transition economies [Hungary, Poland, Romania]: some practical and conceptual difficulties. *CITY D 2000.*

210. **UNGER, D. R. J.** Who pays and when? An analysis of the arrears crisis in Central and Eastern Europe. *TC DUBLIN ML 2001.*

211. **ALTINGER, L. P.** Monetary policy reaction functions in transition economies acceding to the EU. *LONDON (LBS) D 2002.*

212. **KOVACHEV, I. S.** Revival and development strategies for East European economies in transition. *OPEN D 2003.*

213. **BEBLAVÝ, M.** Constrained discretion: monetary policy frameworks, central bank independence and inflation in Central Europe, 1993–2001. *ST ANDREWS D 2004.*

214. **CHIRMICIU, A.** Reforms, institutions, competition and economic performance in transition economies. *CAMBRIDGE D 2004.*

215. **CIRERA, X.** Essays on exchange rate regimes and macroeconomic stability in Central and Eastern European and Baltic countries. *SUSSEX D 2004.*

216. **DOYLE, O.** An economic analysis of voting in Central and Eastern Europe. *TC DUBLIN D 2005.*

217. **ALLAM, M. S.** Adopting the Euro in Central Europe: cross-national variations in the strategies of the Czech Republic, Hungary, Poland and Slovakia. *LONDON (LSE) D 2006.*

218. **MALISZEWSKI, W. S.** Monetary policy in transitional economies. *LONDON (LSE) D 2006.*

Central Asia *(see also under individual countries)*

219. **LUNGER, A. J.** The economic background of the Russian conquest of Central Asia in the second half of the nineteenth century. *LONDON (SSEES) D 1952.*

220. **MAKAROVA, E.** Paradoxes of development in Soviet and post-Soviet Central Asia, with special reference to the role of the *mahalla* Uzbek cities. *MANCHESTER D 1999.*

Czech Republic

221. **KOBRYN, S.** Claims and reality in Czech privatization: a historical-institutionalist analysis. *OXFORD MP 1998.*

222. **UHLIR, D.** Regional transformation in the Czech Republic: internationalization, embeddedness and adaptability. *OPEN D 1999.*

223. **McMASTER, I. A.** Privatisation and transformation in the Czech Republic 1989–1997. *STRATHCLYDE D 2000.*

224. **SIMOVA, J.** Market structure and evolution of the clothing retail sector in the Czech Republic under the specific conditions of a transition economy. *HUDDERSFIELD D 2001.*

Czechoslovakia

225. **KONOVALOV, S. A.** Monetary reconstruction in Czechoslovakia and its effects on economic life. *OXFORD BL 1927.*

226. **DOBES, L.** Czechoslovak economic relations with the developing countries. *OXFORD D 1980.*

227. **FRONKOVÁ, V.** Social preferences and economic constraints on factors influencing the structural evolution of consumer expenditure in the CSSR. *OXFORD ML 1991.*

Estonia

228. **WORTHINGTON, B.** The Estonian travel and tourism industry 1985–1995. *BRADFORD D 1999.*

Georgia

229. **ALTMAN, Y.** A reconstruction, using anthropological methods, of the second economy of Soviet Georgia. *CNAA (MIDDX POLY) D 1983.*

Hungary

230. **GOELLNER, A.** The politics of the Hungarian new economic mechanism. LONDON (LSE) D 1977.

231. **BOROSS, E. A.** The effect of post-war inflation on industrial development in Hungary, 1918–1929. EAST ANGLIA D 1984.

232. **DIETRICH, M. D.** The decentralisation of decision making: a corporate analysis of the Hungarian new economic mechanism. SUSSEX D 1985.

233. **ANTAL, Z.** Privatisation and firm behaviour in national transformation: the case of Hungary. LONDON (LBS) D 1995.

234. **ELAM, P.** The politics of economic transformation in Hungary 1990–93. OXFORD MP 1995.

235. **STEPHAN, J.** Systemic transformation and the conditions of economic development in Hungary with particular reference to the experience from the East German case. BIRMINGHAM D 1997.

236. **TAKSZ, I.** Economic policy implementation in East-Central Europe: industrial privatization in Hungary in the early 1990s. OXFORD D 1997.

237. **BEVAN, A. A.** Computable general equilibrium modelling of the Hungarian economy during transition. HERIOT-WATT D 1998.

238. **COLOMBO, E.** Essays on transitional economics [with special reference to Hungarian firms]. SOUTHAMPTON D 2000.

Kyrgyzstan

239. **TENTIEVA, G. J.** Modelling aspects of macroeconomic behaviour in Kyrgyzstan using system dynamics. SUNDERLAND D 1999.

Latvia

240. **DALE, N. R.** The globalisation of the Latvian economy. CAMBRIDGE D 1996.

241. **SARAJEVS, V.** Macroeconomic issues in a small transition economy: the case of Latvia. LONDON (QUEEN MARY) D 2002.

242. **KAZAKS, M.** Essays on the dynamics of Latvian exchange rates. LONDON (QUEEN MARY) D 2006.

Poland

243. **GAWEL, S. F.** The problem of economic development of backward countries (with special reference to Poland) [NCR]. OXFORD BL 1947.

244. **BLAZYCA, G.** Economic reform in Polish industry: the experience of the 1970s. SUSSEX D 1978.

245. **WANLESS, P. T.** Economic policy and taxation in Poland in the 1970s. STRATHCLYDE D 1981.

246. **ÅSLUND, P. A.** The non-agricultural private sector in the East European economy: the case of Poland and the GDR 1945–1980. OXFORD D 1982.

247. **TROMER, C. E.** Political obstacles to economic reforms in Poland: the reforms of 1956 and 1973. *OXFORD ML 1987.*

248. **BRIEN, L. C.** The response of Polish state owned enterprises to economic reforms. *OXFORD MP 1992.*

249. **VON THADDEN, G. H.** Inflation in the reconstruction of Poland, 1918–27. *LONDON (LSE) D 1995.*

250. **KANDAH, A. S. A.** Privatisation in Poland (1989–1995). *GLASGOW D 1996.*

251. **SPIRO, N.** The politics of economic transition: 'shock therapy' in Poland 1990–1991. *KENT D 1998.*

252. **CAMPBELL, C.** The impact of association with the EU on domestic industrial policy making: the case of Poland 1990–1995. *OXFORD D 1999.*

253. **KAWAI, Y.** The reform of insurance supervisory systems for economies in transition with particular reference to Poland. *CITY D 2000.*

254. **BOOTH, J.** The transformation of professional practices in post-communist Poland: observing the dynamics of globalisation. *OXFORD BROOKES D 2001.*

255. **SHIELDS, S. A.** Globalisation and Poland: transnational forces and the Polish transition to a market economy. *WALES (ABERYSTWYTH) D 2001.*

256. **HAJLASZ, Z.** Development and integration: Poland and Lower Silesia as a case study. *LONDON (UCL) MP 2003.*

257. **GWIAZDA, A.** Europeanisation and Polish competition policy. *TC DUBLIN D 2005.*

258. **SCHWANEBERG, S.** The economic exploitation of the Generalgouvernement in Poland by the Third Reich, 1939 to 1945. *OXFORD D 2006.*

259. **SKULIMOWSKA, M. K.** The evaluation of European Union aid to the candidate countries from Central and Eastern Europe: the case of PHARE aid to Poland. *WALES (ABERYSTWYTH) D 2006.*

260. **WEIS, C.** Inventing a capitalist region: Upper Silesia / Poland economic transformations in old-industrial and post-socialist spaces of Central and Eastern Europe. *OPEN D 2006.*

Romania

261. **SPIGLER, I.** The economic reform in Rumania. *OXFORD BL 1970.*

262. **YOUNG, S.** Romanian regional economic development 1945–1995. *NOTTINGHAM TRENT D 2001.*

263. **CERNAT, L.** From socialism to 'cocktail capitalism': Europeanization, state-societal interactions and economic performance in Romania. *MANCHESTER D 2002.*

264. **RADULESCU, M. -R.** Macroeconomic aspects of transition: an empirical analysis of currency substitution and purchasing power parity in Romania, and growth in 25 transition countries. *NEWCASTLE D 2002.*

265. **SCRIECIU, S. S.** Assessing the economic and environmental impacts of Romania's accession to the Common Agricultural Policy of the European Union. *MANCHESTER D 2005.*

Russia (see also USSR)

266. **MILLER, M. S.** The economic development of Russia from 1905–1914, with special reference to trade, industry and finance. LONDON (SSEES) D 1925.

267. **HURT, E. B.** Russian economic development, 1881–1914, with special reference to the railways and the role of government. LONDON (LSE) D 1963.

268. **HOBSON, J. M.** The tax-seeking state: protectionism, taxation and state structures in Germany, Russia, Britain and America 1870–1914. LONDON (LSE) D 1991.

269. **DOYLE, J.** Russia's *kustar* industry: a chapter in the history of economic ideas, with special reference to the period 1861–1880. OXFORD ML 1992.

270. **KING, F.** The political and economic thought of Vladimir Aleksandrovich Bazarov (1874–1939). EAST ANGLIA D 1994.

271. **LIU, W.** Economic transitions to market economy: a comparative study on economic reform proposals in China and the former Soviet Union. GLASGOW D 1994.

272. **RAMANUJAM, N.** Price mechanism in Russia: its role in the old planning and the new markets. OXFORD D 1995.

273. **HERTZ, N. T.** Russian business relationships in the wake of reform. CAMBRIDGE D 1996.

274. **NAVA, M.** Optimal taxation, tax evasion and rent seeking [in Russia]. LONDON (LSE) D 1996.

275. **SUTHERLAND, D. J.** Regional economic structure and the process of economic transformation in the Russian Federation. BIRMINGHAM D 1997.

276. **CA'ZORZI, M.** Exchange rate instability and economic reform: with specific reference to Russian exchange rate reforms in the early 1990's. WARWICK D 1998.

277. **FLEMMING, W. B. G.** Business-state relations in post-Soviet Russia: the politics of second-phase privatisation, 1995–1997. OXFORD MP 1998.

278. **HARTER, S.** The civilianisation of the Russian economy: a network approach. BIRMINGHAM D 1998.

279. **ANDERS, R. -E.** Globalization and the Russian Far East: propsects for integration. BIRMINGHAM MP 1999.

280. **DENISOVA, I. A.** Monetary policy transmission in Russia (1992–96): the role of industrial enterprise arrears. MANCHESTER D 1999.

281. **VANDYCKE, N.** The economics of the reproduction 'crisis' in transition Europe: the effect of shifts in values, income and uncertainty (with special reference to Russia). LONDON (LSE) D 1999.

282. **ZIMINE, D. A.** Urban economic development policies in Russia: current trends and application of foreign experience. BIRMINGHAM D 1999.

283. **FALTIN, D.** Regional transition in Russia: a study of the free economic zone policy in the Kaliningrad region. LONDON (LSE) D 2000.

284. **KIHLGREN, A.** Small business in Russia: the case of St Petersburg. GLASGOW D 2000.

285. **KIRSANOVA, T.** Three essays on Russian disinflation. OXFORD D 2000.

286. **NAJARIAN, S.** Parameterising the nonlinear dynamics of money demand: a test of Cagan's model applicability: evidence from Russia. OXFORD MP 2000.

287. **FRIEDMAN, R.** A comparative study of regional economic strategy and industrial policy in Russia, 1990–1999. *LONDON (LBS) D 2001.*

288. **GARA, M.** Monetary imbalances and institutional shortcomings in the Russian transition. *BIRMINGHAM D 2001.*

289. **MCCANN, L.** Non-global development in Russia: the case of Tatarstan. *KENT D 2001.*

290. **BUSSE, E. F.** The formal and informal workings of Russian taxation: the case of small and medium sized enterprises in Western Russia. *CAMBRIDGE D 2002.*

291. **ENGMANN, D.** Corruption, taxation and loan conditionality: a contribution to the macroeconomics of reform and transition with reference to Russia. *WARWICK D 2002.*

292. **DOLINSKAYA, I.** Essays on Russian transition. *CAMBRIDGE D 2003.*

293. **MICHAEL, B.** The role of social capital in St Petersburg's developmental state. *OXFORD MP 2003.*

294. **NIKOLIĆ, M.** Money supply — inflation relationship in post-communist Russia. *LONDON (UCL) D 2003.*

295. **MENNICKEN, A. M.** Moving West: the emergence, reform and standardisation of audit practices in post-Soviet Russia. *LONDON (LSE) D 2005.*

296. **SKVIRSKAJA, V.** New economic forms and subjectivity in post-socialist Russia: the case of a rural periphery, Yamal-Nenets Autonomous Region. *CAMBRIDGE D 2006.*

297. **WILSON, E. T.** Building an Arctic community of knowledge: the promotion and reception of Canadian resource management and economic development models in the Russian North. *CAMBRIDGE D 2006.*

Serbia

298. **ZEKIĆ, J.** The role of monetary and financial reform in approaching the European Union: the case of Serbia. *GREENWICH D 2005.*

Slovakia *(see also Czechoslovakia)*

299. **SMITH, A.** Industrial restructuring and uneven regional development in Slovakia: a regulationist approach to 'the transition' in Central and Eastern Europe. *SUSSEX D 1996.*

Slovenia

300. **ČOK, M.** Analysing the distribution of income and taxes in Slovenia with a tax-benefit model. *BRISTOL D 2002.*

Soviet Bloc

301. **DATAR, A. L.** An evaluation of the Eastern Bloc assistance to India (1956–57 to 1965–66). *OXFORD D 1969.*

302. **SHREEVE, D. J.** Economic determinants of integration in the Council for Mutual Economic Assistance [NCR]. *CNAA (WOLVERHAMPTON POLY) MP 1981.*

303. **BAIRAM, E. I.** Returns to scale, technical progress and industrial growth in the USSR and Eastern Europe: an empirical study, 1961–75. *HULL D 1986.*

Ukraine

304. **BLEWETT, L.** The development of a market orientation in a turbulent transitional environment — the case of Ukraine. *ASTON D 2000.*

305. **ROSEVEAR, A. G.** Enterprise restructuring and ownership: the case of Ukraine. *LONDON (LBS) D 2001.*

306. **ZYLA, R. P.** Interactions between the bureaucracy and small independent enterprise in post-socialist Ukraine. *LONDON (UCL) D 2002.*

307. **SERGEYEV, A.** A systemic inquiry into the economic and social transformations of Ukraine. *SUNDERLAND D 2004.*

308. **WYNNYCKYJ, M.** Institutions and entrepreneurs: cultural evolution in the 'de novo' market sphere in post-Soviet Ukraine. *CAMBRIDGE D 2004.*

USSR (see also Russia)

309. **BAYKOV, A. M.** Studies in the development of the national economy of the USSR. *BIRMINGHAM D 1942.*

310. **RONIMOIS, H. E.** Soviet economic life and the general categories of economic analysis. *LONDON (LSE) D 1949.*

311. **DAVIES, R. W.** The development of the Soviet budgetary system, 1917–1941. *BIRMINGHAM D 1954.*

312. **DAY, R. B.** L. D. Trotsky and the economics of Soviet isolation. *LONDON (SSEES) D 1970.*

313. **HANSON, P.** The Soviet consumer sector. *BIRMINGHAM D 1971.*

314. **ELLMAN, M. J.** The optimally functioning Socialist economy: a study in Soviet mathematical economics, 1960–1971. *CAMBRIDGE D 1972.*

315. **JEFFRIES, I.** The Stalinist economic system as a model for underdeveloped countries: the development of Soviet thought since 1953. *LONDON (LSE) D 1974.*

316. **VYAS, A.** The behaviour of real wages in the Soviet economy, 1929–37: a study of the theory and practice of extensive growth. *BIRMINGHAM D 1974.*

317. **WIEDEMANN, P. P.** A consideration of the nature of the objective function in national economic planning, with specific reference to the mathematical modelling of medium-term planning in the Soviet Union and Eastern Europe. *LONDON (LSE) D 1974.*

318. **FILTZER, D. A.** E. A. Preobrazhensky and the theory of expanded reproduction in the USSR during the period of primitive socialist accumulation. *GLASGOW D 1976.*

319. **PEEBLES, G. S.** Money incomes and expenditures of the population of the Soviet Union, 1955 to 1973, and household savings. *GLASGOW ML 1976.*

320. **AROUCA MARQUES DOS SANTOS, L. F.** On the balance of money incomes and expenditures of the population in the USSR. *LONDON (LSE) D 1978.*

321. **DUNMORE, T.** Soviet economic policy-making during the fourth Five Year Plan period (1946–50). *ESSEX D 1978.*

322. **FRERIS, A.** Problems of resource allocation in centrally planned economies, with special reference to the theory of the firm in the Soviet Union. *LONDON (LSE) D 1981.*

323. **THOMAS, W. A.** The Soviet tourist industry. *WALES (SWANSEA) D 1982.*

324. **BRIDGE, R. P.** The recent economic development of the Soviet North, with specific reference to the Yakutskaya ASSR. *CAMBRIDGE D 1986.*

325. **SCHIFFER, J. R.** Postwar Soviet regional economic development policy in Pacific Siberia. *BIRMINGHAM D 1986.*

326. **WALKER, D.** Housing policy in the Soviet Union 1928–1953: 'capital' versus 'commodity' in the housing sector of a high-growth-rate industrialising economy. *CITY MP 1986.*

327. **NADLER, T.** Evolution of central planning in the Soviet Union. *OXFORD MP 1987.*

328. **RUTLAND, P.** The role of the Soviet Communist Party in economic decision making. *YORK D 1987.*

329. **WERDMULLER, O.** The influence of the Soviet model of development on the GDR's economic relations with developing countries. *OXFORD D 1988.*

330. **CRONE BILGER, C.** International and economic policy aspects of the Soviet ocean-going fishing industry. *LONDON (EXTERNAL) D 1990.*

331. **GERON, L.** Soviet foreign economic policy under NEP and perestroika: a comparative analysis. *OXFORD D 1990.*

332. **BURGHART, D. L.** Technology transfer, export control, and economic restructuring in the Soviet Union: the case of Soviet computers. *SURREY D 1991.*

333. **BARNETT, V.** At the margins of the market: conceptions of the market and market economics in Soviet economic theory during the New Economic Policy, 1921–1929. *GLASGOW D 1992.*

334. **TEDSTROM, J. E.** Fiscal federalism and Soviet regionalism, 1988–1991. *BIRMINGHAM D 1994.*

335. **KIM, B. -Y.** Fiscal policy and consumer market disequilibrium in the Soviet Union, 1965–1989. *OXFORD D 1996.*

336. **HAN, Y. -S.** Analysis of the government-directed economy in the USSR: politico-economic model. *GLASGOW ML 1998.*

Yugoslavia (see also under former republics)

337. **HORVAT, B.** Economic theory of associationist socialism: the theory of planned economy [with special reference to Yugoslavia]. *MANCHESTER D 1959.*

338. **BRKIĆ, D.** Industrialisation in Yugoslavia: a study in economic geography. *LONDON (LSE) D 1960.*

339. **MACDONALD, M. B.** Economic development in the backward regions of Yugoslavia, 1953–64. *OXFORD D 1968.*

340. **BENSON, L.** Class, party and the market in Yugoslavia, 1945–1968. *KENT D 1973.*

341. **ŠIŠEVIĆ, B.** Postwar development of Yugoslavia and its regions. *STRATHCLYDE D 1976.*

342. **PROUT, C.** The operation, performance, and evolution of the Yugoslav socialist market system between 1965 and 1974 in the context of federal and republican economic policy. *OXFORD D 1978.*

343. McGLUE, D.   Regional economic policy and regional economic development: the case of Yugoslavia. *SUSSEX D 1980.*

344. RIDLINGTON, S. J.   A survey and reappraisal of wage and price inflation in Yugoslavia, 1955–78. *OXFORD MP 1981.*

345. RAKOVIĆ, M.   The economic disintegration of Yugoslavia. *CAMBRIDGE D 1998.*

346. BEHAN, J.   Yugoslav hyper-inflation: 1992–94 [NCR]. *TC DUBLIN ML 2001.*

6. EDUCATION, YOUTH, SPORT

General and Comparative

347. TUREK, A.   The language method of J. A. Comenius with special reference to the *Janua linguarum reserata. DURHAM MEd 1951.*

348. SADLER, J. E.   The concept of universal education according to J. A. Comenius. *LONDON (EXTERNAL) D 1967.*

349. DOBBIE, A. M. O.   *Panorthosia, or Universal Reform*, by John Amos Comenius, translated from Latin with introduction and commentary. *GLASGOW ML 1972.*

350. BULMORE, B. M.   Moravian education at Fulneck schools, Yorkshire, in the eighteenth and nineteenth centuries. [Includes a chapter on Comenius]. *MANCHESTER D 1992.*

351. LACZIK, A.   School choice from the perspectives of the parents: case studies in Hungary and Russia. *OXFORD D 2005.*

Albania

352. LITA, Z.   Teacher education in Albania: past, present, future. *OPEN D 2003.*

Belarus

353. YAKAVENKA, H.   The role of host educators in the transfer of international knowledge into the education sector within Belarus. *MANCHESTER METROPOLITAN D 2006.*

Bulgaria

354. NEDEVA, M.   Strategies for change: a comparative analysis of the national research system of Bulgaria and the national research system of Britain. *MANCHESTER D 1997.*

355. GIRGINOV, V. G.   Bulgarian sports policy in the 20th century: a strategic relations perspective. *LOUGHBOROUGH D 2000.*

356. SMITH, C. J.   The reform of vocational education and training in Bulgaria. *NOTTINGHAM D 2003.*

357. MICHAIL, D.   Educational disadvantage, trilingualism and social change: the Pomaks of Greek Thrace [NCR]. *LONDON (LSE) D 2004.*

Central and Eastern Europe (see also under individual countries)

358. **TEMPLE, P. R.** Social capital and institutional change in higher education: the impact of international programmes in Eastern Europe. *LONDON (INST EDUC) EdD 2004.*

Czechoslovakia

359. **HUGHES, Z.** Pre-school child care and education in present-day Czechoslovakia: contribution of family and society. *LANCASTER D 1983.*

360. **DIMOND, M. J.** The rise and fall of the falcon: the Sokol gymnastics movement in Czech and Czechoslovak politics, 1862–1955. *WALES (SWANSEA) D 2003.*

Hungary

361. **BALARABE, M.** Motivation and academic attainment among British, Hungarian and Nigerian secondary school pupils. *EDINBURGH D 1989.*

362. **SOLA, Y.** Improving a good school: multi-stakeholder perspectives — England and Hungary. *LEICESTER EdD 2000.*

363. **WEDELL, M.** Managing educational change in a turbulent environment: the ELTSUP project in Hungary 1991–1998. *GLAMORGAN D 2000.*

364. **BALASSA, K.** An investigation into cooperative and collaborative partnerships in Hungarian teacher education. *GLAMORGAN D 2002.*

365. **BUDAI, I.** Some dilemmas in the development of social work education in Hungary. *BOURNEMOUTH D 2004.*

366. **HALÁPI, M.** Ways of improving the teaching of writing in English as a Foreign Language in Hungarian secondary education [NCR]. *GLAMORGAN D 2006.*

367. **MOLNAR, G.** Fighting global uncertainties: a case study of the post-communist migrations of Hungarian professional footballers. *LOUGHBOROUGH D 2006.*

Kosovo

368. **KOSTOVICOVA, D.** The politics of identity and space: Albanian-language education in Kosovo, 1992–1998. *CAMBRIDGE D 2002.*

Latvia

369. **KERSH, N.** Processes of transition in education in Latvia: aspects of policy reforms and development with particular reference to financing and privatisation. *OXFORD D 2000.*

Poland

370. **MALECKA, M. M.** The curriculum of pupils with moderate learning difficulties at secondary level in a small number of special and ordinary schools in France, England and Poland. *NOTTINGHAM D 1989.*

371. **LEWICKI, T.** Theatre / drama in education in the United Kingdom, Italy and Poland. *DURHAM D 1995.*

372. **KRUCZEK-STEIGER, E. A. E.** The Rroma and education. A historical introduction to and a critical comparison of current educational provision for the Rroma in Poland and the United Kingdom. *LOUGHBOROUGH D 1999.*

373. **McMANUS, C.** Democratic consolidation in Poland: Polish higher education as an instrument of democratisation, 1989–1998. *GLASGOW D 1999.*

374. **PIMM, A.** Social and political change in Poland and its influence on foreign language teaching with special reference to the Teaching of English as a Foreign Language. *BIRMINGHAM MP 2001.*

375. **WIŚNIEWSKA, S.** Struggling for change: provision for the professional development of foreign language teachers of young learners in Bydgoszcz, Poland. *NOTTINGHAM D 2004.*

376. **FINKELSTEIN, L.** History of the Rabbinical School of Warsaw from its establishment in 1826 to its closure in 1863. *OPEN D 2005.*

377. **PAWLACZEK, Z.** Physical education in post-communist Poland: a transitory journey. *DURHAM D 2005.*

Romania

378. **VLĂSCEANU, L.** Decision and innovation in the Romanian educational system: a theoretical exploration of teachers' orientation. *LONDON (INST EDUC) D 1976.*

379. **MacGREGOR-HASTIE, R. A. N.** A history of education in Romania. *HULL D 1977.*

380. **ILIES, B. G.** The attitudes towards foreigners of a group of Romanian learners of English and their understanding of foreign cultures. *LANCASTER D 2002.*

381. **ALLEN, J. H. T.** The role of the university manager in a period of change: the case of Romania. *BRISTOL DEd 2005.*

Russia *(see also USSR)*

382. **HANS, N.** History of Russian educational policy, 1801–1917. *LONDON (SSEES) D 1926.*

383. **PILKINGTON, H.** Russia's youth and its culture: a nation's constructors and constructed. *BIRMINGHAM D 1993.*

384. **WEBBER, S. L.** All change? School, reform and society in Russia, 1991–1996. *EXETER D 1997.*

385. **ROSSITER, A. E.** The process of change in classroom practice: a study of change in the teaching of English in post-communist Russia. *BIRMINGHAM D 1999.*

386. **SCHWEISFURTH, M.** A tale of twelve teachers: education and democratisation in Russia and South Africa. *WARWICK D 2000.*

387. **CLARK, A. R.** Higher education reforms in the Russian Federation: institutional and labour market responses. *HERIOT-WATT D 2001.*

388. **TOULTSEVA-MORRIS, V. B.** Innovative trends in higher education in the transition to the market in Russia. *KEELE MP 2001.*

389. **PETROV, G. G.** Decentralisation and re-centralisation in post-1991 Russian higher education: a case study of the Republic of Sakha and Yakutsk State University. *LONDON (INST EDUC) D 2005.*

390. **HAGEN, U.** Heads negotiating school based management in the 1990s: Russian, Norwegian and Scottish stories of change. *LONDON (INST EDUC) D 2006.*

391. **MYCOCK, A.** Post-imperial citizenship and national identity: a comparative study of citizenship and history education in Britain and the Russian Federation. *SALFORD D 2006.*

392. **PENN, J.** Social work in Russia: pedagogy and practice [NCR]. *BATH MP 2006.*

393. **POBEREJNAIA, O. N.** Civic education and the problem of 'imitative modernization' in Russia. *MANCHESTER D 2006.*

Slovakia *(see also Czechoslovakia)*

394. **THOMAS, D.** Culture, ideology and educational change: the case of English language teachers in Slovakia. *LONDON (INST EDUC) D 1999.*

Slovenia

395. **TRATNIK, M.** A comparative analysis of selected aspects of educational change: Slovenia and England. *LONDON (INST EDUC) D 1996.*

396. **ERČULJ, J.** School culture in Slovene primary schools: aspects of the local and the global. *MANCHESTER METROPOLITAN D 2003.*

USSR *(see also Russia)*

397. **KATZ, Z.** Party-political education in Soviet Russia. *LONDON (LSE) D 1957.*

398. **PLOSS, S. I.** The organization of Soviet youth: a history of the All-Union Leninist Communist League of Youth (Komsomol). *LONDON (SSEES) D 1957.*

399. **BRUCE, S. M.** The Commissariat of Education under Lunacharsky (1917–1921). *OXFORD D 1969.*

400. **GRANT, N.** Teacher training in the USSR and Eastern Europe in the post-War period, 1945–1966. *GLASGOW D 1969.*

401. **HOWARD, J. B.** Changing opinions in the Soviet Union about American educational thinkers, 1920–1970. *LONDON (INST EDUC) D 1975.*

402. **O'DELL, F. A.** Soviet child socialisation: children's literature: a case study. *BIRMINGHAM D 1975.*

403. **RIORDAN, J.** Sport in Soviet society: development and problems. *BIRMINGHAM D 1975.*

404. **DUNSTAN, N. J.** Paths to excellence and the Soviet school, with special reference to the period 1958–73. *SHEFFIELD D 1978.*

405. **CANTELON, H.** The social reproduction of sport: a Weberian analysis of the rational development of ice hockey under scientific socialism in the Soviet Union. *BIRMINGHAM D 1981.*

406. **SENTER, C.** The contribution of youth organisations to the educational / socialisation process in the Soviet Union. *HULL MP 1981.*

407. **HAYHOE, R. E. S.** German, French, Soviet and American university models and the evaluation of Chinese higher education policy since 1911. *LONDON (INST EDUC) D 1984.*

408. **Turnbull, M.**   Soviet education and manpower policies in the 1950s. GLASGOW ML 1985.

409. **Aly, A. K. M.**   Political education in Egypt, with reference to England and the Soviet Union. DURHAM D 1986.

410. **Crotty, J. W.**   Professional training and élite identification in sport in the USSR and England. BRADFORD MP 1987.

411. **Evans-Worthing, L. J.**   Physical education for Soviet children and teacher and coach education. BRADFORD D 1987.

412. **Munske, B.**   Images of the enemy — the presentation of the Soviet Union with special reference to selected history textbooks. LANCASTER MP 1987.

413. **Shaw, K. E.**   Change in the Soviet education system: some factors associated with the 1984 reforms. EXETER D 1987.

414. **Settle, A. J.**   Athletics in the Soviet Union [...] with particular attention to the education of coaches and the preparation of élite athletes. BRADFORD MP 1988.

415. **Firth, V. E.**   Moral, political, atheistic/religious education in the Soviet Union and England and Wales. LANCASTER MP 1989.

416. **Suddaby, A.**   The common curriculum and slow learners: an English perspective on Soviet psychopedagogy. LONDON (INST EDUC) MP 1989.

417. **Salwen, R. T.**   Sport and perestroika: the professionalisation of Soviet big-time sport. OXFORD MP 1990.

418. **Bryce, W. J.**   Weightlifting in the USSR and CIS 1917–1992. BRADFORD D 1993.

419. **Blackford, L.**   Musical education in the Soviet Union. SURREY MP 1996.

420. **Fürst, J. C. A.**   Stalin's last generation: youth, state and Komsomol, 1945–1953. LONDON (LSE) D 2003.

421. **Partlett, W.**   Schools as laboratories of revolutionary humanism: Russian revolutions and S. T. Shatskii's rural schools, 1905–1932. OXFORD D 2006.

7. ENERGY

Azerbaijan

422. **Köksal, S.**   Oil pipelines in the CIS: Azeri-Turkish relations. LONDON (GOLDSMITHS) D 2004.

Caucasus (see also under individual countries)

423. **Karagiannis, E.**   The geopolitics of oil transportation in the Caucasus region. HULL D 1999.

424. **Adeebfar, T.**   Geopolitical dimensions of the main export pipeline in the Caspian region: the Baku-Tibilis-Ceyhan pipeline and the events of 11 September 2001. KENT D 2003.

425. **Domjan, P.**   The political and economic impact of energy investment in the Caspian. OXFORD MP 2003.

Central and Eastern Europe *(see also under individual countries)*

426. **Wito, A. G.** Electricity trade in Central Europe [Poland, Hungary and the Czech and Slovak Republics]. EDINBURGH D 1996.
427. **Urbanski, P. T.** Electricity price regulation in the transition economy. LONDON (IMPERIAL) D 2003.

Hungary

428. **Leach, M. A.** Energy sector strategies in Eastern Europe: modelling technological change and policy options [with a case study of Hungary]. LONDON (IMPERIAL) D 1995.

Lithuania

429. **Pasukeviciute, I.** An economic analysis of the impact of EU accession upon crude oil and oil production policy in Lithuania. PLYMOUTH D 2003.

Romania

430. **Pearton, M.** The oil industry in Roumania, 1895–1948: a study in the relationship between the Roumanian state and private capital. LONDON (LSE) D 1965.

Russia *(see also USSR)*

431. **Coopersmith, J. C.** The electrification of Russia, 1880–1925. OXFORD D 1985.
432. **Zaitsev, A.** Gas strategy for Russia, with special reference to the West European market. ABERDEEN ML 1993.
433. **Seck, A. B.** Financing upstream oil and gas ventures in the transitional economies of the former Soviet Union: a study of foreign investment and associate risks. DUNDEE D 1997.
434. **Considine, J. I.** The evolution of the Russian oil industry (1860–2012): a search for a long-run crude oil supply forecasting model. ABERDEEN D 1999.
435. **Seligman, B. J.** Key factors influencing the reliability of trunk gas pipelines in the West Siberian North. CAMBRIDGE D 1999.
436. **Lisurenko, M. A.** Corporate governance, resources and strategy: case of the privatised Russian coal mining enterprises. NOTTINGHAM MP 2002.
437. **Nygaard, C. A. B.** The Russian oil industry in transition — institutional and organisational reform. GLASGOW D 2003.
438. **Sim, L. -C.** The changing relationship between the state and the oil industry in Russia (1992–2004). OXFORD D 2005.
439. **Spatharou, A. D.** Russian oil multinationals: the politics of internationalisation, 1992–2002. CAMBRIDGE D 2005.
440. **Yenikeyeff, S. M.** Bringing the regions back in? Federal corporate groups vs. regional elites in the Russian oil sector. OXFORD D 2005.

South Eastern Europe (see also under individual countries)

441. **WILSON, D. H.**   Information systems strategy in the electricity supply industries of Romania and Bulgaria. EDINBURGH D 1997.

Soviet Bloc

442. **PARK, J. D.**   The oil and gas industries of the Soviet Union and Eastern Europe in relation to the Comecon energy balance and the world petroleum market. GLASGOW D 1977.

443. **WATERMAN, G. J.**   Nuclear energy in the Soviet Union and Eastern Europe, 1917–1976. BIRMINGHAM D 1981.

USSR (see also Russia)

444. **RADFORD, E. A. B.**   Modern developments in the Soviet oil industry. LONDON (LSE) D 1963.

445. **WILSON, D. C.**   The Soviet fuel-energy balance. BIRMINGHAM D 1979.

446. **HISLOP. J. E.**   An example of extraterritoriality in postwar international economic relations: the Siberian pipeline conflict. OXFORD MP 1985.

447. **RYDING, H.**   District heating in the Soviet Union. BIRMINGHAM D 1987.

448. **RICKS, R. A.**   The Siberian pipeline dispute of 1982. OXFORD MP 1988.

449. **DJAMARANI, S. M.**   Local interest representation in Soviet industrial decision-making: development of West Siberian gas resources 1966–1985. LONDON (LSE) D 1989.

450. **PAIK, K. -W.**   Russian and Chinese oil and gas policies in Northeast Asia: international political consequences and implications. ABERDEEN D 1993.

451. **EVTUSHENKO, N.**   The influence of the economic changes on the coal mining industry during Soviet and post-Soviet period and their impact on mining communities in Siberia. NOTTINGHAM MP 2001.

8. FINANCE, BANKING, INVESTMENT

Belarus

452. **KOROSTELEVA, J. A.**   Financial development in transition economies: a case study of Belarus. BATH D 2006.

Bulgaria

453. **PROCOPIS, I.**   Investments of Greek firms in Bulgaria. OXFORD MP 1997.

454. **DILOVA-KIRKOWA, S.**   Banking reforms in transition economies: the case of Bulgaria. BIRMINGHAM D 2000.

455. **O'SULLIVAN, K.**   The effects of financial structure in a transaction cost analysis in the Bulgarian economy. MANCHESTER D 2000.

456. BITZENIS, A. Foreign direct investment (FDI) during the transition from a planned to a market economy: the case of Bulgaria (1989–2001). GLASGOW D 2003.

Central and Eastern Europe *(see also under individual countries)*

457. NUTI, D. M. Problems of investment planning in socialist economies. CAMBRIDGE D 1970.

458. DOUGLAS, R. M. Foreign direct investment in Central Europe: the case of insurance. BRISTOL MP 1993.

459. SCHÜTTE, T. Optimal intertemporal bank lending and firm restructuring policies with applications to Eastern Europe. HERIOT-WATT D 1995.

460. ALI, S. British direct investment in Central Europe: an anlaysis of the motivation and strategies of British firms in Hungary, Poland and the Czech Republic. BRADFORD D 1996.

461. MEYER, K. F. E. Determinants of direct foreign investment in transitional economies in Central and Eastern Europe. LONDON (LBS) D 1996.

462. IMPAVIDO, G. Essays in asymmetric information: institutional response in financial markets with applications to the transition economies of Eastern Europe. WARWICK D 1997.

463. PYE, R. B. K. Foreign direct investment in Central Europe (the Czech Republic, Hungary, Poland, Romania and Slovakia): a study of major Western investors. CITY D 1997.

464. PETRICK, K. J. The role of the banking system in the transitional economies of Hungary and the Czech Republic. LEEDS D 1998.

465. SEVIC, Z. Restructuring banks in Central and East European countries as part of macroeconomic changes towards market-orientated economies. DUNDEE D 1998.

466. SINGH, R. Financial restructuring of transition economies in Central and Eastern Europe. LONDON (BIRKBECK) D 1998.

467. CHAE, S. H. The transfer of Korean passenger car production to East Central Europe: the case of direct investment by Daewoo Motor [in Poland and Romania]. LONDON (UCL) D 1999.

468. NESTOROVA, P. The determinants of foreign direct investment during transition from a centrally-planned to a market economy: the cases of Bulgaria and Hungary. SUSSEX D 1999.

469. ALLEN, M. German direct investment in Central and Eastern Europe. OXFORD MP 2000.

470. CARTY, R. Strategic alliances in emerging markets: an investigation of the effects of culture and emerging market characteristics on the performance of acquisitions in Eastern Europe. CITY D 2000.

471. KASCH-HAROUTOUNIAN, M. Transition equity markets of Central Europe: volatility, predictability, integration [Hungary, Poland and Czech Republic]. CITY D 2000.

472. KOMINEK, Z. W. Speculation and distribution of returns: a simulation and empirical study [with special reference to Poland and Hungary]. LEICESTER D 2000.

473. KONOPIELKO, Ł. Protectionism and reforms in the banking sectors of the Eastern European countries. LONDON (UCL) D 2000.

474. **SOKALSKA, M.** Essays on emerging capital markets in Central and Eastern Europe [Czech Republic, Hungary, Poland]. *CAMBRIDGE D 2000.*

475. **STANCIU, L.** Multinational investment in East Central Europe between 1918–1948. *READING D 2000.*

476. **ASSENOV, I.** Capital account liberalisation and foreign investment in transition economies. *OXFORD MP 2002.*

477. **MANEA, I. C.** Multinational enterprises' strategies and their implications for the processes of transformation and development in Central and Eastern European transition economies. *READING D 2002.*

478. **SCOTT-GREEN, S.** Foreign bank entry into the markets of Poland, Hungary and the Czech Republic. *LEEDS D 2002.*

479. **STOIAN, C. R.** The interplay between foreign direct investment, security and European integration by comparing Poland and Romania. *KENT D 2003.*

480. **GALLAGHER, M.** An analysis of banking efficiency in Central and Eastern Europe. *TC DUBLIN ML 2004.*

481. **DEVIĆ, A.** Essays on corporate finance and ownership in Eastern Europe. *CAMBRIDGE D 2005.*

482. **ZSCHAU, A. Y.** A comparative profile of the Kaliningrad (Russia) and Gdańsk (Poland) regions as investment environments for foreign small to medium-sized enterprises [...]. *OXFORD D 2005.*

Czech Republic

483. **LOW, H.** The role of government in the presence of imperfect capital markets: applications to the Czech Republic. *OXFORD MP 1995.*

484. **DAVIES, E. M. M.** The formation of British-Czech joint ventures: an evaluation of processes and motives during a period of transition to a market economy. *HUDDERSFIELD D 1997.*

485. **GOWER, P. W.** Banking development in the Czech Republic: an analysis of credit allocation. *SUSSEX D 1997.*

486. **ER, M.** An evaluation of financial sector restructuring in the Czech Republic. *BIRMINGHAM D 2001.*

Hungary

487. **TAKSZ, I.** The role of foreign direct investment in economic transition: the case of Hungary, 1989–1993. *OXFORD MP 1994.*

488. **WANG, Z. Q.** Foreign investment and economic development: empirical evidence from Hungary and China. *LIVERPOOL D 1995.*

Kazakhstan

489. **CHARMAN, K. P.** The structure and characteristics of international joint ventures in Kazakhstan. *LONDON (LBS) D 1999.*

Poland

490. **LEBLANC, B. P.** Investment and industrialisation in Poland, 1946–1956. OXFORD D 1964.

491. **PODOLSKI, T. M.** The role of bank credit in financing state enterprises in a socialist economy, with special reference to Poland. BIRMINGHAM D 1970.

492. **YIP, A.** Foreign banks and the banking reforms of Poland: a study of the twinning programme. OXFORD MP 1995.

493. **HEWELT, P. W.** Deregulation and the crisis in transitional banking systems in traditional and newly-established market economies [with special reference to Poland]. NOTTINGHAM TRENT D 1996.

494. **YAU, L.** Simulation analysis of learning and expectations in the stock exchange: a case study of the Warsaw Stock Exchange (WSE). LEICESTER D 1996.

495. **PAWLOWSKA, A. E.** Bank financing of small and medium size enterprises: an empirical investigation of credit rationing in Poland (1989–1995). BIRMINGHAM D 1997.

496. **SHIELDS, K. K.** An econometric analysis of financial markets in Eastern Europe: the case of Poland. LEICESTER D 1998.

497. **AL-JAWHARY, A. G.** Entry strategies for foreign investment and MNCs in transitionary and emerging markets: the case of the top foreign investors in Poland. SHEFFIELD D 1999.

498. **BOUADZE, L.** The essence of banking reforms in a transition economy: the experience of Poland. OXFORD MP 1999.

499. **MAJEROWSKA, E. M.** Portfolio allocation problems and quantity constraints: an analysis of the Warsaw Stock Exchange. LEICESTER D 1999.

500. **DITTSCHAR, B.** The adaptation vs. standardisation paradigm in international financial services marketing: a qualitative analysis focusing on Western banks and their Polish partners. BRUNEL D 2001.

501. **FEAKINS, M. A.** Access to capital for small and medium-sized enterprises in Poland: banks, decisions and economic development in post-socialism. OXFORD D 2001.

502. **FLOYD, D. J.** The impact of the main types of FDI activity on the transition process of the Polish economy. READING MP 2002.

503. **HARDY, J. A.** An institutionalist analysis of foreign investment in Poland: Wrocław's second great transformation. DURHAM D 2002.

504. **CHIDLOW, A.** The motives determining the inflow of foreign direct investment into a transition economy: a study of the Republic of Poland. STAFFORDSHIRE D 2006.

Russia (see also USSR)

505. **READING, P.** Cooperative banking in rural Russia, 1865–1917. BIRMINGHAM D 1986.

506. **GURUSHINA, N.** British private capital exports to late Imperial Russia. OXFORD D 1995.

507. **HOTHERSALL, D. J.** Lending policy in the Russian banking system: government credit, credit to enterprises and corporate governance (1992–1994). OXFORD MP 1996.

508. **SPENCER, T. V.** The emerging property market in Russia. MANCHESTER D 1997.

509. **BARZ, M.**   Foreign direct investment and technology transfer: the case of Russia. SUSSEX D 1998.

510. **BATJARGAL, B.**   New entrepreneurs in post-Soviet Russia. OXFORD D 1998.

511. **JESCHE, K.**   Foreign direct investment in the Tsarist and transitional market economies in Russia: a comparison of its roles and significance. OXFORD MP 1998.

512. **KALEMA-BYAGAGAIRE, V.**   Management and changing uses of credit by selected banks in the former Soviet Union during the years 1991–1996. LONDON (LBS) D 1998.

513. **WILLER, D.**   The development of equity capital markets in transition economies: privatisation and shareholder rights [with special reference to Russia]. LONDON (LSE) D 1998.

514. **CLARK, B.**   The determinants and impact of foreign direct investment in Russia. BRUNEL D 2001.

515. **DE ROSA, D.**   Overdue payments and financial survival strategies in Russian and Ukrainian industry. TC DUBLIN ML 2001.

516. **KOZACHOK, I.**   Setting up and development of interbank financial markets in Russia. MANCHESTER D 2001.

517. **TAYLOR, G. P.**   Entrepreneurship in Novgorod the Great [from 1991] [NCR]. BRUNEL D 2001.

518. **IPPOLITO, F.**   The banking sector rescue in Russia: a missed window of opportunity? [NCR]. OXFORD MP 2002.

519. **SURKOVA, M. A.**   Assessing political risk of investment in the Russian economy. CAMBRIDGE D 2002.

Slovenia

520. **WONG, K. J.**   The inflow of foreign direct investment (FDI) to transition economies: the case of Slovenia. EAST ANGLIA MP 2005.

South Eastern Europe (see also under individual countries)

521. **SALAVRAKOS, I. -D.**   An economic business strategy analysis of joint ventures between Greek enterprises and enterprises in the Balkan countries and Russia, from the Greek parent company perspective. ST ANDREWS D 1997.

522. **SYKIANAKIS, N.**   Foreign direct investment decision making: a case study of a Greek company in the Balkans [NCR]. MANCHESTER D 2002.

523. **CHOROMIDES, C. C.**   Foreign direct investment and Greek companies' internationalisation strategies in the Balkans. EDINBURGH D 2003.

Ukraine

524. **BRIDGEWATER, S.**   The entry mode choices of multinational corporations in turbulent markets: the case of Ukraine. WARWICK D 1995.

525. **BAGRIY, A. I.**   Formation, function and development of the banking system of Ukraine. LOUGHBOROUGH MP 2002.

USSR *(see also Russia)*

526. **CHANDRA, N. K.**   Some problems of investment in a socialist economy, with special reference to the USSR and Poland. *LONDON (LSE) D 1965.*

527. **CAWOOD, M. H.**   Investment decisions in resource development: a comparative study of private corporations and Soviet planning. *LONDON (UCL) D 1976.*

528. **HARRISON, J. W.**   Commercial-financial dealings between the USSR and market-type economies, with special reference to Soviet banking, maritime and trading operations in the West. *GLASGOW D 1978.*

529. **DYKER, D. A.**   The planning of investment in the Soviet Union. *SUSSEX D 1979.*

530. **INCOOM, S. E. K.**   Banking and credit in the USSR, 1917–1937. *BIRMINGHAM MP 1981.*

531. **DONNELLY, J. T.**   The obstacles and uncertainties of joint venturing in the Soviet Union. *OXFORD MP 1991.*

532. **RYAN, J.**   Ideology and Soviet relations with the IMF and World Bank. *OXFORD MP 1991.*

533. **AXELROD, S. J.**   The Soviet Union, the IMF and the World Bank, 1941–1947: from inclusion to abstention. *BIRMINGHAM D 1994.*

534. **PRILL, O.**   Financial sector reform in the Soviet Union / Russia since 1987: options and consequences. *OXFORD D 1995.*

Yugoslavia *(see also under former republics)*

535. **HAVRANEK, V.**   Some aspects of Yugoslav investment policy, 1952–1965. *LONDON (LSE) MP 1975.*

536. **SIMPSON, A.**   The role of the financial system in the development of socialist Yugoslavia to 1965. *OXFORD MP 1980.*

537. **ARTISIEN, P. F. R.**   Joint ventures in Yugoslav industry: an empirical investigation of private foreign investment by Western multinational companies [...] (1968–1980). *BRADFORD D 1982.*

538. **CONNOCK, M. B.**   The effect of labour management on investment policy in developing countries, with special reference to Yugoslavia. *LONDON (LSE) D 1983.*

9. GENDER STUDIES

Azerbaijan

539. **HEYAT, F.**   Career, family and femininity: Sovietisation among Muslim Azeri women. *LONDON (SOAS) D 1999.*

Bosnia-Herzegovina

540. **LINDSEY, R.**   Nationalism and gender: a study of war-related violence against women [with special reference to Bosnia and Croatia]. *SOUTHAMPTON D 2000.*

541. **Hayes, N.** Bosnian women's experience of war, loss and resettlement. LEICESTER DClinPsy 2005.

Bulgaria

542. **Petkova, B.** Cultural discourses and 'womanhood' in Bulgaria before and after Perestroika. BIRMINGHAM D 1996.

Central and Eastern Europe (see also under individual countries)

543. **Djorić, G.** Gender content of social policy changes in East Central Europe since 1989. OPEN MP 2000.

544. **Chiva, M. -C.** Patriarchal transitions: women and democratisation in Hungary and Romania. MANCHESTER D 2002.

545. **Töke, L.** 'Paradoxes to live with': a feminist approach to Eastern European women's films. OPEN MP 2003.

546. **Dumbrell, A. E.** Empowerment in transition: questions of potentiality and women's organisations in Poland and Czechoslovakia. SUSSEX MP 2004.

Czech Republic

547. **Robinson, L. C.** Czech feminism, 1848–1914. LONDON (SSEES) D 1980.

548. **Indruchová, L.** Discourses of gender in pre- and post-1989 Czech culture. LANCASTER D 2002.

549. **Read, R.** Gender and authenticity in a post-socialist institution [in the Czech Republic]. MANCHESTER D 2002.

Hungary

550. **Corrin, C.** The situation of women within Hungarian society. OXFORD D 1987.

551. **Maltby, T.** Women, pensions and social dependency in Britain and Hungary, 1945–1990. SHEFFIELD D 1993.

552. **Jentsch, B. E. K.** Grounds of earnings determination in the new Hungary — the gender dimension. EDINBURGH D 1997.

553. **Lee, S.** Women and transition: a case study of social policy effects in Hungary (1989–1996). ESSEX D 1998.

554. **Barát, E.** A relational model of identity: discoursal negotiations for non-oppressive power relations in (researching) Hungarian women's life narratives. LANCASTER D 1999.

555. **Kalocsai, C.** Conflicts among lesbian representations in Hungary. OPEN MP 1999.

Jews

556. **Porter, C.** Biology as destiny: Jewish women in the Holocaust. NEWCASTLE ML 1993.

Kazakhstan

557. SHREEVES, R. Gender issues in the development of rural areas in Kazakhstan. WOLVERHAMPTON D 2005.

Kosovo

558. SHARAPOV, K. A gender analysis of post-conflict reconstruction in Kosovo: women's access to decision making. GLASGOW D 2006.

Kyrgyzstan

559. JOHNSON, E. Alternative access: mail order brides on the internet. A study of Russian women in Kyrgyzstan. OXFORD MP 1999.

560. HANDRAHAN, L. M. Gendering United States democratic assistance in Kyrgyzstan: understanding the implications and impact of gendered ethnicity. LONDON (LSE) D 2001.

Macedonia

561. THIESSEN, I. T'Ga za Jug — waiting for Macedonia. The changing world of young female engineers in the Republic of Macedonia. LONDON (LSE) D 1999.

Poland

562. READING, A. Socially inherited memory, gender and the public sphere in Poland. WESTMINSTER D 1996.

563. BARRY, T. M. Women and transition in Poland. MANCHESTER MP 2000.

564. SIMPKIN-JAMES, L. Women and the rise of Solidarity in Poland. LEEDS D 2001.

565. KRAMER, A. -M. C. Reproduction and the making of politics in the 'New Poland': gender, nation and democracy in the Polish abortion debate. WARWICK D 2003.

Romania

566. JIANU, A. Women and society in the Romanian principalities 1750–1850. YORK D 2003.

567. SOREA, D. Reading a text on the male body from a British magazine: Romanian female students' social schemata and perceptions of masculinity. LANCASTER D 2004.

Russia (see also USSR)

568. KNIGHT, A. W. The participation of women in the revolutionary movement in Russia from 1890 to 1914. LONDON (LSE) D 1977.

569. EDMONDSON, L. H. Feminism in Russia, 1900–1917. LONDON (SSEES) D 1981.

570. THIELE, E. V. Women and crime in late Imperial Russia. OXFORD MP 1989.

571. LONERGAN, J. M. L. Mikhailov and Russian radical ideas about women, 1847–1865. BRISTOL D 1995.

572. Ó RIAIN, H. C.   Feminism, education and the Russian revolutionary movement 1865–1885. *TC DUBLIN ML 1996.*

573. RENDELL, I.   Sex differences in work attitudes in Northern Ireland, Russia and Japan. *ULSTER MP 1996.*

574. SCHMIDT, R.   On their own terms: gender, discrimination and the role of grassroots women's organisations in contemporary Russian society. *BRADFORD D 1997.*

575. HARDEN, J.   Gender and work in Soviet Russia: the medical profession. *STRATHCLYDE D 1998.*

576. KOROVUSHKINA, I.   Marriage, gender, family and the Old Believer community, 1760–1850. *ESSEX D 1998.*

577. ZHURAVSKAYA, G.   Love as an ideology: the reflections on 'sexual crisis' in Alexandra Kollontai's writing. *OPEN MP 1998.*

578. HILLYAR, A.   Revolutionary women in Russia, 1870–1917. *SOUTHAMPTON D 1999.*

579. ISSOUPOVA, O.   Motherhood and Russian women: what it means to them, and their attitudes towards it. *MANCHESTER D 2000.*

580. RANGER, C. M.   Friendly enemies: Blake, Bakhtin, feminism. *ESSEX D 2000.*

581. BEIGULENKO, Y. V.   Women's experience of home, homelessness and home ownership in Moscow after the Soviet Union. *BRISTOL D 2002.*

582. LODERSTEDT, K.   Post-socialist women in management; a comparative study of women managers in West German companies expanding in Russia and Eastern Germany during the 1990s. *BIRMINGHAM D 2004.*

583. BANTING, M. L.   On seeing, gender and homosexuality: a St Petersburg adventure. *MANCHESTER D 2005.*

584. KANJI, S.   Poverty, inequality and livelihoods: lone mothers and their children in Russia. *LONDON (LSE) D 2005.*

Serbia

585. KEKIĆ, R.   Women, work and the family: changes in gender relations, employment and the family in Belgrade. *LONDON (LSE) D 2000.*

586. JARIĆ, I.   The construction of hegemonic female gender roles in the process of societal deconstruction: women's magazine *Bazar* (Serbia 1979–1999). *OPEN MP 2004.*

South Eastern Europe *(see also under individual countries)*

587. BOSKOVIK, A.   Constructing gender in contemporary anthropology [with ethnographic examples from Slovenia and Macedonia]. *ST ANDREWS D 1997.*

588. MILEVSKA, S.   Gender difference in the Balkans. *LONDON (GOLDSMITHS) D 2006.*

USSR *(see also Russia)*

589. HEITLINGER, A.   Women and social change in socialist societies, with special reference to the Soviet Union and Czechoslovakia. *LEICESTER D 1977.*

590. ALLOTT, S.   Women in the Soviet countryside: towards an analysis of women's roles in rural development in the USSR. *BRADFORD D 1984.*

591. **Browning, G. K.** A consideration of the relationship between the status of women in the USSR and their position in the political leadership, with special reference to the role of Soviet women's groups in raising women's political consciousness. *CNAA (SOUTH BANK POLY) D 1985.*

592. **Evans, J.** Women and family policy in the USSR, 1936–1941. *BIRMINGHAM D 1987.*

593. **Attwood, L.** The new Soviet man and woman: sex-role socialisation in the Soviet Union. *BIRMINGHAM D 1988.*

594. **McDermid, J.** The evolution of Soviet attitudes towards women and the family. *GLASGOW D 1988.*

595. **Kirkham-Lebel, L.** The politics of alienation: current women's issues in the Soviet Union. *OXFORD MP 1991.*

596. **Ilič, M.** Soviet women workers and protective labour legislation, 1917–1941. *BIRMINGHAM D 1996.*

Yugoslavia *(see also under former republics)*

597. **Stanley, P.** Mass rape in war: feminist thought and British press representations of the Balkan conflict, 1991–1995. *WALES (ABERYSTWYTH) D 2002.*

598. **Zadel, A.** Structuring 'nationalist rape': sexual violence in the Yugoslav wars of secession. *OXFORD MP 2003.*

10. GEOGRAPHY, ENVIRONMENT

Bosnia-Herzegovina

599. **Özerdem, A.** An approach to sustainable recovery of urban water supplies in war-affected areas with specific reference to the Tuzla region of Bosnia and Herzegovina. *YORK D 1998.*

Bulgaria

600. **Tejada, M. S.** The unattainability of closure: Bulgaria's democratic consolidation and the Kozloduy nuclear power plant. *OXFORD MP 2004.*

601. **Tejada, M. S.** A history of Bulgaria's environmental movement. *OXFORD D 2006.*

Central and Eastern Europe *(see also under individual countries)*

602. **Pickvance, K.** Environmental movements in Eastern Europe: a comparative study of Hungary and Russia. *KENT D 1995.*

603. **Bektashi, L.** Emerging strategic environmental assessment in Central and Eastern Europe and the newly independent states: driving forces and future integration. *MANCHESTER D 2006.*

Croatia

604. SLADOVIĆ, V. J. R.   Aspects of environmental management problems in the Croatian Adriatic region. BRADFORD MP 2000.

Czech Republic

605. CARTER, F. W.   An industrial geography of Prague: 1848–1921. LONDON (UCL) D 1979.

606. JEHLIČKA, P.   A comparative investigation into the dynamics of environmental politics in Western and Eastern Europe 1988–1993 with special reference to the Czech Republic. CAMBRIDGE D 1998.

607. RIEUWERTS, J. S.   Lead contamination and bioavailability in two industrial towns in the Czech Republic. LONDON (IMPERIAL) D 1998.

608. STEEDMAN, J. M.   An economic analysis of air pollution control in transition economies [with a case study of North Bohemia]. HERIOT-WATT D 1998.

609. BAYER, S. C.   Cleaning up the furnace: patterns of environmental management in the British, Czech and German steel industries. SUSSEX D 2001.

610. SURAPIPITH, V.   Air pollution in northern Czech Republic. EAST ANGLIA D 2002.

611. JEHLICKOVA, B.   The future of biomass as a renewable energy resource in the Czech Republic: the case of waste wood. OPEN MP 2003.

Hungary

612. SWAIN, A.   A geography of transformation: the restructuring of the automotive industry in Hungary and East Germany, 1989–1994. DURHAM D 1996.

613. WEST, E. L.   The environmental programme for the Danube River Basin: an evaluation of Phase I using the policy networks approach [with the role of Hungary as a case study]. BRISTOL D 1998.

614. BIROL, E.   Valuing agricultural biodiversity on home gardens in Hungary: an application of stated and revealed preference methods. LONDON (UCL) D 2004.

Kazakhstan

615. BASABIKOVA, M.   Environmental factors affecting contractor take in emerging countries and a comparison of upstream accounting in Kazakhstan and the UK. DUNDEE D 2002.

Latvia

616. SMITH, G. E.   The Latvian nation: a study in the geography of political integration. GLASGOW D 1978.

Lithuania

617. VYCIUTE-LATSANOVSKY, D.   Understanding wetland management in Lithuania: social, economic, political and ideological context. LONDON (R HOLLOWAY) D 2004.

Moldova

618. CASHIN, S. M. The application of high-resolution imagery and Geographical Information Systems in cadastral mapping: a case study of the Republic of Moldova. *CAMBRIDGE D 2004.*

Poland

619. MAZOWIECKI, M. The political geography of the Poland/USSR boundary of 1945. *LONDON (BIRKBECK) MP 1972.*

620. KARPOWICZ, Z. J. The Polish park system. *BIRMINGHAM D 1987.*

621. RYDER, A. Geographical aspects of reform: growth poles in socialist theory and practice with special reference to Poland. *OXFORD D 1989.*

622. VENEZIANO, F. Environmental issues within the process of integration between Poland and the European Union. *NOTTINGHAM D 2000.*

623. TOWNSEND, E. EU accession: ecological modernisation in Poland. *BATH MP 2002.*

Romania

624. NISTOR, M. M. The development of post-socialist urban areas in Romania. *KENT D 2005.*

Russia (see also USSR)

625. SHAW, D. J. B. Settlement, urbanism, and economic change in a frontier context: the Voronezh Province of Russia, 1615–1800. *LONDON (UCL) D 1973.*

626. PALLOT, J. The geography of enclosure in pre-revolutionary European Russia — Tver', Tula and Samara provinces. *LONDON (UCL) D 1977.*

627. POTTER, S. Eighteenth-century Russian cartography: an aspect of westernisation in Russia. *OXFORD D 1986.*

628. LYNN, N. J. A political geography of the republics of the Russian Federation. *BIRMINGHAM D 1996.*

629. PERROTTA, L. Consumption and urban space in post-Soviet Moscow. *LONDON (LSE) D 1996.*

630. SHAHGEDANOVA, M. Climatology of air pollution in Moscow. *OXFORD D 1996.*

631. TICHOTSKY, J. Natural resources development in the Republic of Sakha: Russia's diamond producing region. *CAMBRIDGE D 1997.*

632. GDANIEC, C. Urban planning and development in Moscow during the economic and political transformation in the 1990s. *BIRMINGHAM MP 1999.*

633. OLDFIELD, J. D. The environmental consequences of societal change in the Russian Federation. *BIRMINGHAM D 1999.*

634. CROTTY, J. The impact of economic transition on pollution control in Russian manufacturing enterprises. *NOTTINGHAM D 2001.*

635. WILSON, E. C. Making space for local voices: local participation in natural resource management, north-eastern Sakhalin Island, the Russian Far East. *CAMBRIDGE D 2002.*

636. **POYNTER, S. E.**   The Neogene evolution of the Amur River and its delta in the Russian Far East. *CAMBRIDGE D 2003.*

637. **WALKER, T. R.**   Terrestrial pollution in the Pechora basin, north-eastern European Russia. *NOTTINGHAM D 2003.*

Serbia

638. **PRODANOVIC, M. P.**   Socio-spatial characteristics of rural and related 'sub-urban' settlements in Serbia. *LONDON (UCL) D 1981.*

639. **GRUBOVIĆ, L.**   Belgrade in transition: an analysis of illegal building in a post-socialist city. *LONDON (LSE) D 2006.*

Slovenia

640. **ANDRIČ, M.**   Transition to farming and human impact on the Slovenian landscape. *OXFORD D 2001.*

Ukraine

641. **NAZAROV, N.**   Development of river pollution control in Ukraine through United Kingdom policy importations. *LONDON (IMPERIAL) D 2001.*

642. **SMITH, S. J.**   Seeking environmental security in Ukraine: reform in selected cases. *LONDON (UCL) D 2003.*

USSR (see also Russia)

643. **ANDRUSZ, G. D.**   Some aspects of housing and urban development in the USSR. *BIRMINGHAM D 1978.*

644. **COONES, P.**   The necessity for determinism in a geographical study of the USSR. *OXFORD D 1981.*

645. **McEVOY, M. B.**   Contemporary developments in Russian nationalism and Soviet environmentalism: a case study. *OXFORD MP 1987.*

646. **HOLT, T.**   The effect of proposed Soviet river diversions in Arctic sea ice processes. *EAST ANGLIA D 1988.*

647. **WHITE, R.**   Air pollution in the former Soviet Union: environmental legacy of a totalitarian state. *SURREY MP 2000.*

Uzbekistan

648. **WEGERICH, K.**   Institutional change in water management at the local and provincial levels in Uzbekistan. *LONDON (SOAS) D 2003.*

Yugoslavia (see also under former republics)

649. **MOODIE, A. E. F.**   The geographical background of political problems associated with the Italo-Jugoslav frontier. *LONDON (BIRKBECK) D 1942.*

650. **GRANZ-BUTINA, D.** The pattern of modern Yugoslav cities: a comparative study of physical and spatial structure in Zagreb and Ljubljana. *CNAA (OXFORD POLY) D 1983.*

11. HEALTH, WELFARE

Albania

651. **GJONÇA, A.** Mortality transition in Albania, 1950–1990. *LONDON (LSE) D 1999.*

Bosnia-Herzegovina

652. **EDMONDS, L. J.** The post conflict integration of persons with disabilities in Bosnia-Herzegovina: the role of community based rehabilitation. *EAST ANGLIA D 2002.*

Bulgaria

653. **BALABANOVA, D. C.** Financing the health care system in Bulgaria: options and strategies. *LONDON (LSHTM) D 2001.*

Central and Eastern Europe (see also under individual countries)

654. **PIKHART, H.** Social and psychosocial determinants of self-rated health in seven countries of Central and Eastern Europe [Russia, Lithuania, Latvia, Estonia, Poland, Czech Republic, Hungary]. *LONDON (UCL) D 2000.*

655. **LINDBERG, G.** Welfare state regimes in East-Central Europe: Western vanity or Eastern reality? A comparative study of the Czech Republic and Hungary. *SUSSEX D 2003.*

656. **REED, T.** The regulation of medicines in Central and Eastern Europe [with case studies of Czech Republic, Hungary and Romania]. *SUSSEX D 2003.*

657. **VANHUYSSE, P.** Divide and pacify: the political economy of the welfare state in Hungary and Poland, 1989–1996. *LONDON (LSE) D 2003.*

658. **WALTON, J.** Continuity or change? The balance of childcare provision in Hungary, Poland, Slovakia and Slovenia 1985–2000. *BATH MP 2003.*

659. **ROSENMÖLLER, M.** Contextual factors of health care reform: the creation of a network of independent physicians in two countries: Czech Republic and Estonia. *LONDON (LSHTM) D 2006.*

Estonia

660. **LANG, K.** Cancer in Estonia. *LONDON (LSHTM) D 2005.*

Hungary

661. **BURG, M. C.** The role of the state in the development of health care in Hungary between 1770–1985. *LONDON (LSE) MP 1989.*

662. **VARVASOVSZKY, Z.** Alcohol policy in Hungary. *LONDON (LSHTM) D 1998.*

663. **VERESS, K.** A framework for informed action: epidemiological approaches to understanding drug use in Hungary. *LONDON (LSHTM) D 2002.*

664. **HOFFER, G.** Defining and exploring the gap in undertaking essential public health functions at local level in Hungary. *LONDON (LSHTM) D 2003.*

665. **SZENDE, A.** Equity in health and health care in Hungary: health status, finance, and delivery of health care. *YORK D 2003.*

666. **GAÁL, P. A.** Informal payments for health care in Hungary. *LONDON (LSHTM) D 2004.*

Kazakhstan

667. **THOMPSON, R.** Informal payments for emergency hospital care in Kazakhstan: an exploration of patient and physician behaviour. *YORK D 2004.*

Kyrgyzstan

668. **NAMAZIE, C. Z.** Welfare and labour markets in transition: the case of the Kyrgyz Republic. *LONDON (LSE) D 2002.*

Latvia

669. **PUTNINA, A.** Maternity services and agency in post-Soviet Latvia. *CAMBRIDGE D 1999.*

Poland

670. **WATSON, M.** The division of labour in child health care: Poland and England & Wales compared. *WARWICK D 1985.*

671. **RUSSELL HODGSON, C.** The provision and uptake of health care in Poland, 1971–1980: an examination of socialist principles in practice. *BIRMINGHAM D 1986.*

672. **BRYKCZYŃSKA, M. M.** Hanna Chrzanowska: portrait of a wise nurse. *LONDON (HEYTHROP) D 2001.*

673. **KLECUN-DĄBROWSKA, E.** Telehealth and information society: a critical study of emerging concepts in policy and practice [in Poland]. *LONDON (LSE) D 2002.*

Romania

674. **MISCA, G. M.** Romania's 'orphans': developmental adjustment of adolescents growing up in childcare institutions in Romania. *NEWCASTLE D 2003.*

675. **PETROVICI, D. A.** A comparative analysis of patterns of food demand in Romania and implications for health and nutrition policy. *NEWCASTLE D 2003.*

Russia (see also USSR)

676. **APPLEBY, J. H.** British doctors in Russia 1657–1807: their contribution to Anglo-Russian medical and natural history. *EAST ANGLIA D 1979.*

677. EISENBARTH, M. Economic transition and the welfare of children in the Russian Federation. OXFORD MP 1995.

678. PROSKURYAKOVA, T. Welfare effects of economic transformation in Russia. OXFORD MP 1995.

679. DENNISON, T. K. Fertility decline in Russia: a cross-sectional study of marital fertility in European Russia, 1897. OXFORD MP 1999.

680. THOMSON, K. R. Services for people with learning difficulties in the Russian Federation: a case study approach to the development of a post-communist welfare system. BIRMINGHAM D 2000.

681. CHUBAROVA, T. V. Occupational welfare in Russia with special reference to health care. LONDON (LSE) D 2002.

682. RICHARDSON, E. C. Health promotion in the field of substance misuse in post-Soviet Russia. BIRMINGHAM D 2002.

683. SMITH, C. The introduction of health insurance in the Russian Federation: an analysis of the reforms in St Petersburg and Volgograd. EDINBURGH D 2002.

684. RUDDY, M. C. Tuberculosis within the prison and civilian sectors of the United Kingdom and Russian Federation. LONDON (KCL) MD 2003.

685. KHLINOVSKAYA ROCKHILL, E. Family discontinuity and 'social orphanhood' in the Russian Far East: children in residential care institutions. CAMBRIDGE D 2004.

686. MAMONOVA, O. N. The self-identity of medical practitioners in Russia in transition. DE MONTFORT MP 2004.

687. RICHTER, K. Household welfare and income shocks: the case of Russia. LONDON (LSE) D 2004.

688. TKATCHENKO, E. V. Exploring the policy process through network analysis: a study of three health policies in Russia. SOUTH BANK D 2004.

689. YURCHENKO, O. V. A sociological analysis of professionalisation of orthodox and alternative medicine in Russia. DE MONTFORT D 2004.

690. HENZE, C. E. Cholera in Saratov, 1892–1910. CAMBRIDGE D 2005.

691. SHAKARISHVILI, G. Analysing the equity of post-Soviet health care systems: evaluation of 1990s health reforms. OXFORD D 2005.

692. BALABANOVA, Y. Tuberculosis in Samara, Russia: diagnosis, epidemiology and risk factors for drug resistance. LONDON (GUY'S, KING'S & ST THOMAS'S MED SCH) D 2006.

693. PERLMAN, F. J. A. Socioeconomic position, self-rated health and mortality in Russia. LONDON (UCL) D 2006.

Slovenia

694. KLAVS, I. National survey of sexual lifestyles and *chlamydia trachomatis* infection in Slovenia. LONDON (LSHTM) D 2002.

Ukraine

695. **Aubrey, J.** An evaluation of the social action process as a mechanism for the transfer of knowledge to facilitate the development of new children's services in Ukraine. DE MONTFORT D 2002.

USSR (see also Russia)

696. **Davis, C. M.** The economics of the Soviet health system: an analytical and historical study, 1921–1978. CAMBRIDGE D 1980.

697. **McKevitt, T.** Medical intervention in pregnancy and childbirth in Britain and the Soviet Union. BIRMINGHAM MP 1982.

698. **Williams, C.** Soviet public health: a case study of Leningrad, 1917–1932. ESSEX D 1989.

699. **Winkelmann, R. A.** Evaluation of cancer surveillance systems in the newly independent states of the former Soviet Union. LONDON (LSHTM) D 1998.

700. **Gilmore, A. B. C.** Tobacco and transition: understanding the impact of transition on tobacco use and control in the former Soviet Union. LONDON (LSHTM) D 2005.

Uzbekistan

701. **Abdullaeva, M.** Women, health and transition in Uzbekistan. KENT D 2004.

702. **Wegerdt, J. F.** Dust exposure and respiratory health in children in Karakalpakstan. NOTTINGHAM D 2004.

12. HISTORY

(For historical treatments of specific subjects,
see the appropriate subject sections)

Albania

703. **Kola, P.** Albania, its isolation and the Albanian national question, with particular emphasis on Kosova, 1941–1992. LONDON (LSE) D 2000.

Armenia

704. **Somakian, M. J.** Tsarist and Bolshevik policy towards the Armenian question, 1912–20. LONDON (SSEES) D 1993.

705. **Malikoff-Missen, L.** Armenia: the struggle for survival. SURREY MP 1999.

706. **Greenwood, T.** A history of Armenia in the seventh and eighth centuries. OXFORD D 2000.

707. **Laycock, J.** Imagining Armenia: Orientalism, history and civilisation. MANCHESTER D 2005.

Azerbaijan

708. DEMIRTEPE, M. T. The quest for a nation-state: the case of Azerbaijan. SHEFFIELD MP 1997.

709. ERGUN, A. State and society in the post-Soviet democratization of Azerbaijan: the republic of old comrades and new citizens. ESSEX D 2002.

Bosnia-Herzegovina

710. OKEY, R. F. C. Cultural and political problems of the Austro-Hungarian administration of Bosnia-Herzegovina, 1878–1903. OXFORD D 1972.

711. BAJRAKTAREVIĆ, M. Bosnia and Hercegovina: acknowledging the past for the sake of the future. SALFORD D 2003.

712. KELLY, R. Liberating memory? The challenges of coming to terms with the past in post-war Bosnia-Herzegovina. BRADFORD D 2003.

Bulgaria

713. GUENTCHEVA, R. P. State, nation and language: the Bulgarian community in the region Banat from the 1860s until the 1990s. CAMBRIDGE D 2001.

Byzantium

714. STEPHENSON, P. A. The Byzantine frontier in the Balkans in the eleventh and twelfth centuries. CAMBRIDGE D 1996.

715. ANDREOU, A. S. Byzantine-Khazar relations c.620–965 [NCR]. OXFORD MP 2000.

Caucasus (see also under individual countries)

716. TCHILINGIRIAN, H. The struggle for independence in the post-Soviet South Caucasus: Karabakh and Abkhazia. LONDON (LSE) D 2003.

Central and Eastern Europe (see also under individual countries)

717. WHEELER, L. M. The SS and the administration of Nazi occupied Eastern Europe, 1939–1945. OXFORD D 1981.

718. HANSEN, P. W. Imperialism, autocracy, nationalism in Eastern Europe: the responses of British radicals, 1900–1914. SHEFFIELD D 1995.

719. BAÁR, M. Historians and the nation in the 19th century: the case of East-Central Europe. OXFORD D 2001.

720. HEALY, J. Central Europe in flux: Germany, Poland and Ukraine, 1918–1922. GLASGOW D 2003.

721. CECERE, G. Maps, frontiers and cultures: defining Europe's Eastern boundaries in the eighteenth century. NUI (DUBLIN) D 2004.

Central Asia *(see also under individual countries)*

722. BURTON, J. A.   Bukharans in trade and diplomacy, 1558–1702. MANCHESTER D 1986.

Croatia

723. DJILAS, A.   Croatian nationalism and Yugoslav unity: the policies of the Communist Party of Yugoslavia towards the Croatian national question, 1919 to 1953. LONDON (LSE) D 1988.

724. TRIFKOVIĆ, S.   The Ustaša movement and European politics, 1929–1945. SOUTHAMPTON D 1990.

725. SIMPSON, C. A.   Pavao Ritter Vitezović [1652–1713]: defining national identity in the Baroque age. LONDON (SSEES) D 1991.

726. BELLAMY, A. J.   A centuries-old dream: the formation of Croatian national identity. WALES (ABERYSTWYTH) D 2001.

727. ROGIĆ, T.   A methodological framework for the recording and evaluation of industrial heritage in Croatia, tested on the example of the tobacco industry. PLYMOUTH D 2006.

Czech Republic *(see also Czechsoslovakia)*

728. ZEMAN, Z. A. B.   The Czechs and the Habsburg monarchy, 1914–1918. OXFORD D 1956.

729. FOWKES, F. B. M.   The policy of the Habsburg monarchy towards the Bohemian question, 1913–1918. LONDON (LSE) D 1967.

730. EVANS, R. J. W.   The court of Rudolf II and the culture of Bohemia, 1576–1612. CAMBRIDGE D 1968.

731. BOSAK, E.   Czech-Slovak relations from 1896 to 1914. LONDON (SSEES) D 1982.

732. OPAČIĆ, Z.   Charles IV and the Emmaus Monastery: Slavonic tradition and Imperial ideology in fourteenth century Prague. LONDON (COURTAULD) D 2003.

Czechoslovakia

733. JOHNSON, S. T.   'A good European and a sincere racist'. The life and work of Professor Charles Saroléa, 1870–1953. [CS had contacts in Czechoslovakia and Poland]. KEELE D 2001.

734. PERRAULT, M.   Interpreting the break-up of Czechoslovakia, 1992. ST ANDREWS D 2001.

England

735. EVANS, J.   England seen by the seventeenth century Bohemian visitors. WALES (SWANSEA) MP 1993.

Georgia

736. GVOSDEV, N. K.   Alliance or absorption: Imperial perspectives and policies towards Georgia, 1760–1819 [NCR]. *OXFORD D 1995.*

737. BROERS, L.   Containing the nation, building the state: coping with nationalism, minorities and conflict in post-Soviet Georgia. *LONDON (SOAS) D 2004.*

Hungary

738. BARCSAY, T.   The Károlyi revolution in Hungary, October 1918–March 1919. *OXFORD D 1971.*

739. RADY, M. C.   Municipal government and jurisdiction in medieval Hungary: the town of Buda from its foundation to the fifteenth century. *LONDON (SSEES) D 1982.*

740. FAIRLEY, I. A.   Criticism in history: the work of György Lukács, 1902–1914. *YORK D 1992.*

741. MITCHELL, S. M.   The image of Hungary and of Hungarians in Italy, 1437–1526. *LONDON (WARBURG) D 1995.*

742. MARK, J.   An oral history of the 1956 generation: the relationship of the individual towards the state in early communist Hungary. *OXFORD MP 1999.*

743. MARK, J. A.   Divided memory, divided society: an oral history of the Budapest middle class and the communist state 1944–56 [NCR]. *OXFORD D 2002.*

744. NORTON, C. V.   Plural pasts: the role of function and audience in the creation of meaning in Ottoman and modern Turkish accounts of the sieges of Nagykanizsa. *BIRMINGHAM D 2005.*

Kazakhstan

745. BAKER, J.   Industrialisation and social change in Kazakhstan, 1917–40. *BIRMINGHAM D 1983.*

746. EDMUNDS, T. P.   Nation-building in a multi-ethnic Kazakstan: identity, power and politics. *SHEFFIELD D 1999.*

Kosovo

747. VEREMIS, M.   Between denial and acceptance: an investigation of the Kosovar Albanian's propensity for secession, 1945–1989. *OXFORD MP 1996.*

Latvia

748. KOTT, M.   Towards an uncivil society: reactions to Soviet and Nazi occupation and the demise of civil society in Riga, 1939–1949. *OXFORD D 2006.*

Lithuania

749. WINAWER, H. M.   The Jewish question in the district of Wilno in 1880–1914 [NCR]. *OXFORD BL 1948.*

750. **ASHBOURNE, A. E. G.**   Lithuania: the rebirth of a nation, 1991–1994. *ST ANDREWS D 1997.*

751. **VASILIAUSKAS, A.**   Local politics and clientage in the Grand Duchy of Lithuania 1587–1632. *LONDON (KCL) D 2001.*

Macedonia

752. **TOKAY, A. G.**   The Macedonian question and the origins of the Young Turk revolution 1903–1908. *LONDON (SOAS) D 1994.*

753. **PSILOS, C.**   The Young Turk revolution and the Macedonian question 1908–1912. *LEEDS D 2000.*

754. **MOUSTAKAS, K.**   The transition from late Byzantine to early Ottoman southeastern Macedonia (14th-15th centuries): a socioeconomic and demographic study. *BIRMINGHAM D 2001.*

755. **HARDING, D. S.**   The Macedonian Question: history, politics and human rights. *BIRMINGHAM MP 2004.*

756. **SISTANI, P.**   Native dilemmas: histories, memories and identities in 'Macedonia'. *BRISTOL D 2004.*

Poland

757. **LESLIE, R. F.**   Polish society and the rebellion of November 1830. *LONDON (SSEES) D 1951.*

758. **SKWARCZYŃSKI, P.**   The origin, history and character of the Pacta Conventa of Henry de Valois, King of Poland. *LONDON (SSEES) D 1953.*

759. **GOBLE, R. V.**   Poland's case against the Teutonic Knights at the Council of Constance, 1414–1418. *OXFORD BL 1957.*

760. **POLONSKY, A. B.**   Piłsudski and parliament: the crisis of parliamentary government in Poland, 1922–1931. *OXFORD D 1967.*

761. **ROSEVEARE, I. M.**   Wielopolski's reforms and the January Uprising. *LONDON (SSEES) MP 1967.*

762. **CIECHANOWSKI, J. M.**   The political and ideological background of the Warsaw Rising, 1944. *LONDON (LSE) D 1968.*

763. **ŁUKOWSKI, G. T.**   The Szlachta and the Confederacy of Radom, 1764–1767/68: a study of the Polish nobility. *CAMBRIDGE D 1976.*

764. **BROWN, M. L.**   The Polish question and public opinion in France, 1830–1846. *CAMBRIDGE D 1977.*

765. **SIEBEL-ACHENBACH, S.**   The social and political transformation of Lower Silesia, 1943–1948. *OXFORD D 1987.*

766. **TOMASZEWSKI, G. M.**   Polish 'normalization': the links between foreign and domestic policy in Poland, 1981–1987. *GLASGOW D 1989.*

767. **DEMUNCK, M. -F.**   War for peace? The unwilling odyssey and exile of Józef S., a Polish citizen, 1939–1989. *BRADFORD MP 1990.*

768. **FROST, R. I.**   The Northern War and the crisis of government in the Polish-Lithuanian Commonwealth, 1655–1658. *LONDON (SSEES) D 1990.*

769. SURASZKA, W.   Centre and provinces in Poland: 1944–1989. OXFORD ML 1991.

770. BUTTERWICK, R. J.   Stanisław August Poniatowski, his circle and English political culture. OXFORD D 1993.

771. SMITH, P. V.   Crusade and society in Eastern Europe: the Hospital and Temple in Poland and Pomerania (1145–1370). LONDON (SSEES) D 1995.

772. NOBLE, A. J.   Propaganda, morale and flight: the Eastern provinces of the German Reich, summer 1944 to spring 1945. LEEDS D 1999.

773. TENDYRA, B. I.   General Sikorski and the Polish government in exile 1939–43: a study of Polish internal émigré politics in wartime. LONDON (LSE) D 1999.

Russia (see also USSR)

774. DUNLOP, D. M.   The history of the Jewish Khazars. GLASGOW DL 1955.

775. HOLMES, J. W. N.   The fall of Novgorod the Great. NOTTINGHAM D 1955.

776. TOKMAKOFF, G. B.   A political evaluation of P. A. Stolypin, 1906–11. LONDON (SSEES) D 1963.

777. DUKES, P.   The Russian nobility and the Legislative Commission of 1767. LONDON (SSEES) D 1964.

778. HANEY, J. V.   Maxim the Greek and the intellectual movements of Muscovy. OXFORD D 1970.

779. McKEAN, R. B.   Russia on the eve of the Great War: revolution or evolution? EAST ANGLIA D 1972.

780. DIMNIK, M.   The life and assassination of Mikhail of Chernigov: an investigation of the sources. OXFORD D 1976.

781. HARGIN, J. C. M.   Muscovy in the Time of Troubles as seen through the diary of Stanisław Niemojewski. GLASGOW ML 1976.

782. DEJEVSKY, N. J.   Novgorod in the early Middle Ages: the rise and growth of an urban community. OXFORD D 1977.

783. SOBEL, L.   Early princely authority in Sweden, Pomerania and Novgorod: a comparative study. LEEDS D 1977.

784. LIEVEN, D. C. B.   The Russian establishment in the reign of Nicholas II: the appointed members of the State Council, 1894–1914. LONDON (SSEES) D 1979.

785. CHERFAS, T. J.   The Third Element and social activities: Russia in the 1890s. OXFORD MP 1980.

786. FRANKLIN, S.   Byzantine historiography in Kievan Russia: a study in cultural adaptation. OXFORD D 1981.

787. WALDRON, P. R.   The Stolypin programme of reform, 1906–1911, with special reference to local government and religious affairs. LONDON (SSEES) D 1981.

788. BARRICK, C. L.   Andrey Yurievich Bogolyubsky: a study of the sources. OXFORD D 1984.

789. DAVIES, M. F. S. R. J. D.   William Gerhardie: a critical biography. CAMBRIDGE D 1986.

790. MYLES, J. E.   The Muscovite ruling oligarchy 1547–1564: its composition, political behaviour and attitudes towards reform. OXFORD D 1987.

791. **BIRKETT, K. E.** The Decembrists in Siberia 1826–1856. *GLASGOW ML 1988.*

792. **CAHALL, C. A.** Paul Miliukov and Liberal tactics. *OXFORD MP 1991.*

793. **HUGHES, M. J.** Moscow Slavophilism 1840–1865: a study in social change and intellectual development. *LONDON (LSE) D 1991.*

794. **SMELE, J. D.** White Siberia: the anti-Bolshevik government of Admiral Kolchak, 1918–1920. *WALES (SWANSEA) D 1991.*

795. **WARTENWEILER, D. M. T.** The Russian university and the emergence of civil society: 1905–1914. *OXFORD MP 1992.*

796. **BROWN, S. P.** Russian church and state influence on nineteenth century Siberian and Russian American colonization. *OXFORD MP 1993.*

797. **HERD, G. P.** General Patrick Gordon of Auchleuchries: a Scot in seventeenth century Russian service. *ABERDEEN D 1994.*

798. **O'ROURKE, S.** Warriors and peasants: the contradictions of Cossack culture 1861–1914. *OXFORD D 1994.*

799. **WILLS, R.** The Jacobites and Russia, 1715-1750. *OXFORD D 1994.*

800. **VOLKOV, V. V.** The forms of public life: the public sphere and the concept of society in Imperial Russia. *CAMBRIDGE D 1995.*

801. **WARTENWEILER, D. M. T.** Civil society in Russia, 1905–1914: academic contributions to the theory and practice of an emancipated society. *OXFORD D 1995.*

802. **LANDIS, E. -C.** Anti-Bolshevism and the origins of the Antonov movement: the Tambov countryside through Revolution and Civil War. *CAMBRIDGE D 1998.*

803. **JONES, R.** Harbin as a Russo-Chinese city 1917–1931. *OXFORD MP 2000.*

804. **LEE, W. C.** Grand ducal role and identity as a reflection on the interaction of state and dynasty in Imperial Russia. *LONDON (UCL) D 2000.*

805. **WERRETT, S. R. E.** An odd sort of exhibition: the St Petersburg Academy of Sciences in enlightened Russia. *CAMBRIDGE D 2000.*

806. **ASSA, N. V.** Authority, society and justice in late Imperial Russia: the case of the Ruling Senate and Zemstvos. *LONDON (UCL) D 2001.*

807. **KOCOUREK, K. A. M.** T. G. Masaryk's *The Spirit of Russia*: Slavophilism, the depiction of the Slav and the construction of a theoretical nation [NCR]. *OXFORD MP 2001.*

808. **BAKER, H. S.** Nicholas II and the Khodynka coronation catastrophe, May 1896: a study of contemporary responses. *LEEDS D 2002.*

809. **SHAKIBI, Z. P.** The King, the Tsar and the Shah: agency and the making of revolution in Bourbon France, Romanov Russia and Pahlavi Iran. *LONDON (LSE) D 2002.*

810. **SKYNER, L.** The separation and consolidation of land ownership in pre 1917 and post 1985 Russia. *CAMBRIDGE D 2002.*

811. **SMIRNOVA, L. I.** Comb-making in medieval Novgorod (950–1450): an industry in transition. *BOURNEMOUTH D 2002.*

812. **GAMSA, M.** The Russian-Chinese encounter in Harbin, Manchuria, 1898–1932. *OXFORD D 2003.*

813. **KARASAC, H.** The torn countries, Turkey and Russia in the post-Cold War era: in search of identity. *KEELE D 2003.*

814. **RENDLE, M.** Identity, conflict and compromise: the Russian nobility, 1917–1924. *EXETER D 2003.*

815. **ADAMOVSKY, E. A.** Land of absence: liberal ideology, the image of Russia and the making of Western identity. *LONDON (UCL) D 2004*.

816. **ALSTON, C.** Russian liberalism and British journalism: the life and work of Harold Williams (1876–1928). *NEWCASTLE D 2004*.

817. **TAZMINI, G.** Parallel histories of development and revolution in Russia and Iran: modernisation from above, revolution from below. *KENT D 2004*.

818. **WELLS, B. T.** The Union of Regeneration: the anti-Bolshevik underground in revolutionary Russia, 1917–1919. *LONDON (QUEEN MARY) D 2004*.

819. **CHARAP, S.** Inside out: Russian domestic political change and foreign policy evolution from Yeltsin to Putin. *OXFORD MP 2005*.

820. **AYLETT, K. S.** Images of Constantinople in Russian history. *LEEDS D 2006*.

821. **KEENAN, P.** Creating a 'public' in St Petersburg, 1703–1761. *LONDON (UCL) D 2006*.

Serbia

822. **FORMHALS, P. K.** Matija Ban and his contribution to the Yugoslav idea, 1844–1862. *NOTTINGHAM D 1980*.

823. **TODOROVIĆ, J.** Entrances and departures: the origins and functions of the ephemeral spectacle in the Archbishopric of Karlovci (1690–1790). *LONDON (UCL) D 2004*.

Slovakia *(see also Czechoslovakia)*

824. **APPLEBY, B. L.** The relations between the Slovaks and the central government of the First Czechoslovak Republic, 1918–1938. *GLASGOW ML 1975*.

825. **BABEJOVÁ, E.** Space, politics and identity in Bratislava, 1867–1914. *CAMBRIDGE D 2000*.

Slovenia

826. **CARMICHAEL, C. D.** Scientific theory, peasant practice and cultural change: interpretations of Lake Cerknica (Slovenia) since the sixteenth century. *BRADFORD D 1993*.

827. **SOVIČ, S.** Peasant communities, local economies and household composition in nineteenth-century Slovenia. *ESSEX D 2001*.

828. **BAJT, V.** From nation to statehood: the emergence of Slovenia. *BRISTOL D 2003*.

829. **BOBIČ, P.** History and myth: nationalism and social memory in Slovenia. *OXFORD MP 2003*.

South Eastern Europe *(see also under individual countries)*

830. **PUŞCARIU, A.** The Danube: its history and its economic and political development. *BIRMINGHAM D 1928*.

831. **METCALF, D. M.** Coinage in the Balkan peninsula, AD 1100–1350: a study of colonial monetary affairs. *CAMBRIDGE D 1959*.

832. **POULTER, A. G.** Moesia Inferior and the Lower Danube, Domitian to Heraclius. *LONDON (INST ARCHAEOL) D 1983*.

833. **Heather, P. J.** The Goths and the Balkans, AD 350–500. *OXFORD D 1987.*

834. **Batty, R. M.** The peoples of the Lower Danube and Rome: settlement, mobility and imperialism to the end of the second century AD. *OXFORD D 1991.*

835. **Sarantis, A. C.** The Balkans during the reign of Justinian: barbarian invasions and imperial responses. *OXFORD D 2005.*

Turkmenistan

836. **Saray, M.** The Turkmens in the age of imperialism: a study of the Turkmen people and their incorporation into the Russian Empire. *WALES (SWANSEA) D 1978.*

Ukraine

837. **Saunders, D. B.** The political and cultural impact of the Ukraine on Great Russia, c.1775–c.1835. *OXFORD D 1978.*

838. **Velychenko, S.** The influence of historical, political and social ideas on the politics of Bohdan Khmelnytsky and the Cossack officers between 1648 and 1657. *LONDON (LSE) D 1981.*

839. **Darch, C. M.** The Makhnovshchina, 1917–1921: ideology, nationalism and peasant insurgency in early twentieth-century Ukraine. *BRADFORD D 1994.*

840. **Vogelsang, I. B.** Narratives of history in Ukraine. *MANCHESTER MP 1996.*

841. **Kuzio, T.** Ukraine: state and nation building. *BIRMINGHAM D 1998.*

842. **Pirie, P. S.** History, politics and national identity in Southern and Eastern Ukraine. *LONDON (SSEES) D 1998.*

843. **Charipova, L. V.** The Library of the Kiev Mohyla Academy (1632–1780) in its historical context. *CAMBRIDGE D 1999.*

844. **Ostryzniuk, E. M.** Revolution in the Ukrainian village: the trans-Dnipro countryside of Ukraine during the Russian revolution from spring 1917 to spring 1919. *CAMBRIDGE D 2000.*

845. **Vogelsang, I. B.** Constructions of the past and trauma in Simferopol, Crimea. *MANCHESTER D 2002.*

846. **Richardson, T. L.** Odessa, Ukraine: history, place and nation-building in a post-Soviet city. *CAMBRIDGE D 2005.*

USSR (see also Russia)

847. **Barber, J. D.** The Bolshevization of Soviet historiography, 1928–1932. *CAMBRIDGE D 1972.*

848. **White, J. D.** M. N. Pokrovsky and the origins of Soviet historiography. *GLASGOW D 1972.*

849. **Talks, F. L.** André Gide's companions on his journey to the Soviet Union in 1936: Jacques Schiffrin, Eugène Dabit, Louis Guilloux, Jef Last and Pierre Herbart. *WARWICK D 1987.*

850. **Thorson, C.** Permitted dissent in Soviet historiography in the Brezhnev era. *OXFORD ML 1987.*

851. **Boekee, N.** Victor Serge and history. *STIRLING ML 1988.*

852. **WEISSMAN, S. C.** Victor Serge: political, social and literary critic of the USSR, 1919–1947. *GLASGOW D 1991.*

853. **COHEN, J. H.** The historiography of the late Stalin period: a case study of war veterans through oral history [NCR]. *OXFORD ML 1993.*

854. **BARON, N.** Sources, methods and the practice and malpractice of history: the historiography of the Soviet Union in the 1930s. *OXFORD MP 1995.*

855. **KERR, S. M.** An assessment of a Soviet agent: Donald Maclean 1940–1951. *LONDON (LSE) D 1996.*

856. **PRITCHARD, G.** German workers under Soviet occupation: working-class politics and Soviet policy in Saxony and Thuringia, 1945–1953. *WALES (SWANSEA) D 1997.*

857. **BARON, N. P.** Soviet Karelia, 1920–1937: a study of space and power in Stalinist Russia. *BIRMINGHAM D 2001.*

858. **LEWIS, D.** Stalinism and empire: Soviet policies in Tuva, 1921–1953. *LONDON (LSE) D 2002.*

859. **MACVARISH, K. A.** Writing the history of the Russian Revolution: historiographical and theoretical approaches. *SUSSEX D 2002.*

860. **TURTON, K.** Forgotten lives: the role of Anna, Ol'ga and Mariia Ul'ianova in the Russian revolution, 1864–1937. *GLASGOW D 2004.*

861. **FLEWERS, P.** The New Civilisation? Assessments of the Soviet Union in Britain, 1929–1941. *LONDON (UCL) D 2005.*

862. **CHILVERS, C. A. J.** 'Something wicked this way comes': the Second International Congress of the History of Science and Technology and the Russian delegation [NCR]. *OXFORD D 2006.*

Uzbekistan

863. **YALÇIN, R.** The rebirth of Uzbekistan: politics, economy and society in the post-Soviet era. *EXETER D 1998.*

Yugoslavia *(see also under former republics)*

864. **CSERENYEY, G.** The assassination of King Alexander of Yugoslavia in 1934, and the political background of the crime. *LONDON (LSE) D 1954.*

865. **SHEPHERD, D.** The royal dictatorship in Yugoslavia, 1929–1934, as seen from British sources. *DURHAM ML 1975.*

866. **HEPBURN, P. A.** The failure of centralism: the centralist system and political relations in Yugoslavia, 1918–1939, with special reference to the period 1934–1939. *LONDON (LSE) D 1987.*

867. **WAINWRIGHT, E.** The sanctity of frontiers: historical development and the case of Yugoslavia 1991–1992. *OXFORD D 1999.*

868. **DJOKIĆ, D.** The politics of agreement: the evolution of the Serb-Croat question in the Kingdom of Yugoslavia 1929–1941. *LONDON (UCL) D 2004.*

869. **KUŠEN, D.** Models of perception in interpreting the conflict in the former Yugoslavia: a cross-cultural study. *LONDON (KCL) D 2005.*

13. INDUSTRY

Austria-Hungary

870. **SCHULZE, M. -S.** The economic development of Austria-Hungary's machine-building industry, 1870–1913. *LONDON (LSE) D 1993.*

Central and Eastern Europe *(see also under individual countries)*

871. **MUELLER, J. D.** Process plant contractors in the Former Soviet Union and Central / Eastern Europe. *DE MONTFORT D 1995.*

872. **JEONG, J. H.** Operating at the margins of industry and geography: Daewoo Motor's entry into the auto industry in Central and Eastern Europe. *OXFORD D 2001.*

Czech Republic

873. **KORNELL, K.** Some aspects of the industrial revolution in the Czech Lands of the Austrian Empire in the 19th century. *LONDON (SSEES) MP 1976.*

874. **SMRČEK, L.** Research, development and manufacturing potential of the general aviation aircraft industry in the Czech Republic. *GLASGOW D 1996.*

875. **CARTER, H.** Post-communist enterprise restructuring in the Czech Republic: seven case studies. *ST ANDREWS D 2003.*

Hungary

876. **PORTES, R. D.** Economic decentralization and the industrial enterprise in Hungary, 1957–1968. *OXFORD D 1969.*

877. **SCOTT, J. M.** Northern Ireland and Hungarian manufacturing industry: an examination of the effects of accession of Central and Eastern European countries to the European Union. *ULSTER D 2002.*

Kazakhstan

878. **SHEVCHIK, N.** The effect of location on the performance of Kazakhstani industrial enterprises in the transition period. *READING D 2003.*

Poland

879. **DAWSON, A. H.** The industrial geography of woollen textile manufacturing in Poland after 1870. *LONDON (UCL) D 1967.*

880. **HARRIS, E. E.** Studies in the industrial history of the occupied territories of Russian Poland during the First World War, 1914–1918. *EDINBURGH D 1979.*

881. **TOPOROWSKI, J. M. T.** Sources of disequilibrium in a centrally planned economy: a study of planning, fluctuations, investment and strategy in Polish industry, 1950–1970. *BIRMINGHAM D 1982.*

882. Husan, R. The Polish motor vehicle industry as a case study in Eastern Europe's transition. OXFORD D 1994.

Romania

883. Ibrahim, G. The structural responses of Romanian industries to transition from a planned to market economy. NOTTINGHAM TRENT D 2000.

Russia (see also USSR)

884. Bater, J. H. The industrial geography of St Petersburg, 1850–1914. LONDON (UCL) D 1969.

885. Jones, R. H. Taylorism and the scientific organisation of work in Russia 1910–1925. SUSSEX D 1988.

886. Kiblitskaya, M. Formal and informal relations: comparative case studies of the privatisation of Russian and British railway repair plants. WARWICK D 1997.

887. Bishop, K. The internationalisation process of manufacturing firms in the former Soviet Union. LONDON (UCL) D 2004.

888. Isachenkova, N. An analysis of industrial company failure in the UK and Russia for the 1990s. BRUNEL D 2004.

889. Adachi, Y. Informal corporate governance practices in Russia in the 1990s: the cases of Yukos Oil, Siberian (Russian) Aluminium, and Norilsk Nickel. LONDON (UCL) D 2005.

Slovenia

890. Turk, J. D. Industrial networks in Slovenia. SUSSEX D 2003.

Soviet Bloc

891. Sobell, V. Industrial co-operation and specialisation in Comecon, 1959–80. OXFORD D 1982.

USSR (see also Russia)

892. Seton, F. The social accounts and industrial structure of the Soviet Union (1934). OXFORD D 1954.

893. Hutchings, R. F. D. Aspects of Soviet industrial development: the influence of inherent factors [...]. LONDON (LSE) D 1958.

894. Hill, M. R. Standardisation policy and practice in the Soviet machine tool industry. BIRMINGHAM D 1970.

895. Cooper, J. M. The development of the Soviet machine-tool industry, 1917–1941. BIRMINGHAM D 1975.

896. Lewis, R. A. Industrial research and development in the USSR, 1924–1935. BIRMINGHAM D 1975.

897. Siemaszko, Z. A. Industrial process control in the Soviet Union. BIRMINGHAM D 1976.

898. **Holmes, L. T.**   A comparative study of the governmental, administrative and political aspects of industrial associations in the USSR and the German Democratic Republic. *ESSEX D 1979*.

899. **Kenney, M.**   A reappraisal of the Soviet industrialization debate. *SUSSEX MP 1983*.

900. **Ilič, M. J.**   The development of the Soviet timber industry, 1926–1940. *BIRMINGHAM MP 1986*.

Yugoslavia (see also under former republics)

901. **Kozul, Z. A.**   Innovation and industrial organization: a comparative study of the Italian and Yugoslav furniture industry. *CAMBRIDGE D 1994*.

14. INTERNATIONAL RELATIONS

Albania

902. **Xhudo, G.**   A critique of United States policy with special reference to Albania and the Bosnian crisis. *ST ANDREWS D 1995*.

Armenia

903. **Nassibian, A.**   Britain and the Armenian question, 1915–1923. *OXFORD D 1982*.

Austria-Hungary

904. **Wayper, C. L.**   The relations between Great Britain and Austria-Hungary from the rising in Herzegovina to the Conference of Constantinople [NCR]. *CAMBRIDGE D 1950*.

905. **Gjurgjević, T. V.**   The Friedjung and Vasić trials in the light of the Austrian diplomatic documents, 1909–1911. *OXFORD D 1956*.

906. **Bridge, F. R.**   The diplomatic relations between Great Britain and Austria-Hungary, 1906–12. *LONDON (INST HIST RES) D 1966*.

907. **Armour, I. D.**   Austro-Hungarian policy towards Serbia 1867–1871, with special reference to Benjamin Kállay. *LONDON (SSEES) D 1994*.

Azerbaijan

908. **Poljak, I.**   A small state with big potential: Azerbaijan's foreign policy, with a focus on relations with Russia, 1992–1996. *OXFORD MP 1997*.

909. **Le Cornu, L.**   A small state's struggle for independence in the post-Soviet period: Azerbaijani-Russian relations, 1991–1999. *OXFORD D 2001*.

910. **Mehdiyeva, N.**   Azerbaijan's foreign policy since 1991: a study of geopolitical dynamics [NCR]. *OXFORD MP 2002*.

911. **Mehdiyeva, N.**   Azerbaijan's foreign policy: perceptions and strategic choices of a small state in great power politics, 1991–2003. *OXFORD D 2006*.

Baltic States *(see also under individual countries)*

912. HIDEN, J. W.   German policy towards the Baltic states of Estonia and Latvia, 1920–1926. *LONDON (SSEES) D 1970.*

913. CHILD, V.   Britain and the question of alliance with Russia in 1939: the Baltic States as a gauge of policy. *OXFORD MP 1991.*

914. CHILD, V.   British policy towards the Soviet Union 1939–42, with special reference to the Baltic States. *OXFORD D 1994.*

915. McMANUS, A. P.   Great Britain, the Baltic Republics and the Soviet Union, 1939–1945. *BRADFORD MP 1994.*

916. ZAJANKAUSKAS, L.   Western attitudes towards the annexation of the Baltic states and the re-establishment of their independence, with special reference to Lithuania. *OXFORD MP 1995.*

917. REDMAN, N. H.   Dilemmas of engagement: Estonian, Latvian and Lithuanian policies towards Russia, 1992–1996. *OXFORD D 1999.*

918. SPOHR, A. R. K.   Unified Germany's Ostpolitik, 1990–2000: the Baltic question in European context. *CAMBRIDGE D 2001.*

919. BERGMAN, A.   Adjacent internationalism: the concept of solidarity and post-Cold War Nordic-Baltic relations. *SUSSEX D 2002.*

920. MOLE, R. C. McK.   National identity and foreign policy: perception of self and other in the post-Soviet international relations of the Baltic states, 1991–99. *LONDON (LSE) D 2003.*

Bosnia-Herzegovina

921. ÜNAL, H.   Ottoman foreign policy during the Bosnian annexation crisis, 1908–1909. *MANCHESTER D 1992.*

922. CHAUDHRY, T. S.   The response of the Organization of the Islamic Conference (OIC) to crisis: the case of the Bosnian conflict from 1992 to 1995. *CAMBRIDGE D 1998.*

923. SIEMENS, C. VON   Russia's policy towards the war in Bosnia-Herzegovina (1992–1995). *OXFORD MP 2001.*

924. SAKIC, S.   The impact of international factors on modern state-building in Bosnia and Hercegovina, 1995–2001 [NCR]. *OXFORD MP 2002.*

925. ZAUM, D.   The sovereignty paradox: policymaking by the international community in Bosnia and Herzegovina. *OXFORD MP 2002.*

926. CONSTANTIAN, C. J.   Tracing the shift: understanding the Clinton Administration's abandonment of 'Lift and Strike' [in Bosnia]. *ST ANDREWS MP 2005.*

927. MENDOZA, A. L.   British relations with the USA during the Bosnian war, 1992–1995. *CAMBRIDGE D 2005.*

928. YOSHITOME, K.   The Western order under quasi-multilateralism: the Bosnian conflict and the West. *LEEDS D 2005.*

929. ZAUM, D.   The sovereignty paradox: norms and the politics of statebuilding by the international community [with special reference to Bosnia-Herzegovina, East Timor and Kosovo]. *OXFORD D 2005.*

Bulgaria

930. **STOKES, A. D.**   Russo-Bulgarian relations in the tenth century. *LONDON (SSEES) D 1959.*

931. **DIMITROV, V. T.**   The failure of democracy in Eastern Europe and the emergence of the Cold War 1944–1948: a Bulgarian case study. *CAMBRIDGE D 1997.*

932. **STANKOVA, M.**   Bulgaria in British foreign policy, 1943–1949. *LONDON (LSE) D 1999.*

933. **TREANOR, P. J.**   British policy and Bulgaria, 1918–1919. *LONDON (SSEES) D 1999.*

934. **KATSIKAS, S.**   Foreign policy making in democratizing states: the case of Bulgaria in the 1990s. *LONDON (UCL) D 2006.*

Byzantium

935. **SHEPARD, J.**   Byzantium and Russia in the eleventh century: a study in political and ecclesiastical relations. *OXFORD D 1974.*

936. **SOPHOULIS, P. P.**   A study of Byzantine-Bulgar relations, 775–816. *OXFORD D 2005.*

Caucasus *(see also under individual countries)*

937. **ÇAĞLAYAN, K. T.**   British policy towards Transcaucasia 1917–1921. *EDINBURGH D 1997.*

938. **KÖK, H.**   The effects of the Caspian oil pipeline issue on Russian foreign policy in the Transcaucasus region. *LEEDS D 1999.*

939. **GOL, A.**   The place of foreign policy in the transition to modernity: Turkish policy towards the South Caucasus, 1918–1921. *LONDON (LSE) D 2000.*

Central and Eastern Europe *(see also under individual countries)*

940. **MAASBURG, L. -M.**   Aspects of the Vatican's Eastern European policy, 1939–1958. *OXFORD ML 1980.*

941. **JORDAN, N. T.**   The Popular Front and the dilemmas of French impotence in Central Europe, 1936–1937. *LONDON (LSE) D 1985.*

942. **BÁTONYI, G.**   Britain and Central Europe, 1918–1932. *OXFORD D 1994.*

943. **CADOGAN, T.**   International society theory reassessed: Poland, the Czech Republic, Slovakia, Bulgaria and the Western European society of states, 1991–93. *OXFORD MP 1994.*

944. **NIBLETT, R.**   The European Community and the Central European Three, 1989–92: a study of the Community as an international actor. *OXFORD D 1995.*

945. **MURPHY, A.**   The European Union and the Visegrád states: governance, order and change. *NUI (DUBLIN) D 1996.*

946. **TEWES, H.**   Germany as a civilian power: policies towards the Visegrád countries between 1990 and 1994. *OXFORD MP 1996.*

947. **SHAFFER, M. R.**   European Union decision-making and the Visegráds: a modified liberal intergovernmentalist analysis of the negotiations for the Europe Agreements. *CAMBRIDGE D 1997.*

948. VACHUDOVÁ, M. A.   Systemic and domestic determinants of the foreign policies of East Central European states, 1989–1994. OXFORD D 1997.

949. WOODWARD, S.   No longer the bridge state? Austrian foreign policy towards Central and Eastern Europe after the Cold War. OXFORD MP 1997.

950. ALI, M.   Eastern Europe foreign policy convergence with Western Europe on the Middle East, 1990–1992. EXETER D 1998.

951. DIMITROVA, A. L.   The role of the European Union in the process of democratization in Central and Eastern Europe: lessons from Bulgaria and Slovakia. LIMERICK D 1998.

952. SEDELMEIER, U.   The European Union's integration policy towards the countries of Central and Eastern Europe: collective EU identity and policy paradigms in a composite policy. SUSSEX D 1998.

953. TEWES, H.   Germany as a civilian power: the western integration of East Central Europe, 1989–1997. BIRMINGHAM D 1998.

954. BILČÍK, V.   Eastern enlargement of the European Union: perspectives and role of the East and West German Länder. OXFORD MP 1999.

955. BUBPASIRI, T.   The fifth enlargement of the European Union: the accession of Central and Eastern European countries. EXETER D 1999.

956. GEBHARDT, B.   European identity and the Eastern borderland of the European Union. EDINBURGH D 1999.

957. PAPADIMITRIOU, D. G.   The European Community and the negotiation of the association agreements with the countries of Central and Eastern Europe: a study of bargaining in iterated games, 1990–92. BRADFORD D 1999.

958. RUPP, M. A.   The European Union's pre-accession strategy towards the Visegrád countries: dynamics of economic and institutional integration. LEEDS D 1999.

959. FEUELL, W. L.   Between transformation and accession in Central and Eastern Europe: contradiction and complementarity [with reference to the Czech Republic, Hungary, Poland and Slovakia]. BIRMINGHAM D 2000.

960. LOJKÓ, M.   Britain and Central Europe, 1919–1925 [Hungary, Poland, Czechoslovakia]. CAMBRIDGE D 2001.

961. ZULEEG, F.   The political economy of the accession process: aspirations of European Union membership leading to divergence within Central and Eastern Europe. EDINBURGH D 2001.

962. GRABBE, H. M. C.   Europeanisation through accession: the influence of the European Union in Central and Eastern Europe. BIRMINGHAM D 2002.

963. HOSKINS, J. A.   Britain and Eastern Europe 1914–1929. BIRMINGHAM MP 2002.

964. INGRAM, P. J.   The US Congress and Eastern Europe, 1945–1992: a study of the dynamics of legislative involvement in foreign policy [NCR]. KEELE D 2003.

965. WU, P. -J.   Change and continuity in German foreign policy: a study of German foreign policy in East Central Europe, 1990–2002. LIVERPOOL D 2003.

966. FRANK, M. J.   Britain and the transfer of the Germans from East Central Europe, 1939–47. OXFORD D 2004.

967. STEFFENS, M. J.   EU Eastern enlargement in theory and practice: a policy of administrative conditionality? SHEFFIELD D 2006.

Central Asia *(see also under individual countries)*

968. **YAPP, M.** British policy in Central Asia, 1830–43. *LONDON (SOAS) D 1959.*

969. **MORRIS, L. P.** Anglo-Russian relations in Central Asia, 1873–1887. *LONDON (SSEES) D 1969.*

970. **WILLIAMS, D. S.** Russian policy in Central Asia in the light of the Pahlen Report of 1908–1909. *LONDON (LSE) D 1969.*

971. **TEALAKH, G. O.** The Russian advance in Central Asia and the British response, 1834–1884. *DURHAM D 1991.*

972. **BAL, I.** Turkey's relations with the West and the Turkic republics of the former Soviet Union: the rise of the 'Turkish Model' (1991–1992). *MANCHESTER D 1997.*

973. **DYANAT, M.** The emergence of the new subordinate system in South-West and Central Asia after the collapse of the USSR. *EXETER D 1998.*

974. **MYER, W. D.** Islam and colonialism: Western perspectives on Soviet Asia. *LONDON (SOAS) D 2000.*

975. **FLAKE, L. S.** Central Asian cooperation: the origin and evolution of the Shanghai Five. *OXFORD MP 2003.*

976. **MISDAQ, N. A.** Political frailty, national integration and external interference: causes and consequences of the communist coup and the Soviet invasion of Afghanistan. *SUSSEX D 2003.*

977. **TORJESEN, S.** Challenging the Great Game: actors and independence in Central Asia, 1996–2001. *OXFORD MP 2003.*

Croatia

978. **AUGTER, S.** Negotiating Croatia's recognition: German foreign policy as two level game. *LONDON (LSE) D 2002.*

979. **SUBAŠIĆ, E.** Croatia's foreign policy towards Bosnia and Herzegovina, 1991–1995. *OXFORD MP 2002.*

Czechoslovakia

980. **MANNION, M.** British policy towards Czechoslovakia, 1936–1939. *NEWCASTLE ML 1971.*

981. **VYSNY, M. P.** A study of Czechoslovak-Russian relations, 1900–1914. *MANCHESTER D 1972.*

982. **CALLCOTT, W. R.** British attitudes to the Czechoslovak state, 1914–1938. *NEWCASTLE D 1986.*

983. **PALMER, K. M.** The Runciman mission to Czechoslovakia, 1938. *QUEENS BELFAST D 1990.*

984. **FAWN, R.** Czechoslovak foreign policy, 1989–1992: the problems of translating ideas into policy. *LONDON (LSE) D 1996.*

985. **PROTHEROE, G. J.** Watching and observing: Sir George Clerk in Central Europe 1919–1926. [British Minister to Czechoslovakia, 1919–1926]. *LONDON (EXTERNAL) D 1999.*

986. **WALLAT, J.** The evolution of Czechoslovak foreign and security policy thinking, 1989–1992. *OXFORD MP 1999.*

987. **WALLAT, J.** Imagining a better Europe. The evolution of Czechoslovak/Czech foreign and security policy: from the Warsaw Pact to NATO 1989–1999. *OXFORD D 2001.*

988. **BROWN, M. D.** Dealing with democrats: decision making and policy formation within the British Foreign Office's Central Department with regard to the Czechoslovak political exiles in Britain and the Czechoslovak question, 1939 to 1945. *SURREY D 2003.*

Finland

989. **CHURCHILL, S.** The East Karelian autonomy question in Finnish-Soviet relations, 1917–1922. *LONDON (LSE) D 1967.*

990. **BAYER, J. A.** British policy towards the Russo-Finnish War, 1939–1940. *LONDON (LSE) D 1976.*

991. **ALLISON, R.** Finland's relations with the Soviet Union 1944–1982: neutrality adjusted to security. *OXFORD D 1982.*

992. **AUSTIN, D. F. C.** Finland's approach: the European Union's border with Russia. *LONDON (EXTERNAL) MP 1998.*

Greece

993. **ANGOURAS, V.** The foreign policy of Greece towards its northern frontier problems (1990–93). *EDINBURGH D 1998.*

994. **VOSKOPOULOS, G.** Greece, common foreign and security policy and the European Union [...]. Case studies: the 1991–1995 Yugoslav crisis and the Greek-FYROM dispute over the latter's name. *EXETER D 2000.*

995. **DEGLERI, A.** The road to St Petersburg 1821–1826: the war in Greece and British diplomacy. *EAST ANGLIA MP 2005.*

Hungary

996. **KOVRIG, B.** The United States and the Hungarian revolution of 1956: a case study of American policies towards East Central Europe from 1945 to 1957. *LONDON (LSE) D 1967.*

997. **KABDEBÓ, T. G.** Francis Pulszky's political activities in England, 1849–60. *LONDON (UCL) MP 1969.*

998. **KABDEBÓ, T.** Joseph Andrew Blackwell (1798–1886): his view of Hungary and his diplomatic missions. *MANCHESTER D 1984.*

999. **GLANT, T.** Through the prism of the Habsburg monarchy: Hungary in American diplomacy and public opinion during the First World War. *WARWICK D 1996.*

1000. **KELLY, M. J.** Hungarian integration into the European Union: the implications for Ireland. *TC DUBLIN ML 1998.*

1001. **ANDERSON, T. K.** The Hungarian uprising of 1956 and Soviet foreign policy. *CAMBRIDGE D 1999.*

1002. **SWIFFEN-CZICZOVSZKI, A. V.** Reinventing regional policy in transitional society: Hungary in the European integration process. *CAMBRIDGE D 2002.*

1003. **Pogatza, Z.** The preparedness of Hungary for the Structural and Cohesion Funds. *SUSSEX D 2004.*

1004. **Kotroczo, D. M.** The Hungarian question in British foreign policy, 1848–1867. *BRADFORD D 2006.*

Italy

1005. **Sluga, G. A.** Liberating Trieste 1945–1954: nation, history and the Cold War. *SUSSEX D 1993.*

Kosovo

1006. **Bohm, T.** Kosovo through Russian eyes: the public debate on NATO's intervention [NCR]. *OXFORD MP 2002.*

1007. **Braun, S.** Pacifists at war: the Kosovo diplomacy of the German EU Presidency (1 January–30 June 1999). *OXFORD MP 2002.*

1008. **Levy, L. R.** The Internet and post-conflict peacebuilding: a study with special reference to Kosovo. *BRADFORD D 2004.*

Latvia

1009. **Morris, H. M.** External actors and the evolution of Latvian nationality policy, 1991–1999. *OXFORD D 2001.*

Lithuania

1010. **Kaminskaite-Salters, G.** Post-communist states and international environmental cooperation: a case study of Lithuania [NCR]. *OXFORD MP 2001.*

1011. **Furmonavičius, D.** Lithuania rejoins Europe. *BRADFORD D 2002.*

1012. **Bielkus, Z. E.** Lithuania's post-Soviet transformation: the role of external actors. *OXFORD MP 2005.*

1013. **Baranauskaite, A.** Explaining Lithuania's policy on EU accession, 1991–2003. *OXFORD MP 2006.*

Macedonia

1014. **Goodman, D. B.** The emergence of the Macedonian problem and relations between the Balkan States and the Great Powers, 1897 to 1903. *LONDON (SSEES) D 1955.*

1015. **Livanios, D.** Bulgar-Yugoslav controversy over Macedonia and the British connection 1939–1949. *OXFORD D 1995.*

1016. **Tziampiris, A.** Greece, European political cooperation and the Macedonian question, June 1991–December 1992. *LONDON (LSE) D 1999.*

Poland

1017. **Grace, W. F. F.** Great Britain and the Polish question in 1863 and the Congress Policy of Napoleon III. *CAMBRIDGE D 1925.*

1018. ŚLIWOWSKI, Z.   Polish-Ukrainian relations, 1919–39   [NCR]. OXFORD BL 1947.

1019. KIMMICH, C. M.   The Weimar Republic and the Free City of Danzig: official German attitudes and policies towards Danzig, 1919–1934. OXFORD D 1964.

1020. BRADY, J. J.   The political implications of Polish-American economic relations between 1957 and 1964. LONDON (LSE) D 1967.

1021. BRYANT, R.   Britain and the Polish settlement, 1919. OXFORD D 1968.

1022. NIECKO, M. J. E. C.   Pro-Polish agitation in Great Britain [1832–1867]. LONDON (QUEEN MARY) D 1968.

1023. ZAWADZKI, W. H.   The views of Prince Adam Jerzy Czartoryski on reconstructing Europe (1801–1830). OXFORD D 1973.

1024. RAFFEL, K.   The German march into Prague and the origins of the British guarantee to Poland of March 1939. OXFORD BL 1974.

1025. ŻUR, S.   British policy and the Polish western frontier, 1941–45. LONDON (QUEEN MARY) D 1974.

1026. COUTOUVIDIS, J.   The formation of the Polish government-in-exile and its relations with Great Britain, 1939–1941. KEELE D 1975.

1027. ŻUROWSKI, M. A.   British policy towards the Polish-Soviet border dispute, 1939–1945. LONDON (LSE) D 1975.

1028. FEDOROWICZ, J. K.   Anglo-Polish relations in the first half of the seventeenth century: a study in commercial diplomacy. CAMBRIDGE D 1976.

1029. ANELAY, T. R.   Debate on Yalta: Poland, the Far East and American domestic politics, 1944–1955. KEELE D 1978.

1030. PRAZMOWSKA, A. J.   Anglo-Polish relations, 1938–1939. LONDON (QUEEN MARY) D 1979.

1031. KULINIAK, M. W.   Polish-American relations during the first Reagan presidency. OXFORD MP 1986.

1032. BOGACKI, A. C. J.   Polish communist foreign policy, 1918–1948: internationalism and the national interest. GLASGOW D 1988.

1033. CATTERSON, J. A.   The significance of the Oder-Neisse border in international politics, 1943–1990. OXFORD MP 1990.

1034. DANGELMAYER, A. M.   French foreign policy towards Poland (1989–1993). OXFORD MP 1995.

1035. SJURSEN, H.   Western policy-making in the Polish crisis (1980–83): the problem of coordination. LONDON (LSE) D 1997.

1036. RAMSEY, L. E.   The Polish Europe agreement: an analysis of implementation and implementation theory in European Union external relations agreements. GLASGOW D 1998.

1037. KUO, M. A.   Contending with contradictions: PRC policy towards Soviet Eastern Europe with special reference to Poland, 1953–1960. OXFORD D 1999.

1038. WICKLUM, E.   Britain and the Second and Third Partitions of Poland. LONDON (LSE) D 1999.

1039. LEŚNIEWSKI, P. A.   Britain and Upper Silesia, 1919–1922. DUNDEE D 2000.

1040. MATYLA, A. J.   The Foreign Office and the Warsaw Uprising of 1944. BIRMINGHAM MP 2000.

1041. ZABOROWSKI, M. The Europeanisation of Polish–(West) German relations: from conflict to cooperation 1944–2000. *BIRMINGHAM D 2001.*

1042. GOLONKA, M. M. International regimes and credibility problems: an assessment of the role played by the EU in locking in Polish trade policy reform. *LONDON (LSE) D 2003.*

1043. GORSKA, J. A. Dealing with a juggernaut: analyzing Poland's policy toward Russia, 1989–2003. *OXFORD MP 2003.*

1044. ŁYSZKOWSKA, D. Domestic politics and international bargaining: the case of Polish accession negotiations with the EU. *OXFORD MP 2003.*

1045. DEEGAN, E. M. A puzzle of peace: Poland's Ukrainian policy at the end of the Cold War. *OXFORD MP 2004.*

1046. SAMUR, H. Challenge of identity formation in the European Union within the context of Eastern enlargement: the case of Poland. *MANCHESTER D 2004.*

1047. BEST, U. German-Polish cross-border co-operation and the politics of transgression. *PLYMOUTH D 2005.*

1048. SZOSTAK, R. Europeanisation and the Polish European policy style, 1989–2004. *CAMBRIDGE D 2006.*

Romania

1049. CABOT, J. M. The Rumanian claims in Hungary before the Peace Conference [NCR]. *OXFORD BL 1924.*

1050. FLORESCU, R. R. N. The origins of Anglo-Roumanian relations: British policy and the problem of the Russian protectorate in the Principalities of Moldavia and Wallachia (1821–1854). *OXFORD BL 1950.*

1051. BRAUN, A. Romanian foreign policy under Nicolae Ceauşescu, 1965–1972: the political and military limits of autonomy. *LONDON (LSE) D 1976.*

1052. LUNGU, D. The problem of Soviet-Romanian relations in Romanian foreign policy under Nicolae Titulescu. *LONDON (QUEEN MARY) D 1976.*

1053. COULTER, L. J. F. The involvement of the English Crown and its embassy in Constantinople with pretenders to the throne of the Principality of Moldavia between the years 1583 and 1620 with particular reference to the pretender Stefan Bogdan between 1590 and 1612. *LONDON (SSEES) D 1993.*

1054. PERCIVAL, M. L. British-Romanian relations 1944–65. *LONDON (SSEES) D 1997.*

1055. HAYNES, R. A. Romanian policy towards Germany, September 1936–September 1940. *LONDON (SSEES) D 1998.*

1056. ARNOLD, R. Germany's economic policy and Romania's economic concessions, August 1936–May 1940. *OXFORD MP 2003.*

1057. BARBU, M. -B. The symbolic presence of the United States in Cold War Romania, 1945–1971. *BIRMINGHAM D 2003.*

1058. GEORGESCU, A. -A. Foreign policy change: the case of Romania. *LIMERICK D 2005.*

Russia (see also USSR)

1059. **Morrow, I. F. D.** The Black Sea question during the Crimean War. *CAMBRIDGE D 1927.*

1060. **Gleason, J. H.** British conceptions of Russia and Russian policy, 1837–41: a study of public opinion and foreign policy. *OXFORD BL 1932.*

1061. **Henderson, G. B.** The European Concert, June 1854–July 1855. *CAMBRIDGE D 1934.*

1062. **Koren, W.** A study of the relationship between the diplomatic and commercial policies of France, Germany, Italy, Russia and Austria-Hungary, 1871–1914. *OXFORD BL 1934.*

1063. **Barnett, R. W.** British foreign policy in relation to the Russo-Japanese War [NCR]. *OXFORD BL 1937.*

1064. **Schenk, H. G.** The social and economic background of attempts at a Concert of Europe from 1804 to 1825. *OXFORD D 1943.*

1065. **Adamiyat, F.** The diplomatic relations of Persia with Britain, Turkey and Russia, 1815–1830. *LONDON (LSE) D 1949.*

1066. **Mosse, W. E. E.** English policy and the execution of the Treaty of Paris, 1856–1857. *CAMBRIDGE D 1950.*

1067. **Lewinson, G.** The Russo-German Reinsurance Treaty, 1887–1890. *LONDON (LSE) D 1953.*

1068. **Palmer, A. W.** Lord Salisbury's attempts to reach an understanding with Russia, June 1895–November 1900. *OXFORD BL 1953.*

1069. **Crisp, O.** The financial aspect of the Franco-Russian alliance [1894–1914]. *LONDON (SSEES) D 1954.*

1070. **Quainton, A. C. E.** French policy and the Russian Revolution, 1917–1924. *OXFORD BL 1958.*

1071. **Alder, G. J.** British policy 'on the roof of the world', 1865–95, with special reference to the Anglo-Russian agreement of 1895. *BRISTOL D 1959.*

1072. **Madariaga, I. de** Anglo-Russian relations during the War of American Independence, 1778–83. *LONDON (SSEES) D 1959.*

1073. **Chavda, V. K.** India, Britain, Russia: a study in British opinion, 1838–1878. *LEEDS D 1961.*

1074. **Gwyn, J. R. J.** The place of Russia in British foreign policy, 1748–1756. *OXFORD BL 1961.*

1075. **Hopwood, D.** Russian activities in Syria in the nineteenth century. *OXFORD D 1964.*

1076. **Preston, A. W.** British military policy and the defence of India: a study of British military policy, plans and preparations during the Russian crisis, 1876–1880. *LONDON (KCL) D 1966.*

1077. **Roberts, H. S.** The Franco-Russian alliance, 1894–1904, with special reference to Great Britain. *LONDON (SSEES) D 1966.*

1078. **Simkin. A. P.** Anglo-Russian-American relations in the Far East, 1897–1904. *LONDON (LSE) D 1967.*

1079. **Spring, D. W.** Anglo-Russian relations in Persia, 1909–15. *LONDON (LSE) D 1968.*

1080. **TENGEY, J. G. K.** The United States and the Russian Provisional Government: the special diplomatic mission to Russia in the summer of 1917. *ABERDEEN ML 1969.*

1081. **SCOTT, G. A. K.** The formation of the Turkestan frontier between Russia and China in the eighteenth century. *OXFORD D 1971.*

1082. **SWEET, D. W.** British foreign policy, 1907–1909: the elaboration of the Russian connexion. *CAMBRIDGE D 1971.*

1083. **CHEN, C. -Y.** The development of relations between China and Russia up to the Treaty of Nerchinsk (1652–1689). *OXFORD BL 1973.*

1084. **McFIE, A. L.** The Straits Question, 1908–1936. *LONDON (BIRKBECK) D 1973.*

1085. **HSU, Y. -T.** The Trans-Manchurian Railway [...]; or: procedure and perception in the making of Chinese foreign policy: a study of the 1896 treaty with Russia. *OXFORD BL 1974.*

1086. **THRASHER, P. A.** The diplomatic career of Pozzo di Borgo [1805–1840]. *LONDON (BIRKBECK) D 1974.*

1087. **PEARSE, D. J.** Reactions of British and French people to Russia from 1815 to 1825. *LIVERPOOL D 1975.*

1088. **OSWALD, J. G.** British public opinion on France, the Entente Cordiale, and the Anglo-Russian Entente, 1903–8. *EDINBURGH D 1976.*

1089. **NEILSON, K. E.** Strategy and supply: Anglo-Russian relations, 1914–1917. *CAMBRIDGE D 1978.*

1090. **SIMKIN, J. E.** Anglo-Russian relations in Persia, 1914–1921. *LONDON (LSE) D 1978.*

1091. **SZAMUELY, H.** British attitudes to Russia, 1880–1918. *OXFORD D 1982.*

1092. **TOUSI, R. R.** Political economy of Persia, 1800–1907, with especial reference to British and Russian influence. *BIRMINGHAM D 1982.*

1093. **LAMBERT, A. D.** Great Britain, the Baltic and the Russian War, 1854–1856. *LONDON (KCL) D 1983.*

1094. **TAYLOR, D. J.** Russian foreign policy, 1725–39: the politics of stability and opportunity. *EAST ANGLIA D 1983.*

1095. **BALI, A.** The Russo-Afghan boundary demarcation 1884–95: Britain and the Russian threat to the security of India. *ULSTER D 1985.*

1096. **KENNEDY, C. G.** Muscovy and the Crimean Khanate: an anatomy of diplomatic relations, 1637–1641. *OXFORD ML 1987.*

1097. **KIM, H. -S.** The Port Hamilton affair and Russo-British rivalry in the Far East, 1876–1905. *GLASGOW D 1989.*

1098. **KROL, G.** The northern threat: Anglo-Russian diplomatic relations 1716–1727. *LONDON (LSE) D 1992.*

1099. **NEUMANN, I. B.** The Russian debate about Europe, 1800–1991. *OXFORD D 1992.*

1100. **UNKOVSKAYA, M. V.** Anglo-Russian diplomatic relations, 1580–1696. *OXFORD D 1992.*

1101. **KLUGE, R.** Russian-German relations: images and perceptions. *OXFORD MP 1994.*

1102. **THOMA, K.** Towards a new foreign policy? Russian foreign policy 1992–1994. *OXFORD MP 1994.*

1103. **BEIM, N.** Democratization and Russian foreign policy, 1991–1996. *OXFORD MP 1996.*

1104. **VAILLANCOURT, L. J. J.** The development of relations between Russia and the European Union. *LONDON (SSEES) D 1996.*

1105. **NIZAMEDDIN, T.** Towards a national foreign policy: Russia and the Middle East, 1991–1996. *LONDON (SSEES) D 1997.*

1106. **VOSKRESENSKII, A. D.** Russia and China: problems of continuity and change in inter-state relations. *MANCHESTER D 1997.*

1107. **EDWARDS, P.** British and Austro-Hungarian diplomatic reporting of the problems facing the Russian monarchy 1894–1914. *LEEDS D 1998.*

1108. **VAHID GHARAVI, A.** The Russian ultimatum to Iran in 1911: Anglo-Russian rivalry in the nineteenth and early twentieth centuries in Iran and the emergence of the Third Power strategy. *BRADFORD D 1998.*

1109. **ZASLAVSKY, A.** The Anglo-Russian Entente and the Straits question, 1907–1909. *OXFORD MP 1998.*

1110. **CROW, S. M.** Fragmented diplomacy: the impact of Russian governing institutions on foreign policy, 1991–1996. *LONDON (LSE) D 1999.*

1111. **GHILCHIK, P.** Russian policy towards Iran: 1991–1998. *OXFORD MP 1999.*

1112. **JOHNSON, R.** The Penjdeh crisis and its impact on the Great Game and the defence of India 1885–1897. *EXETER D 1999.*

1113. **LHO, C.** The transformation of South Korea's foreign policy, 1988–1993: Nordpolitik, Moscow and the road to Pyongyang. *OXFORD D 1999.*

1114. **GÖBEL, D.** The politics of the Russian Foreign Ministry, 1906–1914. *OXFORD D 2000.*

1115. **GRANT, T. D.** Recognition and uncertain statehood: international title to territory in the search for settlement of the crisis of Chechen independence. *CAMBRIDGE D 2000.*

1116. **HEADLEY, J. H.** The Russian Federation and the conflicts in former Yugoslavia, 1992–1995. *LONDON (UCL) D 2000.*

1117. **KUHRT, N. C.** Russian policy towards China and Japan in the El'tsin era, 1991–1997. *LONDON (UCL) D 2000.*

1118. **McMAHON, M. A.** Changing relations: Russia's relations with Ukraine and Belarus. *GLASGOW D 2000.*

1119. **PALMER, M. R.** The British nexus and the Russian liberals, 1905–1917. *ABERDEEN D 2000.*

1120. **SAGRAMOSO, D.** Russia's geopolitical orientation towards the former Soviet states: is Russia able to discard its imperial legacy? *LONDON (UCL) D 2000.*

1121. **TOWNSHEND, W. R.** From new world order to superpower accommodations: political realism and Russian-European security: security risks, objectives and strategies. *LANCASTER D 2000.*

1122. **YOUN, I. J.** Russia's foreign policy towards the Korean peninsula under Yeltsin (1991–96). *GLASGOW D 2000.*

1123. **CHEBANKOVA, E. A.** Russia and the European Union: themes and problems [NCR]. *OXFORD MP 2001.*

1124. JACKSON, N. J.   Russian policy towards the CIS, 1991–1996: debates about the political and military involvement in the Moldova-Transdniestria, Georgia-Abkhazia and Tajikistan conflicts. LONDON (LSE) D 2001.

1125. RONTOYANNI, C. H.   Russia's policies towards Belarus and Ukraine: towards integration or disintegration? GLASGOW D 2001.

1126. ZASLAVSKY, A.   The Anglo-Russian Entente: alliance formation and management. OXFORD D 2001.

1127. BÉRARD, E.   Russian policy towards the South Caucasus since 1992 [NCR]. OXFORD MP 2002.

1128. HOLTOM, P. D.   'A litmus test for Europe'?: constructing Kaliningrad's identity in Moscow, Brussels and Kaliningrad. BIRMINGHAM D 2002.

1129. JACOBSOHN, M.   The making of post-Soviet Russian foreign policy towards Israel, 1991–2001: a decade of de-linkage [NCR]. OXFORD MP 2002.

1130. RANGSIMAPORN, P.   Russia's security perceptions and foreign policy towards China (1996–2001). OXFORD MP 2003.

1131. THORUN, C.   Explaining Russian foreign policy in the Far Abroad from 1993 until 1999: the impact of collective ideas. OXFORD MP 2003.

1132. ANGELAKIS, T. G.   The Russian response to NATO expansion: academic influence and foreign policy, 1993–1997. BRADFORD D 2004.

1133. BELOPOLSKY, H.   Active engagement: Russian strategic alignment with challenger states (China, Iran and Iraq), 1992 to 2002. OXFORD D 2004.

1134. MARSDEN, L.   Bill, Boris and US aid: America's attempt to promote democracy in Russia during the Clinton years. OPEN D 2004.

1135. SPENCE, M. J.   The impact of American democracy promotion in post-Soviet Russia, Ukraine and Kyrgyzstan, 1991–2003. OXFORD D 2004.

1136. ZASLAVSKY, I.   Geopolitics, oil and pipelines: US-Russian relations in the Caspian region. OXFORD MP 2004.

1137. ZIEGNER, G.   Developments of Russian foreign policy towards Germany, 1994–2003. OXFORD MP 2004.

1138. BORE, J. H.   Energy versus security: the dynamics behind US-Russian foreign policies in Central Asia and the Caspian Sea basin. BIRMINGHAM MP 2006.

1139. BUKH, A.   Russia and the construction of Japan's identity: implications for international relations. LONDON (LSE) D 2006.

1140. CARY, D. T.   Russian foreign policy towards Turkey, 1992–2002: the role of domestic and international factors. OXFORD MP 2006.

1141. FILIS, C.   Putin's realpolitik: toward a foreign policy of the possible (March 2000–March 2004). READING D 2006.

1142. KEFFERPÜTZ, R.   Bridging the theoretical divide: Russia's foreign policy towards the European Union. OXFORD MP 2006.

1143. KOCHO-WILLIAMS, A. M.   Culture of Russian and Soviet diplomacy: Lamsdorf to Litvinov, 1900–1939. MANCHESTER D 2006.

1144. MOODGAL, R. N.   Russian-Japanese relations: what role for the Far East? LONDON (LSE) D 2006.

1145. **RANGSIMAPORN, P.** Russia as an aspiring great power in East Asia: perceptions and policies (1996–2003). *OXFORD D 2006*.

1146. **THORUN, C.** Explaining change in Russian foreign policy towards the West, 1992–2004: the impact of collective ideas. *OXFORD D 2006*.

Serbia

1147. **MALCOLM-SMITH, E. F.** The international relations of Serbia from 1848 to 1860. *CAMBRIDGE D 1926*.

1148. **STOJANOVIĆ, M. D.** Serbia in international politics from the insurrection of Herzegovina (1875) to the Congress of Berlin (1878). *LONDON (SSEES) D 1930*.

1149. **FRYER, C. E. J.** The British Naval Mission in Serbia, 1914–1916, with special reference to the work of Rear-Admiral E. C. T. Troubridge. *LONDON (EXTERNAL) D 1985*.

Slovakia *(see also Czechoslovakia)*

1150. **AMBROVICSOVA, A.** Did the European Union play an important role after the end of the Cold War? The case of Slovak-EU relations between 1990–1996. *OXFORD MP 1997*.

Slovenia

1151. **SMITH-WINDSOR, B. A.** The European Union's Common Foreign and Security Policy: the engagement of Slovenia 1991–1996. *LEEDS D 1998*.

1152. **RUSSELL, K. A.** Being Slovene at the East-West frontier: negotiating identities in the borderlands. *LONDON (UCL) D 2002*.

1153. **FARO, J.** EU regional policy and contemporary borderland relations between Italy, Slovenia and Austria. *CAMBRIDGE D 2005*.

South Eastern Europe *(see also under individual countries)*

1154. **MACKENZIE, M. H.** The policy of Lord Palmerston in the Near Eastern question [...1830–1841] [NCR]. *OXFORD BL 1928*.

1155. **BOLSOVER, G. H.** Great Britain, Russia and the Eastern Question, 1832–41. *LONDON (SSEES) D 1933*.

1156. **KHAVESSIAN, E.** Britain and the Eastern Question, 1894–1896. *OXFORD BL 1960*.

1157. **MARZARI, F. O.** The Balkans, the Great Powers, and the European War [1939–40]. *LONDON (LSE) D 1966*.

1158. **MAHER, L. A.** Great Britain and the international control of the Danube, 1856–1883: a study of British policy in South-East Europe with particular reference to the European Commission of the Danube. *OXFORD D 1967*.

1159. **COSGRAVE, P. J.** Sir Edward Grey and British foreign policy in the Balkans, 1914–16: a study in war diplomacy. *CAMBRIDGE D 1971*.

1160. **ROOKE, M. J.** The British Government's relations with the states of South-Eastern Europe, 1934–36. *LONDON (LSE) D 1980*.

1161. ANDRICOPOULOS, Y. The Balkan search for security in the face of the disintegration of the structure of Europe after World War One: the Balkan Entente of 1934. *LONDON (BIRKBECK) D 1983.*

1162. TÜRKEŞ, M. Turkish-Balkan relations in the light of the Balkan Entente, 1930–1934. *MANCHESTER MP 1990.*

1163. CHRISTIDIS, G. Turkey and the ex-communist Balkans. An analysis of bilateral relations between Turkey and the ex-communist Balkans after the end of the Cold War, 1990–1992. *EXETER D 1997.*

1164. SCRASE, G. M. Britain, the Balkans and the politics of the wartime alliance: Great Power collaboration and the pre-percentages agreement of May 1944. *SOUTHAMPTON D 1997.*

1165. DEMETROPOULOU, L. The Europeanisation of the Balkans (EU membership aspiration and institutional adaptation in the Balkan countries) [NCR]. *EDINBURGH D 2001.*

1166. KLEINFELD, R. Diplomacy and development: the European Union's efforts to build the rule of law in South Eastern Europe. *OXFORD MP 2002.*

1167. RATTI, L. Italian foreign policy and NATO expansion to the Balkans: an examination of realist theoretical frameworks. *CARDIFF D 2004.*

1168. BECHEV, D. Constructing South East Europe: the politics of Balkan regional cooperation, 1995–2003. *OXFORD D 2005.*

1169. PAPAHADJOPOULOS, D. Dynamics of regionalism in the post-Cold War era: the case of Southeastern Europe. *LONDON (LSE) D 2005.*

1170. EVGENIOS-PANAGIOTIS, M. The formation of the public image of the Balkans in Britain between 1912 and 1945. *SUSSEX D 2006.*

1171. KISSOUDI, P. Greece, Balkan games and Balkan politics in the interwar years (1929–1939). *DE MONTFORT D 2006.*

Soviet Bloc

1172. TARNOFF, C. L. Evolving structures of Great-Power blocs: the USA and Latin America (1901–1975); the USSR and Eastern Europe (1945–1975). *LONDON (LSE) D 1976.*

1173. HANSON, M. The Conference on Security and Cooperation in Europe: the evolution of a code of conduct in East-West relations. *OXFORD D 1992.*

1174. McKEE, F. A. CSCE — an analysis of its origin, evolution and contemporary role. *ST ANDREWS MP 1993.*

1175. PANAGIOTOU, R. A. The European Community's relations with Comecon. *OXFORD D 1993.*

1176. LYONS, A. J. International relations theory and the end of the Cold War: a retrospective step forwards. *ESSEX D 2001.*

Ukraine

1177. BROOKES, C. J. The development of relations between the Russian Federation and Ukraine, 1992–1998: from multilateral divorce to bilateral cooperation. *OXFORD MP 1998.*

1178. **MORONEY, J. D. P.** Ukraine and the new frontier of East-West relations: dynamics of regional and pan-European policy evolution. *KENT D 2000.*

1179. **KHOROSHILOVA, Y.** British and American relations with independent Ukraine, 1917–1921 and 1991–1994. *NORTH LONDON D 2001.*

1180. **PUGLISI, R.** Power to the pragmatists: the role of the economic elite in relations between Russia and Ukraine, 1994–1998. *GLASGOW D 2001.*

1181. **WOLCZUK, R.** Ukraine's foreign and security policy 1991–2000: the regional dimension. *WOLVERHAMPTON D 2001.*

1182. **CRAMME, O.** Europe's challenge in and to the Eurasian order: exploration of diverging EU identities through the prism of EU relations with Ukraine. *LONDON METROPOLITAN D 2006.*

USSR *(see also Russia)*

1183. **KOCHAN, L. E.** German-Russian relations, 1921–1936. *LONDON (LSE) D 1950.*

1184. **WU, A. K.** Aspects of Sino-Soviet relations. *LONDON (LSE) D 1950.*

1185. **FREUND, G.** Germany's political and military relations with Soviet Russia, 1918–1926: from Brest-Litovsk to the Treaty of Berlin. *OXFORD D 1955.*

1186. **SHERMAN, G.** Soviet policy and Eastern Germany, 1952–1954. *OXFORD BL 1956.*

1187. **OGDEN, G. L.** The Soviet 'Iron-curtain' policy: an examination of its antecedents in the Russian conception of the West. *LONDON (LSE) D 1958.*

1188. **RITTER, G. A.** The British labour movement and its policy towards Russia from the first Russian Revolution until the Treaty of Locarno. *OXFORD BL 1958.*

1189. **ULLMAN, R. H.** British intervention in Russia, November 1917–February 1920: a study in the making of a foreign policy. *OXFORD D 1959.*

1190. **ALLEN, M. N.** The policy of the USSR towards the State of Israel, 1948–1958. *LONDON (LSE) D 1961.*

1191. **IMAM, Z.** Soviet Russia's policy towards India and its effect on Anglo-Soviet relations, 1917–1928. *LONDON (LSE) D 1964.*

1192. **GREGOR, R.** Lenin's foreign policy, 1917–1922: ideology or national interest? *LONDON (LSE) D 1966.*

1193. **ASTER, S.** British policy towards the USSR, and the onset of the Second World War, March 1938 – August 1939. *LONDON (LSE) D 1969.*

1194. **HAMMONDS, E. H.** A study of Soviet and Chinese Communist strategy in sub-Saharan Africa. *LONDON (EXTERNAL) D 1969.*

1195. **JACOBSEN, C. G.** Strategic factors in Soviet foreign policy. *GLASGOW D 1971.*

1196. **PAGE, S. C.** The development of Soviet policies and attitudes towards the countries of the Arabian peninsula. *READING D 1971.*

1197. **LEE, C. D.** The interplay of political and economic factors in Soviet foreign economic relations, with special reference to the period 1945–1953. *LONDON (LSE) MP 1972.*

1198. **MANNE, R. M.** The British government and the question of the Soviet alliance, March 15–August 24, 1939. *OXFORD BP 1972.*

1199. **WHITE, S.** Anglo-Soviet relations, 1917–1924: a study in the politics of diplomacy. *GLASGOW D 1972.*

1200. **CONDREN, P. L. S.** The Soviet Union and conference diplomacy: a study of Soviet attitudes and policy towards international conferences in the period 1933–1939. GLASGOW D 1973.

1201. **EDWARDS, G. R.** Sir Austen Chamberlain's and Sir John Simon's conduct of Anglo-Soviet relations: a case-study in the relationship between the House of Commons and the Foreign Secretary. LONDON (LSE) D 1973.

1202. **LARGE, J. A.** Soviet foreign policy, 1930–1933: the new alignment, with special reference to the non-aggression pact as an instrument of Soviet diplomacy. GLASGOW D 1973.

1203. **RADICE, E. A.** Negotiations for an Eastern security pact, 1933–1936. LONDON (LSE) D 1973.

1204. **STEVENS, C. A.** Relations between the USSR and Africa between 1953 and 1972, with special reference to Ghana, Guinea, Kenya, Mali, Nigeria, Somalia and Tanzania. LONDON (LSE) D 1973.

1205. **GORODETSKY, G.** Anglo-Soviet relations, 1924–1927. OXFORD D 1974.

1206. **JONES, W. D. A.** The British Labour Party and the Soviet Union, 1939–1949. WALES (ABERYSTWYTH) D 1975.

1207. **PETERSON, G. L.** The rapprochement between the Federal Republic of Germany and the Soviet Union, and the policy of international linkage in East-West relations, 1965–1971. LONDON (LSE) D 1975.

1208. **BEAZLEY, K. C.** American and Soviet involvement in the Indian Ocean area, 1968–1975. OXFORD BP 1976.

1209. **FOOT, R. J.** New areas of tension and great power rivalry: Central West Asia and Sino-Soviet relations, 1962–1974. LONDON (LSE) D 1976.

1210. **GOODWORTH, J. K.** Ideology and realpolitik in the history of Sino-Soviet relations. NOTTINGHAM MP 1977.

1211. **HARRIS, P. D.** China's boundary dispute with the Soviet Union: its background and development up to and including the 1969 border clashes. OXFORD BP 1977.

1212. **NASSIBIAN, A.** Attitudes on Clydeside towards the Russian Revolution, 1917–1924. STRATHCLYDE ML 1977.

1213. **DAWISHA, K.** The foundations, structure and dynamics of Soviet policy toward the Arab radical regimes [1955–61]. LONDON (LSE) D 1978.

1214. **EVANS, R. G.** Helsinki, Belgrade and the Soviet monitors. OXFORD BP 1978.

1215. **HASLAM, J. G.** Anglo-Russian relations, 1924–1927. CAMBRIDGE ML 1978.

1216. **RUEBENSAAL, J. D.** The impact of the Sino-Soviet dispute on the Afro-Asian People's Solidarity Organization. LONDON (LSE) MP 1978.

1217. **SURENDAR, T.** Indo-Soviet relations, 1959–1971. GLASGOW D 1978.

1218. **BRIDGES, B. J. E.** Anglo-Soviet relations, 1927–1932. WALES (SWANSEA) D 1979.

1219. **RYAN, H. B.** The vision of 'Anglo-America' and the origins of the Cold War: some aspects of British foreign policy, 1943–1946. CAMBRIDGE D 1979.

1220. **SEGAL, G.** From bipolarity to the Great Power triangle: Moscow, Peking, Washington, 1961–1968. LONDON (LSE) D 1979.

1221. **BURWELL, F. G.** Reaction to revolution: British, French and American policies towards Bolshevik Russia, 1917–1924. OXFORD MP 1980.

1222. **GENOSAR, T.** The 1967 Middle East conflict: Soviet policies and attitudes. *LONDON (LSE) D 1980.*

1223. **SCHULZ, J. J.** Japan and the peace and friendship treaties with Moscow and Peking. *OXFORD D 1980.*

1224. **BELL, M. B.** Anglo-American diplomacy and the problem of the Berlin blockade. *BIRMINGHAM D 1981.*

1225. **CRONIN, P. M.** Soviet-American summit conferences. *OXFORD MP 1981.*

1226. **HEALY, D.** United States' foreign policy-making: détente and grain sales [1971–1981]. *ABERDEEN D 1981.*

1227. **KRANTZ, T. A.** Moscow and the negotiations of the Helsinki Accords, 1972–1975. *OXFORD ML 1981.*

1228. **L'ESTRANGE FAWCETT, L.** The Cold War in the Middle East: Soviet policy towards Iran, 1945–1965. *OXFORD MP 1981.*

1229. **MOHAMMED, A. M. Y.** British policy towards the Soviet Union, from the outbreak of the War, September 1939, to the conclusion of the Anglo-Soviet Alliance, May 1942. *BIRMINGHAM D 1981.*

1230. **KHAN, M. J. R.** Pakistan's relations with the USA, the USSR, China and India from the Sino-Indian War to the Simla Pact. *OXFORD D 1982.*

1231. **MACFARLANE, S. N.** The Soviet Union and national liberation. *OXFORD MP 1982.*

1232. **SHAH, M. A. Z.** Maintaining non-alignment: India's political relations with the super-powers in the 1970s. *LONDON (LSE) MP 1982.*

1233. **STEVENSON, R. W.** The nature of détente: relaxations of tension in US-Soviet relations, 1953–1976. *OXFORD D 1982.*

1234. **CRONIN, P. M.** Soviet-American summit conferences, 1955–1972. *OXFORD D 1983.*

1235. **KINBARA, K.** The development of Japan's economic cooperation with the USSR in Siberia in the 1970s. *OXFORD ML 1983.*

1236. **McLAUGHLIN, A. W.** Khrushchev's reforms in foreign policy: the first phase, 1953–7. *OXFORD MP 1983.*

1237. **SMITH, R.** British policy towards the Soviet Union, 1945–1947. *LIVERPOOL D 1983.*

1238. **SOEDJATI, J.** An analysis of the use and role of a third party in the settlement of international disputes, with special reference to Indonesian-Soviet relations. *LONDON (LSE) D 1983.*

1239. **TURRENT, M. I.** The Soviet Union and Chile's Popular Unity, 1970–1973. *OXFORD ML 1983.*

1240. **WYMAN, F. S.** Soviet-East German relations, 1949–1972: the politics of dependence. *OXFORD MP 1983.*

1241. **CAMPBELL, K. M.** Soviet policy towards South Africa. *OXFORD D 1984.*

1242. **CATHERWOOD, C. M. S.** Turkey in British foreign policy and strategy, with special reference to Turco-Soviet relations, from 1935–1941. *CAMBRIDGE ML 1984.*

1243. **COX, W. H.** Adenauer's interpretation of Soviet policies, 1945–1955. *LONDON (LSE) D 1984.*

1244. **HASLAM, J.** Soviet foreign policy in the 1930s. *BIRMINGHAM D 1984.*

1245. **KURTH, A. E.** The Great Powers and the struggle over Austria, 1945–1955. *OXFORD D 1984.*

1246. **Louis, N.** The Soviet Union and the German question, 1945 to 1973: a study of views and perspectives. OXFORD MP 1984.

1247. **Miller, N. A.** The Soviet Union and Latin America, 1917–1983. OXFORD MP 1984.

1248. **Ongsuragz, C.** Soviet strategy and tactics in ASEAN countries, 1965–1980: political implications of the non-capitalist development theory. LONDON (LSE) MP 1984.

1249. **Roche, J. S.** Soviet foreign policy and Marxist-Leninist ethics. EXETER MP 1984.

1250. **Bennett-Jones, O.** The Soviet foreign policy process. OXFORD MP 1985.

1251. **Blitz, J.** Soviet relations with France, 1958–1968. OXFORD MP 1985.

1252. **Cope, P. J.** Franco-Soviet summits as an instrument of French foreign policy during the presidencies of Georges Pompidou and Valéry Giscard d'Estaing. EXETER D 1985.

1253. **Desjardins, R.** Analyses and interpretations of the Soviet Union in France 1945–1983. OXFORD ML 1985.

1254. **Parker, G.** Soviet foreign policy: relations with Poland 1932–1935. BIRMINGHAM D 1985.

1255. **Stottor, J. L.** The French Popular Front and the Franco-Soviet Pact, 1935–8. LONDON (BEDFORD) MP 1985.

1256. **Gwozdziowski, J. M.** The origins and impact of the Brezhnev Doctrine. OXFORD MP 1986.

1257. **Kamman, E. G.** Soviet perceptions of the first Reagan Administration. OXFORD MP 1986.

1258. **Lehmann, R. A.** The effect of Stalin's death on foreign policy: Churchill's search for a summit, 1951–4. OXFORD ML 1986.

1259. **Light, M.** Soviet theory of international relations 1917–1982. SURREY D 1986.

1260. **Lord, S. M.** Soviet–Vietnam relations, 1969 to 1978. HULL D 1986.

1261. **Miller, N.** Soviet relations with Latin America 1959–1979. OXFORD D 1986.

1262. **Moxham, K. I.** The Labour Party and the Soviet Union, 1945–51. CAMBRIDGE D 1986.

1263. **Rai, S. S.** The political dynamics of Indo-Soviet relations, 1930–1977. YORK D 1986.

1264. **White, B. P.** Britain and East-West détente, 1953–1963. LEICESTER D 1986.

1265. **Ahmed, H. O.** The Soviet Union and the Gulf countries between 1968 and 1980: the impact of Soviet economic aid, military assistance and political influence. EXETER D 1987.

1266. **Elstein, A. C.** Soviet policy towards the Western Alliance: the case of I. N. F.. OXFORD MP 1987.

1267. **Fitton, R.** Interactions between the USA and the USSR in the Third World: a case study of Angola, 1974–76. LEEDS D 1987.

1268. **Pant, G. P.** Foreign aid and economic growth in Nepal, with reference to Chinese and Soviet aid. READING D 1987.

1269. **Patman, R. G.** Intervention and disengagement in the Horn of Africa: the Soviet experience, 1970–1978. SOUTHAMPTON D 1987.

1270. **WHITE, S.** The Genoa Conference and Soviet-Western diplomacy 1921–1922. *OXFORD D 1987.*

1271. **DU TOIT, E. J.** The development of Soviet policy towards the Third World: Mozambique as a case study. *OXFORD MP 1988.*

1272. **EL-DOUFANI, M. M.** Superpower intervention in client-state wars: an analysis of United States and Soviet interventionary behaviour in areas of disputed or uncertain interest symmetry. *LANCASTER D 1988.*

1273. **FROMAN, M. B.** The development of the idea of détente in American political discourse 1952–1985. *OXFORD D 1988.*

1274. **LESTER, J. P.** Cohesion and problems of viability in the GDR's relationship with the Soviet Union. A regional test case: the Bezirk of Halle. *HULL D 1988.*

1275. **PITTMAN, A. A.** The Federal Republic of Germany's political relations with the USSR, 1974–1982. *LANCASTER D 1988.*

1276. **SMITH, M. A.** Soviet perceptions of Latin America, 1959–1987. *OXFORD D 1988.*

1277. **CABLE, J.** The political and strategic dimensions of United States economic relations with the Soviet Union, 1969–1976. *OXFORD D 1989.*

1278. **NEUMANN, I. B.** Soviet perceptions of the European communities, 1950–1988. *OXFORD MP 1989.*

1279. **SIMPSON, M. S. C.** The Soviet Union and Afro-Marxist regimes: the path to the treaties of friendship and co-operation. *LONDON (LSE) D 1989.*

1280. **HANSON, M.** The Conference on Security and Cooperation in Europe: Soviet objectives, 1954–1989. *OXFORD MP 1990.*

1281. **HAZELTON, C. S. R.** Soviet foreign policy during the initial phase of the war with Germany: June–December 1941. *LONDON (LSE) D 1990.*

1282. **TANAKA, T.** Soviet-Japanese normalization talks in 1955–56, with special reference to the attitude of Britain. *LONDON (LSE) D 1990.*

1283. **WALLACE, C. E. G.** Soviet economic and technical cooperation with developing countries: the Turkish case. *LONDON (LSE) D 1990.*

1284. **GINAT, R.** The Soviet Union and Egypt, 1947–1955. *LONDON (LSE) D 1991.*

1285. **GRASSELLI, G.** British and American responses to the Soviet invasion of Afghanistan […]. *BRISTOL D 1991.*

1286. **KHAIRI, K. K. M.** The British perception of Soviet aims and the effect on the diplomatic relations between the two countries 1935–1939. *CNAA (NORTH LONDON POLY) MP 1991.*

1287. **MONEY, J.** The influence of diplomatic precedents and tradition: the Northern Department and Soviet representation, 1921–1927. *LONDON (LSE) MP 1991.*

1288. **WEBBER, M.** Soviet-Angolan relations 1975 to the present. *BIRMINGHAM D 1991.*

1289. **ZHU, J.** A Chinese exploration of Sino-Soviet relations since the death of Stalin, 1953–1989. *GLASGOW D 1991.*

1290. **CHIPMAN, A.** Reappraisal and reaction in Soviet foreign policy toward Western Europe, 1985–1989. *OXFORD MP 1992.*

1291. **DU TOIT, E. J.** Soviet policy towards South Africa, 1974–1991. *OXFORD D 1992.*

1292. **FARROW, R.** Changing Soviet perspectives on Eastern Europe: Khrushchev to Gorbachev. *OXFORD MP 1992.*

1293. **Geranmayeh Rad, M. A.**   Iranian resistance to Soviet pressure: Irano-Soviet relations 1941–1947. *LONDON (SSEES) D 1992.*

1294. **Gunn, T. J.**   Neutrality and alignment: selected aspects of Swedish and Norwegian foreign policies toward the Soviet Union, 1987–1991. *LONDON (LSE) D 1992.*

1295. **Kennedy-Pipe, C. M.**   The Soviet Union and the United States military presence in Europe, 1943–1956. *OXFORD D 1992.*

1296. **Thomas, N.**   A compromised policy: Britain, Germany and the Soviet threat, 1945–1946. *LONDON (QM WESTFIELD) MP 1992.*

1297. **Aldous, R. J.**   Harold Macmillan and the search for a summit with the USSR, 1958–60. *CAMBRIDGE D 1993.*

1298. **Choi, T. K.**   Linkages between domestic and foreign policies under Gorbachev: the case of Korea. *GLASGOW D 1993.*

1299. **Faughnan, S. A.**   The politics of influence: Churchill, Eden and Soviet communism 1951–57. *CAMBRIDGE D 1993.*

1300. **Hara, T.**   East-West relations and the Geneva Summit Conference of 1955. *DUNDEE MP 1993.*

1301. **Podplatnik, T. M.**   The Soviet Far East in international affairs, 1985–1991: the view from Moscow. *OXFORD MP 1993.*

1302. **Roberts, G. C.**   Soviet foreign policy, 1933–1941, with special reference to the pact with Nazi Germany. *LONDON (LSE) D 1993.*

1303. **Taghizadeh, M. R.**   Iran and the Soviet Union: between communism and Commonwealth 1985–1992. *GLASGOW D 1993.*

1304. **Xu Jian**   Sino-Soviet normalization in the 1980s [NCR]. *BRISTOL D 1993.*

1305. **Ashcroft, M. R.**   'Good and bad communists': Australian attitudes towards the Soviet Union 1939–49. *LONDON (INST COMMONWEALTH STUD) D 1994.*

1306. **Dannreuther, R.**   The Soviet Union and the Palestine resistance movement. *OXFORD D 1994.*

1307. **Gökay, B.**   Anglo-Soviet relations and Turkey, 1918–1923. *CAMBRIDGE D 1994.*

1308. **Kerr, D.**   Contrasting Russian and Chinese perspectives on the future of Asia. *GLASGOW D 1994.*

1309. **Leshuk, L. G.**   American perceptions of Soviet economic and military strength 1921–1946. *LONDON (KCL) D 1994.*

1310. **Newton, J. M.**   Soviet policy towards France, 1958–1991: a case study of the Soviet Union's Westpolitik. *OXFORD D 1994.*

1311. **Salzmann, S.**   British Realpolitik and the myth of the Rapallo friendship, 1922–1934. *CAMBRIDGE D 1994.*

1312. **Swann, P. W.**   British attitudes towards the Soviet Union, 1951–1956. *GLASGOW D 1994.*

1313. **Turner, J.**   Soviet new thinking and the Cambodian conflict. *OXFORD MP 1994.*

1314. **Dow, R. M.**   Senator Henry M. Jackson and US-Soviet détente. *OXFORD D 1995.*

1315. **Gwozdziowski, J. M.**   Soviet doctrine justifying military intervention from 1945 to 1989. *OXFORD D 1995.*

1316. **Hong, S. -P.** The USSR-ROK relations (1985–1992): an explanation of the role of elite images and domestic factors in the process of achieving diplomatic recognition. HULL D 1995.

1317. **Ishaq, M. A.** US-Soviet relations 1980–88: the politics of trade pressure. GLASGOW D 1995.

1318. **Bradley, J.** Berlin, NATO and East-West relations: a study of the position of the British and United States governments, 1945–1961 [NCR]. BRUNEL MP 1996.

1319. **Bumpstead, R.** Soviet UN policy 1985–1991 and collective security. OXFORD MP 1996.

1320. **Marlow, S. J.** Personality and policy-making: the case of the Cuban missile crisis. KEELE MP 1996.

1321. **Paszyn, D.** Soviet attitudes to political and social change in Central America (1979–1990): case studies: Nicaragua, El Salvador and Guatemala. LONDON (SSEES) MP 1996.

1322. **Braddick, C. W.** Japan and the Sino-Soviet alliance, 1950–1964. OXFORD D 1997.

1323. **Folly, M. H.** British government attitudes to the USSR, 1940–1945. LONDON (LSE) D 1997.

1324. **Jackson, I. R. W.** Co-operation and constraint: Britain's influence on American economic warfare policy on CoCom 1948–54. QUEENS BELFAST D 1997.

1325. **Pierpoint, D.** British policy in Iran and relations with the Soviet Union, 1945–46. BIRMINGHAM MP 1999.

1326. **Ralph, J. G.** From the 'security dilemma' to the 'emancipation dilemma': a critical perspective on US policy towards the Soviet Union 1983–1991. LONDON (KCL) D 1999.

1327. **Ruotsila, M. M.** The origins of Anglo-American anti-Bolshevism, 1917–21. CAMBRIDGE D 1999.

1328. **Souyad, A.** The Soviet Union in Syria's foreign policy 1970–1980: ideology versus regime interest. EXETER D 1999.

1329. **Azrieli, N.** Soviet economic diplomacy, 1941–1947. OXFORD D 2000.

1330. **Bar-Noi, U.** Anglo-Soviet relations during Churchill's peacetime administration 1951–55: Cold War politics, propaganda, trade and détente. LONDON (LSE) D 2000.

1331. **Newman, K. P.** Britain and the Soviet Union: the search for an interim agreement on Berlin, November 1958–May 1960. LONDON (LSE) D 2000.

1332. **Sheeran, P. D.** Altered states in international relations: the role of counterculture in the disintegration of the Soviet Union. NOTTINGHAM TRENT D 2000.

1333. **Bain, M. J.** Soviet / Cuban relations 1985–1991. GLASGOW D 2001.

1334. **Bisley, N. L.** Historical sociology and great power vulnerability: the end of the Cold War and the collapse of the Soviet Union. LONDON (LSE) D 2001.

1335. **O'Brien, J. G.** Return to the centre: personalities, bureaupolitical styles and world-views: the evolution of Reagan's early Soviet policy, 1981–1985. LIMERICK D 2001.

1336. **Shaw, L. G.** Attitudes of the British political élite towards the Soviet Union, May 1937–August 1939. LONDON (KCL) D 2001.

1337. **Anderson-Jaquest, T. C.** Restructuring the Soviet-Ethiopian relationship: a case study in asymmetric exchange. LONDON (LSE) D 2002.

1338. **Foo, Y. W.** Wartime diplomacy at the Chinese embassy in Moscow 1943–1945: Ambassador Fu BingChang. *LINCOLN D 2002*.

1339. **Hilali, A. Z. A.** US-Pakistan partnership in response to the Soviet invasion of Afghanistan 1979–88: causes, dynamics and consequences. *HULL D 2002*.

1340. **Hughes, G. A.** The Wilson Government, the USSR and British foreign and defence policy in the context of East-West détente: 1964–1968. *LONDON (KCL) D 2002*.

1341. **Mizumoto, Y.** Counselling America, involving the Soviet Union: Winston Churchill's strategy for Britain's revival, 1951–1955. *KEELE D 2002*.

1342. **Worth, O.** (De-) constructing hegemony: a study of hegemony and counter-hegemony in the global political economy with reference to the former USSR. *NOTTINGHAM TRENT D 2002*.

1343. **Hofmann, A.** Willy Brandt, John F. Kennedy and the emergence of détente. *LONDON (LSE) D 2003*.

1344. **Elsby, A. W.** British foreign policy towards the Soviet Union over Germany in the immediate post-World War Two period: a causal analysis. *SUSSEX D 2004*.

1345. **Dannenberg, J. von** The fruits of daring diplomacy: the making of the Moscow Treaty, 12 August 1970. *OXFORD D 2005*.

1346. **Jones, S. H.** Lyndon Johnson, the Atlantic alliance and the pursuit of détente, 1966–1969. *CAMBRIDGE D 2005*.

1347. **Radchenko, S.** The China puzzle: Soviet policy towards the People's Republic of China in the 1960s. *LONDON (LSE) D 2005*.

1348. **Stevens, T.** Chess in the Cold War. [International chess competition between the US and USSR, 1945–1975]. *KEELE D 2005*.

1349. **Beytullayev, E.** Soviet policy towards Turkey, 1944–1946. *CAMBRIDGE D 2006*.

1350. **Megas, A.** Soviet policy towards the German Democratic Republic: domestic politics and the international system. *LEEDS D 2006*.

Yugoslavia (see also under former republics)

1351. **Mansbach, R. W.** The Soviet-Yugoslav rapprochement of 1955–8: its ideological and political implications. *OXFORD D 1967*.

1352. **Wheeler, M. C.** The War, the Yugoslavs, and British foreign policy, 1940–1943. *CAMBRIDGE D 1978*.

1353. **Kay, M. A.** The British attitude to the Yugoslav Government-in-Exile, 1941–45. *SOUTHAMPTON D 1986*.

1354. **Heuser, D. B. G.** Yugoslavia in Western Cold War policies, 1948–1953. *OXFORD D 1987*.

1355. **Lane, A. J.** The policy of the British Foreign Office towards Yugoslavia, 1945–1949. *LONDON (LSE) D 1988*.

1356. **Fitzgerald, J.** Changing courses: Britain, America and Yugoslavia 1945–1949. *LONDON (SSEES) D 1989*.

1357. **Williams, J. C.** The concept of legitimacy in international relations: lessons from Yugoslavia. *WARWICK D 1997*.

1358. **Terret, S. T.** The dissolution of Yugoslavia and the Badinter Arbitration Commission. *LIVERPOOL D 1998*.

1359. **BELLOU, F.** American leadership image and the Yugoslav crisis (1991–1997). *LONDON (KCL) D 2000.*

1360. **BOTH, N.** From indifference to entrapment: the foreign policy of the Netherlands with regard to the Yugoslav crisis between 1990 and 1995. *SHEFFIELD D 2000.*

1361. **CAPLAN, R. D.** Political conditionality and conflict management: the European Community's recognition of new states in Yugoslavia. *LONDON (KCL) D 2000.*

1362. **NIKOLIĆ, I. A.** Anglo-Yugoslav relations: 1938–41. *CAMBRIDGE D 2001.*

1363. **GRBIN, C. A.** The role of Britain in Yugoslavia and its successor states: 1991–1995. *GLASGOW D 2004.*

1364. **HUNT, L.** The European Union and the former Yugoslavia: the development of European foreign policy? *LOUGHBOROUGH D 2004.*

1365. **RAJAK, S.** Yugoslav-Soviet relations, 1953–1957: normalization, comradeship, confrontation. *LONDON (LSE) D 2004.*

1366. **MILOVAC-CAROLINA, S. M.** The Romantic Zeitgeist in post-Cold War international relations and the disintegration of Yugoslavia. *LONDON (LSE) D 2006.*

15. LABOUR

Central and Eastern Europe *(see also under individual countries)*

1367. **HIRIS, L.** The determinants of East-West labour migration in the context of EU enlargement. *WEST OF ENGLAND D 2004.*

Czech Republic

1368. **WISEMAN, R. V.** Civil society, policy-making and the quality of democracy: trade unions in the Czech Republic. *SHEFFIELD D 2002.*

Georgia

1369. **BERNABÉ, S. L.** Informal labour market activity: a social safety net during economic transition? The case of Georgia. *LONDON (LSE) D 2005.*

Hungary

1370. **SZIRÁCZKI, G.** Labour market in a socialist economy: labour process, subcontracting and dismissals in Hungary. *CAMBRIDGE D 1989.*

1371. **FINE, C. R.** Post-socialist Hungarian industrial relations development and industrial dispute resolution: the first six years. *LEEDS D 1997.*

1372. **SZIVAS, E.** A study of labour mobility into tourism: the case of Hungary. *SURREY D 1997.*

1373. **PITTAWAY, M. D.** Industrial workers, socialist industrialisation and the state in Hungary, 1948–1958. *LIVERPOOL D 1998.*

1374. O'HAGAN, E.   Industrial relations within the integrating European Union: a comparative study of two peripheral economies, Ireland and Hungary. QUEENS BELFAST D 1999.

1375. SCHARLE, Á.   Self-employment in Hungary. OXFORD D 2001.

1376. ROSSI, M.   Government–trade union relations and Europeanisation in Hungary from 1990–2000. STRATHCLYDE D 2003.

Kazakhstan

1377. VERME, P.   Transition, recession and labour supply in Kazakhstan (1990–1996). LONDON (LSE) D 2000.

1378. MUSSUROV, A.   Human capital, screening and discrimination in Kazakhstan [NCR]. WALES (ABERYSTWYTH) D 2006.

Macedonia

1379. MOJSOSKA-BLAŽEVSKI, N.   The public employment service, education and labour markets in Macedonia. STAFFORDSHIRE D 2006.

Poland

1380. LEHMANN, H.   Labour market flows and labour market policies in the British Isles, Poland and Eastern Germany since 1980. LONDON (LSE) D 1993.

1381. PERRY, M.   The measurement of unemployment in Europe with particular reference to Britain, France and Poland. WOLVERHAMPTON D 1993.

1382. KLUVE, J.   Evaluation of active labour market policies in Poland — an application of matching estimators. TC DUBLIN ML 1998.

1383. HETRICK, S. R.   Globalisation, convergence and human resource management: a study of multinational corporations in Poland 1996 to 1999. CITY D 2001.

1384. DUFFY, F.   Essays on regional restructuring and the Polish labour market. TC DUBLIN D 2002.

1385. PASTORE, F.   A study of the regional distribution of unemployment in Poland's economic transition. SUSSEX D 2003.

1386. SIBLEY, C. W.   Industrial structures and labour market outcomes: an examination of Poland in transition. TC DUBLIN D 2005.

Romania

1387. TAGLE, F.   Labour policy in Rumania, with special reference to wages and manpower policies. OXFORD BL 1977.

Russia (see also USSR)

1388. PALAT, M. K.   Labour legislation and reform in Russia, 1905–1914. OXFORD D 1973.

1389. ASHWIN, C. S. J.   Complaining in corners: Russian mineworkers and the transition from communism. WARWICK D 1997.

1390. **ACQUISTI, A.** Labour dynamics in the Russian Federation. *TC DUBLIN ML 1999.*

1391. **RICHTER, A.** Over-employment, labour immobility, distress work and firm start-ups: four economic themes of Russia's slow transition to the market. *OXFORD D 1999.*

1392. **ROBERTSON, A.** The social impact of employment restructuring in Kuzbass. *WARWICK D 1999.*

1393. **BORISOV, V. A.** Strikes in Russia: the case of the coal-mining industry. *WARWICK D 2000.*

1394. **BOUEV, M.** Labour supply, informal economy and Russian transition. *OXFORD MP 2001.*

1395. **GERRY, C. J.** Wage inequality, wellbeing and the labour market: Russia 1994–2000. *ESSEX D 2003.*

1396. **LUKE, P. J.** Russian and Estonian labour markets during the 1990s — an investigation of insider-power in Russia and segmented labour markets in Estonia. *HERIOT-WATT D 2004.*

1397. **LYU, H.** The foiled quest for a democratic factory order: a study in factory relations in Petrograd during the Russian Civil War, 1918–1921. *ESSEX D 2004.*

1398. **SCHWARTZ, G.** Recasting the labour collective: the social determination of wages, employment and labour relations in Russia, 1999–2002. *WARWICK D 2004.*

1399. **BOUEV, M. V.** Essays on labour markets in Russia and Eastern Europe. *OXFORD D 2006.*

USSR (see also Russia)

1400. **FAKIOLAS, R. E.** Aspects of Soviet industrial employment. *LONDON (LSE) D 1961.*

1401. **MATTHEWS, W. H. M.** Youth employment in the USSR, 1946–58. *OXFORD D 1961.*

1402. **MCAULEY, M.** The settlement of labour disputes in the USSR, 1957–1965. *OXFORD D 1968.*

1403. **SHUE, V. B.** Ideology in Communist politics: a case study of mental and manual labour in China and the USSR. *OXFORD BL 1969.*

1404. **FLENLEY, P. S.** Workers' organizations in the Russian metal industry, February 1917–August 1918: a study in the history and sociology of the labour movement in the Russian Revolution. *BIRMINGHAM D 1982.*

1405. **DALE, J. P.** Industrial workers and the party-state in the USSR, 1928–1932. *ESSEX D 1984.*

1406. **ARNOT, R. J.** The Shchekino experiment: the question of control over the Soviet industrial workforce. *GLASGOW D 1985.*

1407. **WARD, C.** Russian cotton workers and the New Economic Policy. *ESSEX D 1985.*

1408. **RUSSELL, J.** The role of socialist competition in establishing labour discipline in the Soviet working class, 1928–1934. *BIRMINGHAM D 1987.*

1409. **AVES, J. J.** Industrial unrest in Soviet Russia during War Communism and the transition to the New Economic Policy: 1918–22. *LONDON (SSEES) D 1989.*

1410. **BARR, G.** Trotsky's views on the trade unions: 1919–1929. *EXETER MP 1991.*

1411. POSPIELOVSKY, A. Suppression of worker militancy during the NEP, 1921–1928: the worker, the unions, the Party and the secret police. LONDON (SSEES) D 1999.

Uzbekistan

1412. LUBIN, N The ethnic/political implications of labor use in the Uzbek SSR. OXFORD D 1981.

Yugoslavia (see also under former republics)

1413. BARZEY, A. Economic development, technical change, productivity and the vertical division of labour in Yugoslav worker-managed society. LEEDS D 1995.

1414. KRSTIĆ, G. An empirical analysis of the formal and informal labour markets in FR Yugoslavia (1995–2000). SUSSEX D 2002.

16. LANGUAGE, LINGUISTICS

General and Comparative

1415. ELLIS, J. O. The structure of neologisms in Russian and Czech. LONDON (SSEES) D 1948.

1416. BECHER, R. A comparative study of primary spatial prepositions in modern literary Russian and Polish. GLASGOW BL 1955.

1417. LEWIS, B. E. A comparison of verbal aspect in Russian and Czech. LEEDS MP 1969.

1418. GUILD, D. G. The development of the aorist and imperfect in some Baltic and Slavic languages. EDINBURGH D 1972.

1419. BIRD, N. A critical evaluation of an inventory of Polish and Russian root morphemes of native origin. LONDON (EXTERNAL) D 1985.

1420. TSONEVA-MATHEWSON, S. Verbal property predication in Russian and Bulgarian. ST ANDREWS D 2006.

Albanian

1421. KALLULLI, D. The comparative syntax of Albanian: on the contribution of syntactic types to propositional interpretation. DURHAM D 1999.

1422. PERTA, C. Language of decline and death in three Arbëresh communities in Italy: a sociolinguistic study. EDINBURGH D 2004.

1423. HOXHALLARI, L. Learning to read and spell in Albanian, English and Welsh: the effect of orthographic transparency. WALES (BANGOR) D 2006.

Belorussian

1424. SADOŬSKI, J. A linguistic analysis of the four Books of Kings printed by Skaryna in 1518. LONDON (SSEES) D 1967.

1425. McMILLIN, A. B.   A study of the vocabulary of the White Russian literary language in the nineteenth century. *LONDON (SSEES) D 1971.*

1426. TAMUSHANSKI, R. J.   German loan words in Middle Byelorussian. *LONDON (SSEES) D 1974.*

1427. AKINER, S.   The religious vocabulary of the British Library Tatar-Byelorussian *Kitab*. *LONDON (SSEES) D 1980.*

Bulgarian

1428. MACROBERT, C. M.   The decline of the infinitive in Bulgarian. *OXFORD D 1980.*

1429. POPOVA, D.   Developing English for science and technology in the Bulgarian context. *SURREY D 2000.*

1430. POPOVA, G. D.   Aspect in the morphological paradigm: a case study of Bulgarian. *ESSEX D 2006.*

Caucasian

1431. CRISP, S.   Language planning and the development of written Avar syntax. *OXFORD D 1982.*

1432. LALOR, O. F.   Languages in contact in north-west Caucasian communities. *LONDON (BIRKBECK) D 1990.*

Czech

1433. HLUBÍK, T.   The recent development of the Czech language in relation to the changes in the structure of society. *OXFORD D 1962.*

1434. PALYZA, M. M.   The intonation of contemporary standard Czech. *LONDON (UCL) D 1979.*

1435. NUNNEY, V. J.   Machek's Gambit: heterophones in etymology. *LONDON (SSEES) D 1989.*

1436. DANKOVIČOVÁ, J.   The linguistic bases of articulation rate variation in Czech. *OXFORD D 1998.*

Estonian

1437. HIIETAM, K.   Definiteness and grammatical relations in Estonian. *MANCHESTER D 2003.*

1438. ASU, E. L.   The phonetics and phonology of Estonian intonation. *CAMBRIDGE D 2004.*

Finnic

1439. BAKER, R. W.   Innovation and variation in the case system of contemporary Komi dialects. *EAST ANGLIA D 1984.*

1440. MOSELY, C. J.   Language attrition and death: Livonian in its terminal stage. *LONDON (SSEES) MP 1993.*

German

1441. **WHITEHEAD, R. N.**   Between two languages: language shift among the Germans of Russia. OXFORD MP 1993.

Hungarian

1442. **JONES, F. R.**   Going it alone: self-instruction in adult foreign-language learning [of Hungarian]. NEWCASTLE D 1996.

1443. **KISS-GULYAS, J.**   The acquisition of English restrictive relative clauses by Hungarian learners of English. ESSEX D 1999.

1444. **PAPP, S.**   The acquisition of focus by adult English learners of Hungarian. EDINBURGH D 1999.

1445. **ENEVER, J.**   The politics of non-decision making in language policy in Hungary. BRISTOL D.ED 2001.

1446. **BABARCZY, A.**   A path from broader to narrower grammars: the acquisition of argument structure in English and Hungarian. EDINBURGH D 2002.

1447. **WEDGWOOD, D.**   Predication and information structure: a dynamic account of Hungarian pre-verbal syntax. EDINBURGH D 2003.

1448. **CHISARIK, E. Z.**   Structure of Hungarian noun phrases: a lexical-functional approach. MANCHESTER D 2005.

Latvian

1449. **LOWMAN, G. S.**   The phonetics of the Lettish language. LONDON (UCL) D 1931.

1450. **ALKSNIS, P.**   A study of the lexical relationship between Russian and Latvian, based on R. Trautmann's *Baltisch-slavisches Wörterbuch*. LONDON (SSEES) MP 1968.

1451. **KRESLINS, K.**   A stemming algorithm for Latvian. LOUGHBOROUGH D 1996.

1452. **SINKA, I.**   The development of tense and agreement in Latvian and English bilingual children. READING D 1999.

Polish

1453. **WESTFAL, S. S.**   The genitive singular masculine in modern literary Polish. LONDON (SSEES) D 1953.

1454. **ULATOWSKA, H. K.**   A textual study of translation equivalents in English and Polish. EDINBURGH D 1961.

1455. **KONNOVA, V. F.**   Semantic differences between Polish dialects as a means of establishing patterns of semantic change. OXFORD ML 1978.

1456. **WEAVER, Z.**   A semantic analysis of comparative structures in the modern Polish language. NOTTINGHAM D 1980.

1457. **GIEJGO, J. A.**   Movement rules in Polish syntax. LONDON (UCL) D 1981.

1458. **GORAYSKA, B. M.**   The semantics and pragmatics of English and Polish, with reference to aspect. LONDON (UCL) D 1985.

1459. **MUIR, E.**   The strategies of language acquisition in bilingual Polish/English children. READING D 1986.

1460. **JAWORSKA, E.** Aspects of the syntax of prepositions and prepositional phrases in English and Polish. *OXFORD D 1987.*

1461. **STYŚ, M. E.** A processing model of information structure in machine translation processor text [with reference to English and Polish]. *CAMBRIDGE D 1998.*

1462. **REID, A.** The combinatorial lexicon: psycholinguistic studies of Polish morphology. *LONDON (BIRKBECK) D 2001.*

1463. **SZCZERBIŃSKI, M.** Learning to read and spell single words: a case study of a Slavic language [i.e. Polish]. *LONDON (UCL) D 2001.*

1464. **BARANIUK, K.** Morphological generation and analysis, case study on Polish language. *ULSTER D 2002.*

1465. **KOWALUK, A.** The development of pronouns and determiners in the second language: a study of Polish learners of English. *CAMBRIDGE D 2002.*

1466. **RENC-ROE, J.** Discourses on women in the Polish parliamentary debates: dominance and resistance in critical and feminist linguistic perspective. *OPEN MP 2003.*

1467. **GŁOWACKA, D.** The role of alignment in morphology and prosody: the case of Polish. *LONDON (UCL) D 2005.*

1468. **KIBORT, A.** Passive and passive-like constructions in English and Polish. *CAMBRIDGE D 2005.*

Romanian

1469. **STEFANOVICI, I. O.** Comparative phonetics of English and Roumanian. *LONDON (UCL) D 1927.*

1470. **HURREN, H. A.** A linguistic description of Istro-Rumanian. *OXFORD D 1971.*

1471. **MALLINSON, G.** Complex structures and deletion in English and Romanian syntax. *EXETER D 1974.*

1472. **DELETANT, D. J.** A textual study of the Ieud Manuscript. *LONDON (SSEES) D 1976.*

1473. **COPOSESCU, L. -R.** The construction of meaning in the interaction between native speakers of English and Romanians. *LANCASTER D 2002.*

1474. **KOUFOGIORGIOU, A.** Vlach-Aromanian in Metsovo: a sociolinguistic investigation of a case of language shift in Greece. *ESSEX D 2003.*

1475. **IETCU, I.** Dialogicality and ethical perspective in Romanian intellectual discourse after 1989: a study of H.-R. Patapievici. *LANCASTER D 2004.*

1476. **CUSEN, G.** Investigating vocabulary learning strategies: a case study of Romanian undergraduates with a professional interest in learning English as a foreign language. *LANCASTER D 2005.*

1477. **SCHULTE, K.** Pragmatic causation in the rise of the Romance prepositional infinitive: a statistically-based study with special reference to Spanish, Portuguese and Romanian. *CAMBRIDGE D 2006.*

Russian

1478. **HINGLEY, R. F.** The stress of Russian nouns in -a/ -ja. *LONDON (SSEES) D 1952.*

1479. **FURNISS, G.** Diminutive formations in modern literary Russian. *CAMBRIDGE D 1953.*

1480. **Du Feu, V. M.** The relative in 17th-century Russian. LONDON (SSEES) D 1956.

1481. **Mickley, B. D. G.** The composition and usage of the Russian vocabulary in the first quarter of the eighteenth century, with special reference to the relationship between its Russian and Church Slavonic elements. CAMBRIDGE D 1957.

1482. **Leeming, H.** Polish-Latin loanwords in pre-Petrine Russian. LONDON (SSEES) D 1961.

1483. **Drage, C. L.** Palatalization of consonants before palatalized consonants in contemporary standard Russian. LONDON (SSEES) D 1963.

1484. **Pennington, A. E.** The language of Kotoshikhin. OXFORD D 1964.

1485. **Gardiner, S. C.** Old Russian diplomatic vocabulary: a study based on the documents of the Posol'skiy Prikaz relating to the Holy Roman Empire, 1488–1699. LONDON (EXTERNAL) D 1965.

1486. **Le Fleming, L. S. K.** The language of Chekhov's later stories. CAMBRIDGE ML 1967.

1487. **Yates, D. M.** A linguistic model for Russian-English machine translation, and its use in the synthesis of the English output. LONDON (UCL) D 1967.

1488. **Bivon, R.** Sequence of elements of clause structure in contemporary written Russian: a comparison of the language of the humanities and the natural sciences. ESSEX D 1969.

1489. **Ryan, W. F.** Astronomical and astrological terminology in Old Russian literature. OXFORD D 1969.

1490. **Sherwood, P. M.** German loanwords in Russian, 1700–1725. MANCHESTER D 1969.

1491. **Thomas, G.** Middle Low German loan words in Russian (1200–1500). LONDON (SSEES) D 1969.

1492. **Miller, J. E.** Tense and aspect in Russian. EDINBURGH D 1970.

1493. **Morley, G. D.** A systemic description of the process-participant relationships in selected types of Russian clause. ESSEX D 1970.

1494. **Berg, D. J.** Semantics and word-formation of neologisms designating material objects in the Russian lexicon since 1953. LONDON (SSEES) D 1971.

1495. **Roberts, C. B.** A historical analysis of the meanings of Russian verbal prefixes [...]. EDINBURGH D 1971.

1496. **Comrie, B. S.** Aspects of sentence-complementation in Russian. CAMBRIDGE D 1972.

1497. **Sussex, R. D.** Aspects of the syntax of Russian adjectives. LONDON (SSEES) D 1972.

1498. **Baldwin, J. R.** A formal analysis of the intonation of modern colloquial Russian. LONDON (UCL) D 1973.

1499. **Clarke, J. E. M.** Karamzin's linguistic ideas, with particular reference to his conception of the Russian literary language. OXFORD BL 1973.

1500. **Kilby, D. A.** Deep and superficial cases in Russian. EDINBURGH D 1973.

1501. **Sowerby, J. G.** The pronunciation of groups of three or more consonants in modern Moscow Russian. LONDON (SSEES) D 1975.

1502. CORBETT, G. G.　Problems of adjectival agreement in Russian. BIRMINGHAM D 1976.

1503. WADE, T. L. B.　Meanings of extent and purpose in modern Russian primary prepositions. STRATHCLYDE D 1977.

1504. WAIGHT, T.　The pronunciation of words of foreign origin in standard modern Russian. LONDON (SSEES) D 1977.

1505. DUNN, J. A.　The construction 'nominative + infinitive' in Russian. OXFORD D 1978.

1506. HAIGH, O. A.　Aksyonov's use of slang and colloquial language in his literary work of the nineteen-sixties and early nineteen-seventies. LONDON (SSEES) MP 1978.

1507. TROMAN, W. M. J.　The formation of Christian terminology in modern Russian. LONDON (SSEES) MP 1978.

1508. BEEDHAM, C.　The passive aspect in English, German and Russian. SALFORD D 1979.

1509. HERON, P. A.　The underlying grammar in a language course (with a special reference to Russian). ASTON D 1979.

1510. MAYO, P. J.　The morphology of aspect in seventeenth century Russian (based on texts of the *smutnoe vremja*). SHEFFIELD D 1981.

1511. RUSCHOFF, B. -H.　Russian verb-based nominal compounds: a semantic and morphological study. LONDON (SSEES) D 1982.

1512. THOMPSON, D. F.　German loan words in 19th century Russian. OXFORD D 1983.

1513. WHITTALL, S.　A study of English nautical loanwords in the Russian language of the eighteenth century. MANCHESTER MP 1984.

1514. DE BRAY, H. T.　Nouns pertaining to clothing and accessories not recorded in published Soviet monolingual dictionaries. OXFORD ML 1986.

1515. LAGERBERG, R. J.　The relationship between stress and affixation in Russian. LONDON (SSEES) D 1992.

1516. RYAZANOVA, L. I.　The development of skills in the use of Russian emotional and evaluative lexis for English-speaking students at an advanced level. [*In Russian*]. STRATHCLYDE D 1992.

1517. STEELE, M. H.　Paragraph structure and translation: theory and practice of paragraph and other high level structures in English and Russian narrative and the effect of the translation process [...]. GLASGOW D 1992.

1518. MELLOR, M. D.　Aspects of aspectual verbs in English and Russian. EDINBURGH D 1995.

1519. SMITH, M.　The influence of French on eighteenth-century literary Russian in the writings of D. I. Fonvizin. LONDON (SSEES) D 1996.

1520. HIPPISLEY, A.　Declarative derivation: a network morphology account of Russian word formation with reference to nouns denoting 'person'. SURREY D 1997.

1521. RAVENHALL, S. R.　The reflection of recent political and economic change in the lexis of Russian financial literature. WALES (BANGOR) MP 1997.

1522. UKIAH, N. J.　Stress in modern Russian inflection: patterns and variation. LONDON (SSEES) D 1997.

1523. **BROWN, D.**   From the general to the exceptional: a network morphology account of Russian nominal inflection. *SURREY D 1998.*

1524. **DAVIE, J. D.**   Making sense of the nonstandard: a study of borrowing and word-formation in 1990s Russian youth slang, with particular reference to the language of the fanzine. *PORTSMOUTH D 1998.*

1525. **RAJEWSKY, A.**   Changes in the Russian terminology of economic law since perestroika. *OXFORD D 1998.*

1526. **CHEW, P.**   A computational phonology of Russian. *OXFORD D 1999.*

1527. **TRONENKO, N. G.**   Regularities in the behaviour of Russian phrasal idioms. *OXFORD D 2000.*

1528. **WHITTAKER, E. W. D.**   Statistical language modelling for automatic speech recognition of Russian and English. *CAMBRIDGE D 2000.*

1529. **SAMOILOVA, N.**   The adaptation of Baltic Finnic loanwords in Russian. *ST ANDREWS D 2001.*

1530. **BEER, R. D. S.**   'The hygiene of souls': languages of illness and contagion in late Imperial and early Soviet Russia. *CAMBRIDGE D 2002.*

1531. **BARRY, S. M. E.**   Temporal correlates of the voicing contrast in Russian. *LONDON (UCL) D 2003.*

1532. **SMITH, K. L.**   The translation of advertising texts: a study of English-language printed advertisements and their translations in Russian. *SHEFFIELD D 2003.*

1533. **KOTEYKO, N.**   Bias in presenting the business world: English loanwords in Russian print media. *BIRMINGHAM D 2006.*

Serbo-Croat

1534. **DE BRAY, R. G.**   A study in Serbo-Croat accent and intonation. *LONDON (SSEES) D 1958.*

1535. **IZAKOVIĆ, V.**   Acoustic cues for the distinction between palatalized and non-palatalized voiceless affricatives in Serbo-Croatian. *LONDON (SSEES) MP 1967.*

1536. **YARWOOD, D.**   The vocabulary of knowledge and understanding in Serbo-Croat and English. *EDINBURGH D 1973.*

1537. **HERRITY, P.**   The literary language of Emanuil Janković. *LONDON (SSEES) D 1974.*

1538. **BELL, G.**   The struggle for a standard Serbo-Croat literary language as reflected in literary journals in Serbia and Croatia in 1850–1900. *NOTTINGHAM D 1979.*

1539. **RISTICH, V.**   The literary language of Pavle Julinac. *LONDON (SSEES) D 1980.*

1540. **BRALA, M.**   English, Croatian and Italian prepositions from a cognitive perspective: when 'at' is 'on' and 'on' is 'in'. *CAMBRIDGE D 2000.*

1541. **TRENKIĆ, D.**   The acquisition of English articles by Serbian speakers. *CAMBRIDGE D 2000.*

1542. **PEROVIC, A.**   Knowledge of binding in Down syndrome: evidence from English and Serbo-Croatian. *LONDON (UCL) D 2004.*

1543. **NOVAKOVIĆ, N.**   Developmental issues in the acquisition of word order in L2 Serbo-Croatian with special reference to second-position clitics. *CAMBRIDGE D 2005.*

1544. SEVA, N.   Exploring the facilitating effect of diminutives on the acquisition of Serbian noun morphology. STIRLING D 2006.

Slavonic

1545. GALTON, H.   The phonological system of original Old Slav and its genesis. LONDON (SSEES) D 1951.

1546. HUNTLEY, D. G.   A semantic analysis of Old Church Slavonic verbs of motion and their compounds. LONDON (EXTERNAL) D 1968.

1547. PRESS, J. I.   *Jery* in the Slavonic languages. LONDON (SSEES) D 1978.

1548. ROLFE, G. C.   Graeco-Latin lexical elements in Russian and Czech. ULSTER D 1978.

1549. CLEMINSON, R. M.   *Stefanit" i Ikhnilat"*: the grammar of Russian Church Slavonic as represented by Bodl. MS. Russ. e.1, [...] with a full critical edition of the text. OXFORD D 1983.

1550. CAINK, A. D.   The lexical interface: closed class items in South Slavic and English. DURHAM D 1998.

1551. BRACKNEY, N. C.   The origins of Slavonic: language contact and language change in ancient Eastern Europe and Western Eurasia. ST ANDREWS D 2004.

1552. OVEN, P. C.   The development of special characters in Slavonic languages, with the emphasis on the orthographic reforms in Slovenian and Croatian language. READING D 2004.

1553. TURNER, S.   A pragmatic approach to constituent order in early East Slavonic sources. OXFORD D 2005.

Slovene

1554. LIMON, D. J.   A contrastive analysis of the finite verb phrase in Slovene and English based on a corpus of translated texts. EXETER MP 1987.

1555. POPOVIĆ, M.   Implementation of a Slovene language-based free-text retrieval system. SHEFFIELD D 1991.

1556. ČINKOLE, B.   Fo patterns in Slovene pitch-accents. NOTTINGHAM D 1993.

1557. GRAHEK, S.   Argument structure in Slovene. LEEDS D 2006.

Sorbian

1558. BRIDGWATER, W. P.   Veneti-Wenden: an ethnological and onomastic study. OXFORD BL 1956.

1559. STONE, G. C.   Lexical developments in the Upper Sorbian literary language, 1827–1927. LONDON (EXTERNAL) D 1969.

1560. GEBEL, K.   Language and ethnic / national identity in Europe: the importance of Gaelic and Sorbian to the maintenance of associated cultures and ethno-cultural identities. MIDDLESEX D 2002.

South Eastern Europe

1561. PRESTON, T. R. N.   Topographical elements in the Balkan lexicon: a descriptive and historical study of vocabulary pertaining to the mountains, lowland and littoral of South-Eastern Europe. LONDON (SSEES) D 1993.

Ukrainian

1562. CYMBALISTYJ, P.   Ukrainian linguistic elements in the Russian language, 1680–1760. LONDON (SSEES) D 1991.

1563. TAYLOR, J. E. P.   The position of the Ukrainian language in Ukraine. LONDON (SSEES) D 1999.

USSR

1564. KERAWALLA, G. J.   A comparative study of factors influencing the language policies in India and the USSR. LONDON (EXTERNAL) D 1975.

1565. REZNIK, V.   From Saussure to sociolinguistics: the evolution of Soviet sociology of language in the 1920s and 1930s. EXETER D 2004.

Yiddish

1566. ESTRAIKH, G.   Origin and features of Soviet Yiddish. OXFORD D 1995.

17. LAW, HUMAN RIGHTS

General and Comparative

1567. GÜNDÜZ, A.   Security and human rights in Europe: the CSCE process. ESSEX MP 1993.

1568. O'NIONS, H.   A case study on the protection of human rights. Human rights and legal wrongs: the Roma in Europe. LEICESTER D 1999.

Albania

1569. ALIMEHMETI, E.   The concept of effective remedies in the Albanian legal system, particularly as regards meeting its obligations under the European Convention on Human Rights (art. 13). OPEN MP 2000.

Baltic States (see also under individual countries)

1570. ZIEMELE, I.   State continuity and nationality in the Baltic states: international and constitutional law issues. CAMBRIDGE D 1999.

Bosnia-Herzegovina

1571. Cox, D. M. The making of a Bosnian state: international law and the authority of the international community. CAMBRIDGE D 2002.

Bulgaria

1572. SMILOV, D. Judicial discretion in constitutional jurisprudence: doctrines and policies of the Bulgarian Constitutional Court. OXFORD D 2003.

Central and Eastern Europe (see also under individual countries)

1573. MORLEY, A. H. The new constitutions of Europe: a comparative study of post-war European constitutions with special reference to Germany, Poland, Czechoslovakia, The Kingdom of the Serbs, Croats and Slovenes, and the Baltic States [NCR]. OXFORD BL 1925.

1574. PIOTROWICZ, R. W. The post-war settlement in Central Europe: legal aspects of frontiers and citizenship. GLASGOW D 1987.

1575. WILLIAMS, P. R. International law and the resolution of Central and East European trans-boundary environmental disputes [with the Gabčíkovo-Nagymaros Project as primary case study]. CAMBRIDGE D 1998.

1576. VOICULESCU, A. Prosecuting history: political justice in post-communist Eastern Europe. LONDON (LSE) D 1999.

1577. VENEAU, M. H. D. The role of fundamental rights in the enlargement of the European Union to Central and Eastern European countries. BIRMINGHAM D 2000.

1578. SENGAYEN, M. Behind the curtain: the true nature of the 'revolution' within the Central European product liability regimes. WESTMINSTER D 2004.

1579. SLAVOVA, S. S. Institutional and legal aspects of financial development in transition economies. LONDON (LSE) D 2005.

Estonia

1580. NURMELA, I. Viability of litigation in resolving international commercial business-to-business disputes in the EU, in particular England and Estonia. CAMBRIDGE D 2006.

Hungary

1581. ZSUPPAN, F. T. Electoral reform in Hungary, 1916–1919. LONDON (LSE) D 1972.

Kazakhstan

1582. DOSMUKHAMEDOV, E. K. The legal regulation of foreign direct investment in transitional states: the case of the Republic of Kazakhstan in comparative perspective. OXFORD D 1999.

1583. KURMANBAYEV, M. -A. An analysis of the development of copyright law and practice in Kazakhstan. WARWICK D 2005.

Poland

1584. LASOK, D.   The Polish Constitutions of 1947 and 1952: a historical study in constitutional law. LONDON (LSE) D 1954.

1585. PUCHALSKA-TYCH, B. A.   Property in Great Britain and Poland: a comparison. Property regime in transition — the Polish case. LANCASTER D 1999.

1586. FIJALKOWSKI, A. A.   Rule of law revived: the Polish judiciary 1918–1998. LONDON (QM WESTFIELD) D 2000.

Romania

1587. MUNTEANU, G.   The constitution of Rumania. LONDON (LSE) D 1935.

Russia (see also USSR)

1588. HARTLEY, J. M.   The implementation of the laws relating to local administration, 1775–1796, with special reference to the guberniya of St Petersburg. LONDON (SSEES) D 1980.

1589. WAGNER, W. G.   The development of the law of inheritance and patrimonial property in post-emancipation Russia and its social, economic and political implications. OXFORD D 1980.

1590. POMERANZ, W. E.   The emergence and development of the Russian 'Advokatura' 1864–1905. LONDON (SSEES) D 1990.

1591. POPKINS, G.   The Russian peasant *volost* court and customary law 1861–1917. OXFORD D 1995.

1592. YOSHIDA, I.   Comparative study of international commercial arbitration in England, Japan and Russia. EDINBURGH D 2000.

1593. MULCAHY, R. G.   Canon law in medieval Russia: an examination of the *Kormchaia kniga* as a source of law. LONDON (UCL) MP 2001.

1594. LUCAS, S. B.   Foundations of the law on industrial organisations in Russia and the former republics of the USSR — 1985–1990. LONDON (UCL) D 2002.

1595. VENDIL, C.   The Russian legitimation formula 1991–2000. LONDON (LSE) D 2002.

1596. RAISKIN, J.   The role of law in Russian international business transactions. OXFORD D 2003.

1597. SUNDARA RAJAN, M. T.   Moral rights and creative freedom: a study of post-communist law reform in Russia. OXFORD D 2003.

1598. VERESHCHAGIN, A. N.   The development of judicial law-making in the Russian legal system. ESSEX D 2004.

1599. BADYKOV, M. R.   Private international law rules of the Russian Civil Code and the European Convention on the Law Applicable to Contractual Obligations: a comparative analysis. ESSEX D 2005.

1600. BYKHOVSKAYA, E.   State immunity: Russian perspective in the context of international practice. ESSEX D 2005.

1601. DOBATKIN, D.   Company law in Russia: problems of transformation. OXFORD D 2005.

1602. LEONIDOV, I. Comparative and international legal study on the position of irregular migrants in the United Kingdom, Russia and South Africa. *LONDON (INST ADV LEGAL ST) D 2005.*

1603. UTYASHEVA, L. Non-judicial methods of human rights protection: the ombudsman and non-governmental organisations — the experience of the UK and Russia. *NEWCASTLE D 2006.*

Serbia

1604. LALONDE, S. N. *Uti possidetis* and internal administrative boundaries [with special reference to the Serbia/Croatia and Serbia/BiH boundaries]. *CAMBRIDGE D 1997.*

Soviet Bloc

1605. ŠEBEK, V. The attitudes of the East European states to the law of the adjacent marine and submarine areas. *LONDON (LSE) D 1974.*

Ukraine

1606. WAGNER, K. A. Towards orange litigation: judicial politics and the Supreme Court in Ukraine. *OXFORD MP 2006.*

USSR (see also Russia)

1607. RUDDEN, B. A. Soviet insurance law. *WALES (ABERYSTWYTH) D 1965.*

1608. GROVE, E. Soviet commercial contract in the light of economic reform. *LONDON (KCL) MP 1973.*

1609. OLAJUMOKE, W. O. Legal aspects of the forms of international co-operation between the Soviet Union and African states. *EDINBURGH D 1974.*

1610. MAKEPEACE, R. W. Marxist ideology and Russian reality as reflected in Russian criminal legislation, 1917–1977. *LONDON (LSE) D 1978.*

1611. HUSKEY, E. E. The formation of the Soviet legal profession (*advokatura*), 1917–1939. *LONDON (LSE) D 1983.*

1612. FITZPATRICK, R. S. The Helsinki Final Act and human rights in Soviet-American relations. *EDINBURGH D 1989.*

1613. PRINCE, K. P. Consumer protection in the Soviet Union. *OXFORD MP 1990.*

1614. ISSACOVITCH, A. Public international law in the Soviet Union since 1985. *OXFORD MP 1991.*

1615. BATTARBEE, A. P. The politics of legal reform in the Soviet Union: the development and implementation of the concept of the *pravovoe gosudarstvo* (law-governed state) [NCR]. *OXFORD ML 1992.*

1616. GORLIZKI, Y. De-Stalinization and the politics of Russian criminal justice, 1953–1964. *OXFORD D 1992.*

1617. CALLUM, D. R. Soviet society and law: the history of the legal campaign to enforce the constitutional duty to work. *GLASGOW D 1995.*

1618. O'HALLARON, C. M.   American human rights policy toward the Soviet Union in the Conference on Security and Cooperation in Europe 1975–1989: the Belgrade, Madrid and Vienna review meetings. CAMBRIDGE D 1995.

1619. CAMPBELL, J. M.   Is there a case for socialist jurisprudence? [With special reference to the former Soviet republics]. GLASGOW D 1997.

1620. LEE, K. -G.   The law of state succession in the post-decolonisation period with special reference to Germany and the former Soviet Union. CAMBRIDGE D 1998.

Yugoslavia (see also under former republics)

1621. CORONNA, E. M.   The joint-ventures of the Yugoslav legal system. LONDON (KCL) D 1981.

1622. NEOCLEOUS, I.   International Tribunal for the Former Yugoslavia. SUSSEX MP 1999.

1623. CARTER, D. J.   International law and state failure: Somalia and Yugoslavia. SOUTHAMPTON D 2000.

1624. HIRSH, D.   The coming of age of cosmopolitan law: crimes against humanity and their prosecution [with case studies of action in Yugoslavia]. WARWICK D 2001.

1625. KERR, R. C.   The International Criminal Tribunal for the Former Yugoslavia: law, diplomacy and politics. LONDON (KCL) D 2001.

1626. BAROS, M.   International law and the resolution of the Yugoslav conflicts: application or creation? NOTTINGHAM D 2002.

1627. PUPAVAC, M.   The International Criminal Tribunal for the Former Yugoslavia and the rule of law in international relations. NOTTINGHAM D 2003.

18. LITERATURE

General and Comparative

1628. GÖMÖRI, G.   The development of Polish and Hungarian poetry in the post-war period, 1945–56. OXFORD BL 1962.

1629. PAYNE, J. W.   Continuity in Georg Lukács' theory of literary realism. EDINBURGH D 1976.

1630. TAN, S. S. B.   Bakhtin and discourse stylistics. NOTTINGHAM D 1996.

1631. LARSEN, M. D. H.   The Bakhtinian chronotype: origins, modifications and additions. KENT D 1997.

1632. TIHANOV, G. V.   Bakhtin and Lukács: the theory of the novel as social philosophy. OXFORD D 1997.

1633. POPESCU-SANDU, O.   Bodily textures: generic inscriptions and ideological markings in Russian and Romanian fantastic literature. OPEN MP 1999.

1634. RENFREW, A.   Material, representation and the problem of genre in Bakhtin. SHEFFIELD D 2000.

1635. LEŠIĆ-THOMAS, A.   Barthes, Bakhtin, structuralism: a reassessment. LONDON (QUEEN MARY) D 2001.

1636. **GARDNER, C. B.** Versions of interactivity: a theoretical and empirical approach to the study of hypertext function [Bakhtin Centre]. *SHEFFIELD D 2002.*

1637. **KLUJBER, A. R.** Snow and window: archetypes of imagination [including Hungarian and Russian literature]. *CAMBRIDGE D 2002.*

1638. **ZBINDEN, K.** The cross-cultural transmission of works by Mikhail Bakhtin and the Bakhtin Circle: missing sociality. *SHEFFIELD D 2002.*

1639. **CHITNIS, R. A.** Liberation and the authority of the writer in the Russian, Czech and Slovak fiction of the Changes. *LONDON (UCL) D 2003.*

1640. **ROBINSON, R.** Border space: Central and Eastern Europe in the writings of Italo Svevo, Joseph Roth, Rebecca West and James Joyce. *EAST ANGLIA D 2003.*

1641. **BUGAN, C.** Poetics of exile: East European poetry in translation and Seamus Heaney's *Ars poetica. OXFORD D 2004.*

1642. **DRAGNEVA, D. V.** Conceptions of decay in Czech and Bulgarian national mythology. *LONDON (UCL) D 2006.*

1643. **THOMAS, A. C.** St Petersburg in three works of contemporary non-Russian writing: narratives of a city in transition. *BATH D 2006.*

1644. **ZORIĆ, V.** Literature beyond exilium: inscriptions of enforced displacement. *NOTTINGHAM D 2006.*

Bulgarian

1645. **PINTO, V. DE S.** The Narodnik movement in Bulgarian literature, and the influence on that movement of Russian literature and thought. *LONDON (SSEES) D 1952.*

Caucasian

1646. **CLOGG, R.** Abkhazian cultural identity in the twentieth century: the case of Fazil ' Iskander. *OXFORD D 1999.*

Czech

1647. **WOODWARD, J. A.** Reflections of West European literature, especially English, French and German, in Czech literature from 1860 to 1918, with special reference to Jaroslav Vrchlický. *LONDON (SSEES) D 1953.*

1648. **BRADBROOK, B.** Karel Čapek and the Western world. *OXFORD D 1958.*

1649. **DOMIN, J. P. C.** Czech social poetry of the late nineteenth and early twentieth centuries [NCR]. *GLASGOW ML 1970.*

1650. **DOWDING, L. M.** The treatment of contemporary society and the individual in the Czech novel from 1948–68. *OXFORD BL 1972.*

1651. **HORSFALL, S.** Some critical attitudes to the plays of Karel Čapek in Czechoslovakia, 1920–1963. *LEEDS MP 1972.*

1652. **HARDS, P. W. G.** The concept of revolution in Czech writing, 1918–1938. *CAMBRIDGE D 1975.*

1653. **NAUGHTON, J. D.** The reception in nineteenth-century England of Czech literature and of the Czech literary revival. *CAMBRIDGE D 1978.*

1654. **Thomas, A.** The Czech chivalric romances *Vévoda Arnošt* and *Lavryn* in their literary context. CAMBRIDGE D 1987.

1655. **Chirico, D. D.** Karel Hlaváček and the decadent intertext. CAMBRIDGE D 1995.

1656. **Cooke, M. G.** Disillusion and the myth of the victim in American and Czech fiction since World War II. LONDON (QM WESTFIELD) D 1997.

1657. **Hayes, K.** The prose and polemics of Karel Matěj Čapek-Chod. LONDON (SSEES) D 1997.

1658. **Miljević, R.** Notions of identity in the work of Egon Hostovský. LONDON (UCL) D 2000.

1659. **Keat, J.** Projections in black and white: cinematic construction / construction of a cinematic in Czech Poetist prose of the 1920s. OXFORD D 2001.

1660. **Rowlands, S. P.** Marginal politics: the aesthetic and the essayistic in selected writings by Twm Morys, Václav Havel and Bohumil Hrabal. OXFORD D 2002.

1661. **Woods, M.** Lost letters: translating Milan Kundera's Czech fiction. TC DUBLIN D 2002.

1662. **Pickett, V.** Consciousness of fiction: structures of narrative uncertainty in the prose of Richard Weiner. OXFORD D 2006.

1663. **Şandru, C. E.** 'The West and the rest': Eastern Europe, postcolonialism and the fictions of Milan Kundera and Salman Rushdie. WALES (ABERYSTWYTH) D 2006.

English

1664. **Dunn, D.** Shaw's Russia: a study of the attitudes, ideas and beliefs of George Bernard Shaw as they affected, and were modified by, the development of Soviet Russia. LONDON (LSE) D 1984.

1665. **Nicholson, S. J.** The portrayal of communism and the Soviet Union in selected plays performed in Great Britain, 1917–1945. LEEDS D 1991.

1666. **Goldsworthy, V.** Representations of the Balkans in English literature, their Romantic origins and their development between 1894 and 1965. LONDON (BIRKBECK) D 1996.

1667. **Howlett, B. -Y.** Cultural transfer in translation with particular reference to Russian and Chinese translations of Dickens' *David Copperfield*. LEEDS D 1996.

1668. **Williams, S. J.** An analysis of the readings of cultural indicators embedded in children's literature texts [from teaching English children's literature to Czech students]. COVENTRY D 1998.

1669. **Labon, J.** English literary responses to 1930s Europe in Rebecca West's *Black Lamb and Grey Falcon: A Journey Through Yugoslavia in 1937* (1941) and Storm Jameson's *Europe to Let: The Memoirs of an Obscure Man* (1940). LONDON (BIRKBECK) D 2000.

1670. **Guyver, L.** Post-Cold War moral geography: a critical analysis of representations of Eastern Europe in post-1989 British fiction and drama. WARWICK D 2001.

1671. **Lobytsyna, M.** The impact and presence of the writings of Laurence Sterne in eighteenth-century Russia. GLASGOW ML 2001.

1672. **Hammond, A. N.** The debated lands: British travel writing and the construction of the Balkans. WARWICK D 2002.

Hungarian

1673. **Egger, M.** A comparative study of the English, Scottish and Hungarian popular ballad. *LONDON (KCL) D 1928.*

1674. **Rubin, A.** Social criticism in the Hungarian novel (1820–1850). *LONDON (EXTERNAL) D 1945.*

1675. **Cushing, G. F.** Széchényi, Kossuth, and national classicism in Hungarian literature. *LONDON (SSEES) D 1952.*

1676. **Leader, N. A. M.** The main Hungarian classical ballads [...] with particular reference to English and Scottish ballads. *CAMBRIDGE D 1962.*

1677. **Czigány, L. G.** The reception of Hungarian literature in Great Britain from Bowring's *Poetry of the Magyars* to the novels of Jókai. *LONDON (SSEES) D 1965.*

1678. **Rynd, A.** Georg Lukács: aspects of a social aesthetic. *ESSEX D 1975.*

1679. **Aczel, R.** National character and European identity in Hungarian literature 1772–1848. *LONDON (SSEES) D 1990.*

1680. **Jones, G. A.** Urban narratives in Hungarian literature: the prose fiction of Budapest, 1873–1939. *LONDON (UCL) D 2006.*

1681. **Minier, M.** Translating *Hamlet* into Hungarian culture: a case study in rewriting and translation [NCR]. *HULL D 2006.*

Jewish

1682. **Moseley, M. G. M.** Jewish autobiography in Eastern Europe: the pre-history of a literary genre. *OXFORD D 1990.*

Latvian

1683. **Rubess, B. N.** Jānis Rainis and the problem of nationalism. *OXFORD D 1982.*

Polish

1684. **Pietrikiewicz, J.** A comparative study of English lyric poetry from a Polish point of view [...] . *LONDON (KCL) D 1947.*

1685. **Bienkowska, D. I.** An analytical study of the early literary work of Stefan Żeromski, its cultural background, and its critical reception in Poland. *LONDON (SSEES) D 1965.*

1686. **Hultberg, P.** The literary style of Wacław Berent's early works. *LONDON (SSEES) D 1967.*

1687. **Welsh, D. J.** The art of Henryk Sienkiewicz, with special reference to the *Trilogy*. *LONDON (EXTERNAL) D 1967.*

1688. **Halikowska, T.** A comparative study of Polish and English emblem literature of the seventeenth century, with special reference to the works of Zbigniew Morsztyn and Francis Quarles. *OXFORD BL 1968.*

1689. **Cwiakala, J.** Some English and Polish women novelists of the inter-war period, 1918–1939. *OXFORD BL 1969.*

1690. **Kumiega, J.** Grotowski within Poland. *BRISTOL ML 1978.*

1691. Dudek, J. The poetics of W. B. Yeats and K. Wierzynski: a parallel. OXFORD D 1979.

1692. Gibbs, L. Latin achievement and vernacular ambition: the *Elegiae* of Jan Kochanowski, Books I & IV. OXFORD MP 1989.

1693. Gorell, E. Urban themes in Polish Baroque literature between 1597 and 1696. OXFORD D 1990.

1694. Malkiewicz, G. Literature as a medium for self-understanding. A study with particular reference to the writings of Witold Gombrowicz. OXFORD D 1991.

1695. Tighe, C. Dilemmas of the literary left in Poland, 1945–89: Polish writers and post war politics. MANCHESTER D 1994.

1696. Bates, J. M. The PUWP's preferences in the contemporary Polish novel, 1959–1985. GLASGOW D 1997.

1697. Grudzien, A. Death and suffering in the poetry of John Donne and Mikołaj Sęp Szarzyński. OXFORD D 1999.

1698. Sanders, B. Jan Kochanowski's *Psałterz Dawidów* in the context of the European tradition. ST ANDREWS D 2001.

1699. Jajdelski, W. Structuralist transformations in Polish literary theory after 1956. OXFORD D 2004.

Romanian

1700. Giuran, M. -I. Mihail Eminescu: an exponent of Romanian romanticism. LONDON (SSEES) MP 1991.

1701. Feetam, C. R. The influence of Germanic writing and thought on the philosophy, drama and literary work of Lucian Blaga. LONDON (EXTERNAL) D 1993.

1702. Drace-Francis, A. J. Literature, modernity, nation: the case of Romania, 1829–1890. LONDON (UCL) D 2001.

1703. Şerban, A. Audience design in literary translations from Romanian into English: a corpus-based analysis of deixis and presupposition. HERIOT-WATT D 2003.

1704. Cinpoes, N. 'As a stranger, give it welcome': Romania's Hamlet. WARWICK D 2005.

Russian

1705. Dennis, C. P. L. The complete poems of Aleksey Vasil'evich Kol'tsov, translated from the Russian with an introduction and commentary. LONDON (EXTERNAL) D 1922.

1706. Gerhardi, W. A. Anton Chekhov: a critical study [NCR]. OXFORD BL 1923.

1707. Godinski, L. Le roman russe en France à la fin du dix-neuvième siècle considéré au point de vue de l'influence exercée par Tolstoi sur Paul Margueritte et Romain Rolland. LONDON (R HOLLOWAY) D 1923.

1708. Matthews, W. The influence of Byron on Russian poetry. LONDON (SSEES) D 1926.

1709. Webb, M. P. The life and poetry of Tyutchev. LONDON (SSEES) D 1927.

1710. Iovetz-Tereshchenko, N. Some problems of the 'Tale of the expedition of Igor', a Russian poem of the twelfth century [NCR]. OXFORD BL 1928.

1711. BEASLEY, I. M. The dramatic art of Ostrovsky. LONDON (SSEES) D 1931.

1712. HILL, E. M. The growth of the Russian psychological novel from its origins to 1864. LONDON (SSEES) D 1931.

1713. GILL, R. The poetry of Alexander Blok. LONDON (EXTERNAL) D 1938.

1714. GUERSHOON, A. Certain aspects of Russian proverbs. LONDON (SSEES) D 1938.

1715. REEDY, L. D. Russian realism and the development of the English novel, 1880–1914: a study in literary influence. TC DUBLIN D 1938.

1716. MUKHERJEA, S. K. The influence of Byron on Lermontov. OXFORD BL 1945.

1717. HEMMINGS, F. W. J. The influence of the Russian novel on French writers and thinkers, with particular reference to Tolstoy and Dostoevsky. OXFORD D 1949.

1718. LANG, D. M. Alexander Nikolaevich Radishchev and his contacts with contemporary French and German thinkers. CAMBRIDGE D 1949.

1719. LEWITTER, L. R. A study of the academic drama in Russia and the Ukraine in the seventeenth and eighteenth centuries, with special reference to its Polish origins. CAMBRIDGE D 1950.

1720. DAVIE, D. A. The English idea of Russian fiction since 1828. CAMBRIDGE D 1951.

1721. FENNELL, J. L. I. The history of the conflict between the 'Possessors' and the 'Non-Possessors' in Russia and its reflection in the literature of the period — the end of the fifteenth century and the first half of the sixteenth century. CAMBRIDGE D 1951.

1722. DONCHIN, G. The influence of French symbolism on Russian poetry. LONDON (SSEES) D 1953.

1723. PARTRIDGE, M. A. Alexander Herzen: a study of his years in Russia [1812–1847]. LONDON (EXTERNAL) D 1953.

1724. RAPP, H. Ivan Goncharov and his relation to the intelligentsia. LONDON (SSEES) D 1953.

1725. VLASTO, A. P. M. M. Heraskov: a study in the intellectual life of the age of Catherine the Great. CAMBRIDGE D 1953.

1726. HORVAT, J. A. The poetry of Alexander Blok: a critical analysis. CAMBRIDGE D 1954.

1727. JOHNSON, D. J. L. The sources of Pushkin's *Songs of the Western Slavs*. BIRMINGHAM D 1954.

1728. FUTRELL, M. H. Dickens and three Russian novelists: Gogol', Dostoyevsky, Tolstoy. LONDON (SSEES) D 1955.

1729. GREENE, M. Some aspects of Scottish authors in Russian literature in the first half of the nineteenth century. EDINBURGH D 1955.

1730. RIASANOVSKY, A. V. Social and aesthetic views of Nicholas Chernyshevsky. OXFORD BL 1955.

1731. BEDFORD, C. H. The development of the ideas of Dmitriy Merezhkovskiy. LONDON (SSEES) D 1956.

1732. FREEBORN, R. H. Trends of development in the Russian nineteenth-century realistic novel (1830–1880). OXFORD D 1957.

1733. MITCHELL, J. H. Some aspects of the problem of guilt, with special reference to Kafka, Kierkegaard and Dostoevsky. EDINBURGH D 1958.

1734. **RUKALSKI, Z.** Anton Chekhov and Guy de Maupassant: a comparative study. CAMBRIDGE D 1958.

1735. **EVANS, R. J. M.** Antiokh Kantemir: a study of his literary, political and social life in England, 1732–1738. LONDON (EXTERNAL) D 1959.

1736. **PYMAN, A.** The Russian decadents, 1890–1905, with special reference to D. S. Merezhkovsky. CAMBRIDGE D 1959.

1737. **RICHARDS, D.** Zamyatin: life and works. OXFORD BL 1959.

1738. **DEBRECZENY, P.** A study of Gogol''s literary style. LONDON (SSEES) D 1960.

1739. **PEACE, R. A.** N. G. Pomyalovsky: a literary, biographical and social study. OXFORD BL 1961.

1740. **CHRISTA, B.** Andrey Bely as a symbolist poet. CAMBRIDGE D 1963.

1741. **PIPER, D. G. B.** V. A. Kaverin: a study of his literary techniques and of the relationship of his prose writings to the Russian 'Left Art' movement during the period 1921–1939. CAMBRIDGE D 1964.

1742. **WOODWARD, J. B.** Leonid Andreyev: a study of his thought and art. OXFORD D 1964.

1743. **ITA, J. M.** The significance of Russian literature for the work of Thomas Mann. CAMBRIDGE D 1965.

1744. **JONES, M. V.** Dostoevsky and German idealist philosophy. NOTTINGHAM D 1965.

1745. **PARSONS, N. S.** S. Ya. Nadson (1862–1887): a biographical and critical study. OXFORD BL 1965.

1746. **THOMSON, R. D. B.** A critical study of the work of Leonid Leonov. OXFORD D 1965.

1747. **CROSS, A. G.** N. M. Karamzin's contribution to Russian letters (1783–1803). CAMBRIDGE D 1966.

1748. **TURNER, C. J. G.** Boris Tomashevsky (1890–1957): his literary theory and some examples of his critical methods. OXFORD BP 1966.

1749. **WILLIAMS, G.** The life and works of A. I. Kuprin, 1870–1938. OXFORD BL 1966.

1750. **CANNELL, R. H.** The work of N. A. Dobrolyubov as a literary critic. LONDON (SSEES) MP 1967.

1751. **THOMPSON, A. H.** The *Skazanie o tsarstve Tsarya Fedora* as the literary culmination of the Dimitry legend. OXFORD BL 1967.

1752. **BARRATT, G. R.** An exegesis of the verse of E. A. Baratynsky in the context of the movements of his time. LONDON (SSEES) D 1968.

1753. **BINYON, T. J.** Valery Yakovlevich Bryusov (1873–1924): life, literary theory, poetry. OXFORD D 1968.

1754. **BRIGGS, A. D. P.** A critical study of the original lyric poetry of A. A. Fet. LONDON (SSEES) D 1968.

1755. **DAVIES, J.** The life and works of Sergei Esenin, 1916–1925. MANCHESTER D 1968.

1756. **ELSWORTH, J. D.** The novels of Andrey Bely. CAMBRIDGE D 1968.

1757. **HIPPISLEY, A. R.** Simeon Polotsky as a representative of the baroque in Russian literature. OXFORD D 1968.

1758. **McVAY, G.** The life and works of Sergei Esenin (1895–1925). OXFORD D 1968.

1759. RICKWOOD, T. M.   Themes and style in the poetry of Kondratiy Ryleyev. LIVERPOOL D 1968.

1760. JORDAN, M.   Andrei Platonov (1899–1951): a study. MANCHESTER D 1969.

1761. LANDSMAN, N. B.   An analysis of the political and aesthetic aspects in the early work of Bestuzhev-Marlinsky. LONDON (SSEES) D 1969.

1762. LARY, N.   Dickens and Dostoevsky. SUSSEX D 1969.

1763. LLEWELLYN SMITH, V.   Women in Chekhov's work and life. OXFORD D 1969.

1764. RUBENSTEIN, R.   Virginia Woolf's response to Russian literature. LONDON (BIRKBECK) D 1969.

1765. STABLEFORD, M. T.   The life and works of N.A. Ostrovskij. LEEDS MP 1969.

1766. WOSIEN, M. G.   The Russian folktale: some structural and thematic aspects. LONDON (SSEES) D 1969.

1767. ARMES, K.   The early novels of Konstantin Fedin. CAMBRIDGE D 1970.

1768. CHAPLIN, M. J.   Mikhail Prishvin, 1873–1954: the link between man and nature in the works of Mikhail Prishvin. LONDON (EXTERNAL) MP 1970.

1769. DAVISON, R.   Camus' interest in Dostoevsky: the impact of Dostoevsky's novels on the Camus of Le Mythe de Sisyphe. LEEDS MP 1970.

1770. HAMMOND, K. G.   The metrical and rhythmical development of the Russian fable in the eighteenth century. LONDON (SSEES) D 1970.

1771. LANE, R. C.   The life and work of F. I. Tyutchev. CAMBRIDGE D 1970.

1772. PAVLOV, A.   The work of Yuriy Kazakov. ULSTER MP 1970.

1773. WEST, J. D.   Vyacheslav Ivanov and the Russian Symbolist aesthetic. CAMBRIDGE D 1970.

1774. BARNES, C. J.   The poetry of Boris Pasternak, with special reference to the period 1913–1917. CAMBRIDGE D 1971.

1775. COLLINS, P.   Turgenev and his French literary associates. OXFORD BL 1971.

1776. GRAHAM, S. D.   The lyric poetry of A. K. Tolstoy. EDINBURGH ML 1971.

1777. HAIGHT, A. C.   Anna Akhmatova: life and work. LONDON (SSEES) D 1971.

1778. LUKER, N. J. L.   The life and works of Alexander Grin, with special reference to his novels. NOTTINGHAM D 1971.

1779. McDUFF, D. W.   The poetry and aesthetics of Innokenty Annensky. EDINBURGH D 1971.

1780. OKAI, J. D. A.   Dostoyevsky: his artistic rearrangement of reality as manifested in the development of his literary style, with particular reference to his earlier works. LONDON (SSEES) MP 1971.

1781. RECK, V. T.   Boris Pil'nyak: the literary scandals of 1926 and 1929. LONDON (SSEES) D 1971.

1782. TAIT, A. L.   The literary works of A. V. Lunačarskij (1875–1933). CAMBRIDGE D 1971.

1783. TALBOTT, N. S.   Mayakovsky Agonistes: the myth of self in the poetry of Vladimir Mayakovsky. OXFORD BL 1971.

1784. BEAUMONT, B. J.   Flaubert and Turgenev: an examination of the parallels in their intellectual and literary development. LEICESTER D 1972.

1785. **GARLIŃSKI, J. E. J.**   Chekhov in France, 1893–1939. *LONDON (SSEES) MP 1972.*

1786. **KATZ, M. R.**   The literary ballad in early nineteenth-century Russian literature. *OXFORD D 1972.*

1787. **LITTLE, T. E.**   P. A. Vyazemsky as a critic of Russian literature. *LONDON (SSEES) D 1972.*

1788. **WADDINGTON, P. H.**   Courtavenel: the history of an artists' nest and its role in the life of Turgenev. *QUEENS BELFAST D 1972.*

1789. **WILKS, R.**   K. N. Batyushkov (1787–1855): a critical and biographical study. *LONDON (SSEES) D 1972.*

1790. **WILSON, D. N.**   A study of the works of Mikhail Prishvin in the period 1906–1928. *OXFORD BL 1972.*

1791. **BAINES, J. C. A.**   The poetry of Mandel´shtam. *OXFORD D 1973.*

1792. **COOPER, B. F.**   The history and development of the ode in Russia. *CAMBRIDGE D 1973.*

1793. **DEWEY, J.**   Dostoevsky and Hesse. *NOTTINGHAM MP 1973.*

1794. **GRAYSON, J.**   A comparison of Vladimir Nabokov's Russian and English prose: an investigation of those works of which versions exist in both languages. *OXFORD D 1973.*

1795. **HACKEL, S.**   Aleksander Blok and *The Twelve*: a study in iconography. *SUSSEX D 1973.*

1796. **PATRON, J. F. M.**   Valentin Katayev: a biographical and critical study. *OXFORD D 1973.*

1797. **TULLOCH, J. C.**   Anton Chekhov: a case study in the sociology of literature. *SUSSEX D 1973.*

1798. **DUNWOODIE, P.**   Camus et Dostoïevski: une étude comparée. *EDINBURGH D 1974.*

1799. **GŁOWACKI-PRUS, X.**   The literary significance of S. T. Aksakov's memoirs. *LONDON (EXTERNAL) MP 1974.*

1800. **HASLETT, D. M.**   The influence of populist ideas on the literary works of V. G. Korolenko. *CAMBRIDGE D 1974.*

1801. **LAFFERTY, V.**   A.S. Serafimovich: a study of his works with a biographical introduction. *LONDON (SSEES) D 1974.*

1802. **NICHOLSON, M. A.**   Aleksandr Solzhenitsyn and the Russian literary tradition. *OXFORD D 1974.*

1803. **RATHBONE, C.**   Problems of pattern in Lermontov's verse and prose. *OXFORD D 1974.*

1804. **RULLKÖTTER, B.**   The depiction of the hero in Soviet Russian scientific fantasy: aspects of alienation in a peripheral genre. *GLASGOW ML 1974.*

1805. **SKLAR, S.**   The relationship between social context and individual character in the naturalist drama, with special reference to Chekhov, D. H. Lawrence, and David Storey. *LONDON (UCL) D 1974.*

1806. **TUDGE, O. E.**   V. M. Garshin (1855–1888) and his works in Russian and Soviet literary criticism. *OXFORD BL 1974.*

1807. **BRADBURY, D. L.**   The narrative structure of *Besy* by F. M. Dostoevsky: a formal analysis. *EDINBURGH ML 1975.*

1808. **ELLIOT, E. M.** The early prose works of Fedor Sologub. OXFORD D 1975.

1809. **GILL, L. F.** Chekhov's concept of dramatic time. LONDON (SSEES) MP 1975.

1810. **KITCH, F. C. M.** An analysis of *pletenije sloves* in Russian with special reference to Epifanij Premudryj. LONDON (SSEES) D 1975.

1811. **MANGO, A.** Derzhavin and the poetry of enlightened absolutism in the reigns of Catherine II and Paul. LONDON (EXTERNAL) MP 1975.

1812. **MARTIN, D. W.** Stylistic devices and narrative technique in Chekhov's short stories, 1888–1903. OXFORD BL 1975.

1813. **MILNE, L. M.** The emergence of M.A. Bulgakov as a dramatist. CAMBRIDGE D 1975.

1814. **BARRATT, A.** Personal and literary relations of Maksim Gorky and Leonid Andreyev, 1898–1919, with particular reference to the revolution of 1905. DURHAM D 1976.

1815. **BUDGEN, D. E.** The works of F. A. Emin (1735–70): literary and intellectual transition in eighteenth-century Russia. OXFORD D 1976.

1816. **BURNETT, L. P.** Dimensions of truth: a comparative study of the relationship between language and reality in the works of Wordsworth, Coleridge, Zhukovsky, Pushkin, and Keats. ESSEX D 1976.

1817. **DOYLE, P.** Mikhail Bulgakov. MANCHESTER D 1976.

1818. **GILES, S.** The problem of action in modern European drama: a comparative study with special reference to Büchner, Ibsen and Chekhov. EAST ANGLIA D 1976.

1819. **KAY, S. E.** Saltykov's theory and practice of writing: an analysis of the work of M. Ye. Saltykov-Shchedrin, 1868–1884. LONDON (SSEES) D 1976.

1820. **KNIGHT, C. D.** Past, future and the problem of communication in the work of V. V. Khlebnikov. SUSSEX MP 1976.

1821. **KNIGHT, S. C.** The function of quotation in Dostoevsky. ESSEX D 1976.

1822. **McNAIR, W. J. M.** N. G. Garin-Michajlovskij: a study in the rhetoric of his fiction. EDINBURGH D 1976.

1823. **MUCKLE, J. Y.** The Protestant spirit in the works of Nikolay Leskov. LEEDS D 1976.

1824. **SOBEL, R.** Gogol's *Selected passages* and its contemporary critics. LEEDS D 1976.

1825. **THOMAS, C. G.** Aleksandr Grin: life and works. MANCHESTER D 1976.

1826. **WHITE, N. M.** V. V. Vorovsky's life and thought, with special reference to his literary criticism. GLASGOW ML 1976.

1827. **HUGHES, A. C.** From a didactic to an exploratory conception of literature: trends in recent Soviet prose fiction. LANCASTER D 1977.

1828. **JENKINS, M.** A study of A. F. Pisemsky and his fate in Russian literature. LONDON (EXTERNAL) D 1977.

1829. **NEWTON, J. R.** The role of Stalin in the Second World War as portrayed in Soviet Russian prose fiction, 1941–72. OXFORD D 1977.

1830. **ROSSLYN, W. A.** The original poetry of Eduard Bagritsky (1913–1934): forms and images. LONDON (SSEES) MP 1977.

1831. **SMITH, G. S.** The stanza form of Russian poetry from Polotsky to Derzhavin. LONDON (EXTERNAL) D 1977.

1832. STUPPLES, P. C.   Aspects of the political and ideological evolution of Il'ya Erenburg as reflected in some of his post-war writings. LEEDS MP 1977.

1833. EDWARDS, T. R. N.   The irrational in the work of Zamyatin, Pil'nyak and Bulgakov. BRISTOL D 1978.

1834. GOTTLIEB, V. A. R.   Chekhov: from farce to tragi-comedy. BRISTOL ML 1978.

1835. MARKOVIĆ, B.   The applications of theories of psychology by English and American critics to the novels of Dostoevsky from 1937 to the present. LONDON (WESTFIELD) MP 1978.

1836. McCURRY, R. M.   Dostoyevsky: the image of virtue in his work after 1864. LONDON (SSEES) MP 1978.

1837. NG, M. -S.   The intellectual hero in Chinese fiction of the nineteen-twenties and early 'thirties, in relation to Russian influences. OXFORD D 1978.

1838. PROCHAZKA, H. Y.   Military prose narratives in Old Russian literature. LONDON (SSEES) D 1978.

1839. RITTER, A. C.   Velimir Khlebnikov: poetry and prose. OXFORD D 1978.

1840. WEST, D. M.   Mandelstam's *Egipetskaya marka*: its relationship to his other prose and to his poetry from 1912 to 1933. DURHAM D 1978.

1841. GAMBLE, C. E.   The English Chekhovians: the influence of Anton Chekhov on the short story and drama in England. LONDON (R HOLLOWAY) D 1979.

1842. HENDERSON, I.   Study of the development of Lermontov as a poet through his different versions of *The Demon* written between 1829 and 1839. OXFORD D 1979.

1843. INGHAM, D.   Psychological criticism of Dostoyevsky in the English language, with special reference to the period since 1952. NOTTINGHAM MP 1979.

1844. MacGRATH, M. A.   The servant in nineteenth-century Russian prose fiction. EXETER D 1979.

1845. MARSH, C. E. A.   M. A. Voloshin — artist-poet: an investigation into the synaesthetic aspects of his poetry. LONDON (SSEES) D 1979.

1846. RICHARDS, S. M.   Alexander Solzhenitsyn: the literary and didactic conflict in his prose, 1954–1971. OXFORD D 1979.

1847. RUSSELL, R.   The works of Valentin Kataev. EDINBURGH D 1979.

1848. SICHER, E. R.   The works of I. E. Babel' (1894–?1941), with special reference to tradition and innovation in the style of his narrative prose of the 1920s. OXFORD D 1979.

1849. WEST, T. G.   The novel in transition: a study of J. K. Huysmans' *À rebours*, R. M. Rilke's *Die Aufzeichnungen des Malte Laurids Brigge* and Andrej Belyj's *Peterburg*. MANCHESTER D 1979.

1850. DOWSETT, C. F.   A study in conceptual and expressive spontaneity: the prose of Marina Ivanovna Tsvetaeva. ESSEX MP 1980.

1851. HUGHES, D. N. M.   Moral problems in the works of Vladimir Tendryakov [NCR]. ESSEX MP 1980.

1852. JOHAE, A.   In two minds: a study of dream and symbolism in Dostoevsky and Kafka [NCR]. ESSEX D 1980.

1853. KEENAN, W. L.   The early work of N. S. Leskov: a study of the writer's development. LONDON (SSEES) D 1980.

1854. LANE, C. A.   Tolstoy the dramatist. LONDON (SSEES) MP 1980.

1855. **OKOLE, M.** Boris Pil'nyak: an evaluation of his work in the light of the criticism of his contemporaries. CNAA (PORTSMOUTH POLY) MP 1980.

1856. **WARE, R.** A Russian literary journal and its public: *Otechestvennye zapiski*, 1868–84. OXFORD D 1980.

1857. **MUREDDU, D.** The influence of the poetry of Petrarch on Russian literature, 1900–1930. ESSEX D 1981.

1858. **PATON, W. S.** The beginnings of Russian Marxist literary criticism, with special reference to G. V. Plekhanov. LONDON (EXTERNAL) D 1981.

1859. **PILGRIM, H. M.** A study of the novels and stories of Dmitrii Furmanov. EXETER D 1981.

1860. **ROTHERAY, B. C.** Dualism, synthesis, and tradition in the novels of Ivan Aleksandrovich Goncharov. LEEDS D 1981.

1861. **SMITH, T. G.** Duality and dualism in Dostoevsky and Camus. NOTTINGHAM MP 1981.

1862. **TARRY, D. M.** The utopian vision of the total state in the 20th century, with special reference to Zamyatin, Aldous Huxley and George Orwell. LONDON (LSE) D 1981.

1863. **WELLS, R. J.** The theme of science and technology in Soviet literature of the post-Stalin period (1953–64). OXFORD D 1981.

1864. **COOKE, O. M.** The grotesque in Andrej Belyj's 'Moscow' novels. LONDON (SSEES) D 1982.

1865. **CURTIS, J.** Mikhail Bulgakov: literature and the writer (1929–40). OXFORD D 1982.

1866. **DODD, W. J.** Kafka and Dostoevsky: influences and affinities. LEEDS D 1982.

1867. **DOUGLAS, R. C. C.** Philosophical themes in the poetry of Nikolai Zabolotsky and their development through the poetic image. OXFORD D 1982.

1868. **FOX, S.** Nationalism in the lives and works of W. B. Yeats and Alexander Blok: a comparative study. MANCHESTER D 1982.

1869. **MARSHALL, T.** Private and public spaces: narrative strategies in Dostoyevsky and Conrad. EAST ANGLIA D 1982.

1870. **MAY, S. R.** The image of rural women in contemporary Soviet prose. OXFORD ML 1982.

1871. **O'NEILL, P. G.** A benevolent Salieri: from Russian formalism to structuralism in literary scholarship [NCR]. ESSEX MP 1982.

1872. **SIMPSON, P. A.** A study of the tragic doctrine of mystical anarchism within the Russian literary intelligentsia, 1905–1909. ESSEX D 1982.

1873. **SUGDEN, J. N.** Thomas Mann and Dostoevsky: a study of *Doctor Faustus* in comparison with *The Brothers Karamazov*. CAMBRIDGE D 1982.

1874. **AVERRE, D. L.** The historical novels and stories of the Soviet writer Yurii N. Tynyanov. MANCHESTER D 1983.

1875. **BOLL, R. W.** Dostoevsky and the English novel. BRISTOL D 1983.

1876. **COCKRELL, R.** A study of the stories and literary theories of Aleksandr Fadeev, 1922–1932. EXETER D 1983.

1877. **COOKE, R.** The poetic world of Velimir Khlebnikov: an interpretation. SUSSEX D 1983.

1878. **CORNWELL, N. J.** The life and works of V. F. Odoyevsky (1804–1869). QUEENS BELFAST D 1983.

1879. **DAVIDSON, P.** Vyacheslav Ivanov and Dante: reflections of medieval tradition in the poetic imagination of a Russian symbolist. OXFORD D 1983.

1880. **JONES, C. R.** A study of guilt in the fiction of Dostoevsky, Conrad and Kafka. LANCASTER MP 1983.

1881. **JONES, S. W.** The function of simile and metaphor in a selection of Remizov's prose. OXFORD ML 1983.

1882. **SLATER, A. J.** Dostoyevsky's attitude to institutionalized religion. LIVERPOOL D 1983.

1883. **TEJERIZO, M. H.** Dostoevsky's reception in the Hispanic world with particular reference to Pío Baroja. STRATHCLYDE ML 1983.

1884. **AIZLEWOOD, R.** Verse form and meaning in the poetry of Vladimir Mayakovsky, with special reference to: 'Vladimir Mayakovsky. Tragediya'; 'Oblako v shtanakh'; 'Fleita-pozvonochnik'; 'Chelovek'; 'Lyublyu'; and 'Pro eto'. OXFORD D 1984.

1885. **BARRATT, W. B.** Chateaubriand in Russian life and literature of the nineteenth century. BIRMINGHAM ML 1984.

1886. **CAMBRAY, C. B.** The work of Vasil' Bykov from 1949 to 1969. MANCHESTER MP 1984.

1887. **DURRANT, J. S.** The life and works of Vikentiy Vikent'evich Veresaev, 1867–1945. LONDON (SSEES) D 1984.

1888. **GILLESPIE, D. C.** Man and Soviet society in the works of Vasily Belov and Valentin Rasputin, 1960–81. LEEDS D 1984.

1889. **McCAREY, P.** Hugh MacDiarmid and the Russians: Dostoevsky, Solovyov, Blok, Mayakovsky and Shestov; with a preliminary chapter on Ossian, Scott and Byron in Russian literature. GLASGOW D 1984.

1890. **NETHERCOTT, F. M.** A survey of the memoirs of Nadezhda Mandel'stam. OXFORD MP 1984.

1891. **RANSOME, M. G.** N. A. Nekrasov's narrative poetry on the theme of the Russian peasantry: a critical reappraisal. BRISTOL D 1984.

1892. **TLUSTY, I.** Anna Akhmatova and the composition of her 'Poema bez geroya', 1940–1962. OXFORD D 1984.

1893. **TURTON, L. G.** Turgenev and the context of English literature, 1850–1900. WARWICK D 1984.

1894. **KELLY, C. H. M.** Innokenty Fedorovich Annensky and the classical ideal: poetry, translations, drama and literary essays. OXFORD D 1985.

1895. **MAKIN, M. L.** The rewriting of the inherited text in the poetic works of Marina Tsvetaeva. OXFORD D 1985.

1896. **PITTMAN, R. H.** Mikhail Bulgakov: the theme of evil in *Master i Margarita*. EDINBURGH D 1985.

1897. **POLUKHINA, V.** The poetry of Joseph Brodsky: a study of metaphor. KEELE D 1985.

1898. **SKILLEN, D. H.** Urban and rural images and ideas in post-revolutionary Russian literature, 1917–1924. LONDON (SSEES) D 1985.

1899. **FOXCROFT, N. H.** The principle of conflict in certain historical and lyrical works of A. S. Pushkin: a thematic and linguistic investigation. SHEFFIELD MP 1986.

1900. **GILROY, M.** The ironic vision in Lermontov's *A Hero of Our Time*. STRATHCLYDE D 1986.

1901. **GONZALEZ, J. G. G.** The search for exemplary morality in Russian literature during the 1930s. OXFORD MP 1986.

1902. **HARVEY, B. D.** Boris Pilniak's 1931 trip to the USA. OXFORD MP 1986.

1903. **HODGSON, A. C.** The minor archipelago: Solzhenitsyn's portrayal of women. OXFORD ML 1986.

1904. **HUTCHINGS, S. C.** A semiotic analysis of the short stories of Leonid Andreyev, 1900–1909. DURHAM D 1986.

1905. **KOENIG, L.** *Tarusskie stranitsy*: a literary-political case study. OXFORD MP 1986.

1906. **MACKINNON, J. E.** All things human: Pasternak on art and the artist. EXETER MP 1986.

1907. **THOMPSON, D. E. O.** *The Brothers Karamazov* and the poetics of memory. CAMBRIDGE D 1986.

1908. **CARTER, S.** The political and social thought of F. M. Dostoevsky (with special reference to *The Devils*). LONDON (LSE) D 1987.

1909. **ISSA, I.** Secularization of passion and resurrection in certain plays of Strindberg, Chekhov, Bond and Howard. ESSEX D 1987.

1910. **KEYS, R. J.** The reluctant modernist: Andrei Belyi and the development of Russian fiction, 1902–1914. CAMBRIDGE D 1987.

1911. **LEHMAN, C.** Literary responses to Russian populism in the 1870s. OXFORD MP 1987.

1912. **MYERS, D.** Time, space and art in Mandelstam's poetic perception. LONDON (SSEES) D 1987.

1913. **WHITEHEAD, S. G.** English pre-Romantic and Romantic influences in the poetry of V. A. Zhukovskii. EAST ANGLIA D 1987.

1914. **APLIN, H. A.** M. S. Zhukova and E. A. Gan: women writers and female protagonists 1837–1843. EAST ANGLIA D 1988.

1915. **BRADLEY, E. R. J.** A comparison of the shorter prose works of Anton Chekhov and Arthur Schnitzler. EDINBURGH D 1988.

1916. **GIBSON, A. C.** Russian poetry and criticism in Paris from 1920 to 1940. LONDON (QUEEN MARY) MP 1988.

1917. **GILLESPIE, P. A.** Elements of continuity in the prose of Georgy Vladimov. OXFORD MP 1988.

1918. **LUCK, C. D.** Figures of war: two cycles of stories by Isaak Babel'. SUSSEX D 1988.

1919. **THOMPSON, P. W.** The will to believe in the age of post-naturalism: Gorky, Strindberg, Maeterlinck and Chekhov. EAST ANGLIA D 1988.

1920. **WELLS, D.** Akhmatova and Pushkin: a study of a literary relationship. OXFORD D 1988.

1921. **DAVIES, P. J.** The early prose fiction of Boris Leonidovich Pasternak. NOTTINGHAM MP 1989.

1922. HIRSCHKOP, K. The novel and dialogism in the work of M. M. Bakhtin. OXFORD D 1989.

1923. KUZMINSKY, I. The 'language of women'? A study of three women writers: Marina Tsvetaeva, Ingeborg Bachmann and Monique Wittig. OXFORD D 1989.

1924. MUTTALEB, F. A. Shakespeare, Chekhov and the problem of the Russian Hamlet. ESSEX D 1989.

1925. YOUNG, S. B. Chekhov on the British stage: reactions to a theatrical tradition. CAMBRIDGE D 1989.

1926. BAKER, R. Problems of social change as reflected in selected major works of Andrei Platonov and Valentin Rasputin. OXFORD MP 1990.

1927. BUCHWALD, E. A. J. Ideals of womanhood in the literature of Finland and Russia 1894–1914. LONDON (SSEES) D 1990.

1928. ELLIS, N. J. Vasiliy Grossman: the genesis and evolution of heresy. BRISTOL D 1990.

1929. GREENHILL, R. Stylistic and lexical devices in the language of I. Ilf and E. Petrov's novels *Twelve Chairs* and *The Golden Calf.* LONDON (SSEES) D 1990.

1930. McPHAIL, A. The poetry of N. M. Yazykov: a re-evaluation. EDINBURGH D 1990.

1931. ROMANYK, T. The heroic ethos in the *Slovo o polku Igoreve*: a comparative study in the light of early Western European epic. LONDON (SSEES) D 1990.

1932. SHEPHERD, D. G. Metafiction in Soviet literature, with particular reference to works by Leonid Leonov, Marietta Shaginyan, Konstantin Vaginov and Veniamin Kaverin. MANCHESTER D 1990.

1933. CROWE, N. J. The pastoral theme in the literature of eighteenth- and nineteenth-century Russia. CAMBRIDGE D 1991.

1934. MARYNIAK, I. W. M. Religious perspectives in Soviet prose fiction, 1964–1988: the animist/totemist dichotomy. LONDON (SSEES) D 1991.

1935. REPEC, M. A. Manifestations of the Muse, or inspiring female figure, in Russian literature. OXFORD MP 1991.

1936. RIEDER, R. The novels of Maksim Gorky's literary period on Capri, 1906–1913. HULL MP 1991.

1937. THOMPSON, S. A. The prose of Iurii Trifonov: a writer and his time. CAMBRIDGE D 1991.

1938. WILLIAMS, J. From Lermontov to Dostoevsky: a study in the development of psychological realism in Russian literature. BIRMINGHAM MP 1991.

1939. HODGSON, K. Russian Soviet war poetry 1941–45. CAMBRIDGE D 1992.

1940. KAHN, A. The classical Roman tradition in Russia c. 1750–1840: studies in its sources and character. OXFORD D 1992.

1941. ROBERTS, G. H. J. The metafiction of Konstantin Vaginov, Aleksandr Vvedensky and Daniil Kharms. OXFORD D 1992.

1942. SPIEKER, S. Figures of memory and forgetting in Andrei Bitov's prose. OXFORD D 1992.

1943. SWARTZ, H. M. The Soviet-Afghan war in Russian literature. OXFORD D 1992.

1944. TROTT, S. B. B. M. Eikhenbaum 1918–1929: literary theory and cultural change. LONDON (SSEES) D 1992.

1945. **BERRY, R. J.** Conrad and Dostoevsky: an unsuspected brotherhood. *STIRLING D 1993.*

1946. **DI BARTOLOMEO, L. M.** The female characters of Fyodor Mikhailovich Dostoevsky. *GLASGOW ML 1993.*

1947. **EGERTON, K. A.** Rhyme in the poetry of Joseph Brodsky. *OXFORD ML 1993.*

1948. **JABBOURY, H. A.** Constance Garnett, Aylmer Maude, S. S. Koteliansky: Russian literature in England, 1900–1930. *SHEFFIELD D 1993.*

1949. **MYLES, E.** A comparative study of Ivan Bunin's *The Gentleman from San Francisco* and Thomas Mann's *Death in Venice* [NCR]. *ST ANDREWS MP 1993.*

1950. **POLONSKY, R.** The role of English and American literature in Russian poetry and aesthetics *c.* 1890–1910. *OXFORD D 1993.*

1951. **SMITH, A.** Tsvetaeva's interpretation of Pushkin's life and work. *LONDON (SSEES) D 1993.*

1952. **SMITH, G. E.** Andrei Platonov — constant idealist of a fickle revolution. *LONDON (SSEES) MP 1993.*

1953. **TEJERIZO, M. H.** Exoticism and familiarization: studies in Hispano-Russian literary relations. *GLASGOW D 1993.*

1954. **CROFT, M. E.** From Siberia to the underground: the thought of Dostoyevsky in the early 1860s. *BRISTOL D 1994.*

1955. **HOLOHAN, D. M.** Collectivization and the utopian ideal in the works of Boris Andreevich Mozhaev. *BATH D 1994.*

1956. **NICHOLLS, D.** Verbal and non-verbal communication in the short stories of Anton Chekhov 1898–1904. *CAMBRIDGE ML 1994.*

1957. **WILCOCKS, L.** Looking at the sun: confrontation with death in Tolstoy's fiction. *KEELE MP 1994.*

1958. **REYNOLDS, A. W. M.** 'The burden of memories': towards a Bloomian analysis of influence in Osip Mandelstam's *Voronezh Notebooks. OXFORD D 1995.*

1959. **SMIRNOVA, O. A.** Opyt vdokhnoveniia v poezii Aleksandra Bloka. *KEELE D 1995.*

1960. **DOBSON, J.** The theatre of the self: poetic identity in the plays of Hélène Cixous and Marina Tsvetaeva. *NOTTINGHAM D 1996.*

1961. **FARRELL, A. J.** Ivan Konevskoy (1877–1901): a reconstruction of integral identity. *DURHAM D 1996.*

1962. **SWANN, S. P.** Metaphor and metonymy in the prose works of Nikolai Gogol'. *STRATHCLYDE MP 1996.*

1963. **WOOD, C.** The modernity of Ivan Bunin. *BRADFORD D 1996.*

1964. **BRUNTON, A. J.** The addressed poems of Alexander Pushkin: categorisation and criticism. *BIRMINGHAM D 1997.*

1965. **CAVENDISH, P. J.** Evgenii Zamiatin and the literary stylization of Rus'. *LONDON (SSEES) D 1997.*

1966. **CHRISTIAN, N. C.** Emancipating the eccentric: an examination of the dominant themes in the life and works of Vasilii Shukshin. *BRISTOL D 1997.*

1967. **FARMER, R. S.** The life and works of Vladimir Voinovich: the satirist as exile. *NOTTINGHAM D 1997.*

1968. FRENCH, J. A study of the childhood theme as interpretive key to the works of Tatiana Tolstaia in the 1980s. *BRISTOL D 1997.*

1969. BAIKOVITCH, G. O. F. Fedor Abramov and the poetics of Russian village prose. *BATH D 1998.*

1970. BEN-AMOS, A. Imagination and literature in the Russian prose of Valdimir Nabokov. *ESSEX D 1998.*

1971. BROOKS, C. Vasilisk Gnedov's futurism. *LONDON (SSEES) MP 1998.*

1972. CARSTEN, S. Divided loyalties: the generation of the 1960s in Soviet literature. *BRADFORD D 1998.*

1973. CHRISTMAS, S. Ideal motives: self-perfection and self-knowledge in the work of Dostoevsky. *CAMBRIDGE D 1998.*

1974. DABBS, N. The development of language and characterisation in selected Russian plays of the period 1781–1836. *BIRMINGHAM MP 1998.*

1975. FAURE, I. Solzhenitsyn's *Krasnoe koleso* and the philosophy of the Russian spiritual renaissance. *OXFORD D 1998.*

1976. ROGATCHEVSKI, A. Eduard Limonov: a critical study. *GLASGOW D 1998.*

1977. SEALEY RAHMAN, C. Levels of reality in the plays of Aleksandr Nikolaevich Ostrovsky. *BIRMINGHAM D 1998.*

1978. TOSI, A. The forgotten years: Russian prose in the age of Alexander I, 1801–1825. *CAMBRIDGE D 1998.*

1979. BULLOCK, P. R. The feminine in the work of Andrey Platonov. *OXFORD D 1999.*

1980. DEARMAN, V. The reality of time, history and life in the prose of Ivan Bunin. *SHEFFIELD D 1999.*

1981. KINGMAN, J. P. Boris Pil'niak and the crisis of subjectivity: an intertextual approach. *SHEFFIELD D 1999.*

1982. MILLS, S. N. Poet vs. poetess: feminine images in the poetry of Anna Akhmatova. *LONDON (SSEES) MP 1999.*

1983. SMITHSON, S. M. Author, narrator and reader in the artist-tales of N. V. Gogol'. *SHEFFIELD MP 1999.*

1984. WILLIAMS, P. The thought and art of Iurii Dombrovskii. *WALES (SWANSEA) MP 1999.*

1985. ZAFFT, T. W. Nina Katerli: the discovered chameleon. *BATH D 1999.*

1986. FITT, T. H. Novodvorskii-Osipovich: a writer out of time. *KEELE D 2000.*

1987. GRÜNEWALD, H. Rethinking dramatic action on the basis of an intertextual reading of Chekhov's *Tri sestry* and *Vishnevyi sad*, Kharms's *Elizaveta Bam* and Petrushevskaia's *Tri devushki v golubom* in relation to the theatre of the absurd. *NOTTINGHAM D 2000.*

1988. HICKS, J. G. Mikhail Zoshchenko and the poetics of 'Skaz'. *LONDON (UCL) D 2000.*

1989. HOBSON, M. E. Griboedov's *Gore ot uma* in the context of his life and other writings. *LONDON (UCL) D 2000.*

1990. MAUDE, E. Pushkin's imagery of dreams and flying. *LONDON (UCL) MP 2000.*

1991. MILLER, D. Economies of time and allegory in the major works of Fedor Dostoevskii and Mikhail Bakhtin. *SHEFFIELD D 2000.*

1992. **Moseley, N. A.**   Peter Aleshkovskii: answering the accursed Russian question. *birmingham mp 2000*.

1993. **Semenchenko, O.**   The 'Ukrainian' stories of Nikolai Gogol´ in English-language translations. Problems of cultural transfer with particular reference to *Taras Bul´ba*. *leeds d 2000*.

1994. **Weatherlake, S.**   Dreams and epiphanies: their narrative function in L. N. Tolstoy's major fiction up to 1880. *manchester d 2000*.

1995. **Wyllie, B. E.**   A study of the work of Vladimir Nabokov in the context of contemporary American fiction and film. *london (ucl) d 2000*.

1996. **Aiello, L.**   The reception of Fedor Dostoevskii in Britain (1869–1935). *sheffield d 2001*.

1997. **France, R.**   Mikhail Zoshchenko's *Michel Siniagin*. A critical study and translation. *glasgow d 2001*.

1998. **Hudspith, S. F.**   Dostoevskii and Slavophilism: a new perspective on unity and brotherhood. *sheffield d 2001*.

1999. **Jackson, S. K.**   A memorable time: the prose of Vladimir Makanin, 1987–1995. *sheffield d 2001*.

2000. **Shellard, J. M.**   The representation of the Cheka in Soviet Communist literature of the early 1920s. *bristol d 2001*.

2001. **Tardivo, M. -A.**   Aleksandr Solzhenitsyn's *The Gulag Archipelago*: the self before the law. *keele d 2001*.

2002. **Whitehead, C. E.**   Theory and practice of the fantastic in French and Russian prose fiction of the nineteenth century. *bristol d 2001*.

2003. **Adlam, C.**   Transgressive identities in the prose fiction of Valeriia Narbikova, Liudmila Petrushevskaia and Nina Sadur. *sheffield d 2002*.

2004. **Barber, S.**   Insanity in nineteenth century Russian literature. *keele mp 2002*.

2005. **Carnighan, R.**   Somewhere between eschatology and literature: F. M. Dostoevsky and romantic realism. *st andrews mp 2002*.

2006. **Golden, N.**   Varlam Shalamov's *Kolyma Tales*: a formalist analysis. *keele mp 2002*.

2007. **Morris, J. B.**   Living in the *pod"ezd*: the alternative writing of Evgenii Popov. *sussex d 2002*.

2008. **Tilly, H. L.**   Lidiia Chukovskaia: an examination of her literary career with reference to the values of the Russian intelligentsia. *bristol d 2002*.

2009. **Barrand, R.**   The poetry of Mariia Shkapskaia, 1903–1925. *leeds d 2003*.

2010. **Fasey, R. J.**   Writers in the service of revolution: Russia's ideological and literary impact on Spanish poetry and prose 1925–36. *st andrews d 2003*.

2011. **Glynn, M. A.**   A novelist of delusion: Vladimir Nabokov's Bergsonian and Russian Formalist affinities. *exeter d 2003*.

2012. **Katz, E. M.**   Representations of 'the Jew' in the writings of Nikolai Gogol´, Fyodor Dostoevsky and Ivan Turgenev. *southampton d 2003*.

2013. **Rulyova, N. E.**   Joseph Brodsky: translating oneself. *cambridge d 2003*.

2014. **Stock, U. B. C.**   The ethics of the poet: Marina Tsvetaeva's art in the light of conscience. *cambridge d 2003*.

2015. **BARRETT, R.** Women in nineteenth-century Russian literature: representations and identities. *KEELE MP 2004*.

2016. **BYFORD, A.** Literary academia in late Imperial Russia (1870s-1910s): rituals of self-representation. *OXFORD D 2004*.

2017. **KALTENBACH, J. A.** Literary *biznes*: sketches from Tula and other Eastern Europes. *CARDIFF D 2004*.

2018. **MOSS, J. D.** The whole truth? War in Viktor Astaf′ev's prose fiction. *BIRMINGHAM D 2004*.

2019. **PEELING, S.** Values and identities for post-Soviet Russia in the prose fiction of Vladimir Sorokin, Viktor Pelevin, Vladimir Makanin and Lyudmila Petrushevskaya. *OXFORD MP 2004*.

2020. **SKOMP, E. A.** Women and violence in postwar Russian literature. *LONDON (UCL) D 2004*.

2021. **BACONOVÁ, J.** Russian drama at the turn of the 19th and 20th centuries. *GLASGOW ML 2005*.

2022. **FILOSOFOVA, T.** Christian folk poetry in the manuscript tradition of the Russian Old Believers. *ST ANDREWS D 2005*.

2023. **FRANK, S.** The function of theatre in the works of Vladimir Nabokov. *OXFORD D 2005*.

2024. **LYGO, E.** Leningrad poetry, 1953–75. *OXFORD D 2005*.

2025. **NICOLSON, J. McK.** Petersburg literature: towards a definition. *BRISTOL D 2005*.

2026. **SUMMANEN, L.** Russian psychological fiction in the twentieth century: Nabokov, Bunin, Zamiatin. [*In Russian*]. [NCR]. *BATH D 2005*.

2027. **TITOV, A. S.** Lev Gumilev, ethnogenesis and Eurasianism. *LONDON (UCL) D 2005*.

2028. **BARRON, A. H.** A secret sharing: a comparative study of Conrad and Dostoevsky. *KENT D 2006*.

2029. **BEASLEY-MURRAY, T.** Mikhail Bakhtin and Walter Benjamin: experience and form. *LONDON (UCL) D 2006*.

2030. **BERRY, B. A.** Language caught between cultures: Andreï Makine's oeuvre as an example of border writing. *LEEDS METROPOLITAN D 2006*.

2031. **GRIGORIAN, N.** The use of myth in European Symbolism, with reference to selected examples of Symbolist poetry and painting in France, Germany and Russia. *OXFORD D 2006*.

2032. **MACPHAIL, D. J.** The anecdote in modern Russian fiction. *CAMBRIDGE D 2006*.

2033. **SYKES, T. M. J.** Textual fragmentation as a response to time in Russian modernism after the Revolution. *LONDON (UCL) D 2006*.

2034. **WILLIAMS, D. -A.** Poethics: twentieth-century apologia in T. S. Eliot, Joseph Brodsky, Seamus Heaney and Geoffrey Hill [NCR]. *OXFORD D 2006*.

Serbo-Croat

2035. **SUBOTIĆ, D.** Serbian traditional folk-poetry in England, France and Germany in the nineteenth century [NCR]. *OXFORD BL 1927*.

2036. **TORBARINA, J.** The influence of Italian literature on Ragusan poetry in the XVIth century. *LONDON (SSEES) D 1930.*

2037. **JAVAREK, V.** English influence on the works of Dositej Obradović: its extent and importance. *LONDON (SSEES) D 1954.*

2038. **GOY, E. D.** Serbian Russophilism and the infiltration of Russian literature and thought into Serbia in the second half of the nineteenth century. *CAMBRIDGE D 1955.*

2039. **JOHNSON, B. S.** A study of the poetry of Zaharija Orfelin. *NOTTINGHAM D 1960.*

2040. **ĆURČIĆ, N.** The religious element in the works of the principal poets of Ragusan literature of the 15th to 18th centuries. *LONDON (SSEES) MP 1968.*

2041. **WILLIAMS, E. C.** Change and continuity in contemporary Serbian poetry. *LONDON (SSEES) MP 1969.*

2042. **GRAHOR, O.** France in the work and ideas of A.G. Matoš. *LONDON (SSEES) MP 1972.*

2043. **ĆURČIĆ, N. M. J.** The ethical elements in the works of Dositej Obradović. *LONDON (SSEES) D 1974.*

2044. **McGREGOR, G. F.** Aspects of the development of Miroslav Krleža as a novelist. *NOTTINGHAM MP 1975.*

2045. **NORRIS, D. A.** Time in the novels of Miloš Crnjanski. *NOTTINGHAM D 1989.*

2046. **SCHULTE, M. B.** Images of women in the works of Desanka Maksimović. *OXFORD ML 1990.*

2047. **ŠIŠIĆ, A.** The portrayal of female characters in the work of three contemporary writers of the former Yugoslavia: Meša Selimović, Ivan Aralica and Slobodan Selenić. *LONDON (SSEES) D 1997.*

2048. **RANKOVIĆ, S.** The distributed author and the poetics of complexity: a comparative study of the sagas of Icelanders and Serbian epic poetry. *NOTTINGHAM D 2006.*

Slovak

2049. **TAYLOR, E.** Milo Urban: the style of his novels [NCR]. *OXFORD ML 1986.*

Slovene

2050. **DENTON, D. S.** The life and works of Ciril Kosmač. *NOTTINGHAM D 1984.*

USSR

2051. **MURRAY, J.** The Union of Soviet Writers: its organization and leading personnel, 1954–1967. *BIRMINGHAM D 1973.*

2052. **SHUKMAN, A. M.** Structuralist literary criticism in the Soviet Union, 1962–1970, with special reference to the work of Yu.M. Lotman. *OXFORD D 1974.*

2053. **KEMP-WELCH, A.** The origins and formative years of the Writers' Union of the USSR, 1932–1936. *LONDON (LSE) D 1976.*

2054. **ALDWINCKLE, L. D.** The politics of *Novyi mir*, 1950–1970. *LONDON (LSE) D 1977.*

2055. **STARZA, A.** Children's literature in the Soviet Union, 1917 to 1934. *NOTTINGHAM D 1983.*

2056. **METCALF, A. J.** Literary journals and literary politics (1921–1932): the early years of the new Soviet literature, with particular reference to the journal *Novyi mir. HULL D 1984.*

2057. **NOBLE, R. A.** Aleksander Fadeyev and the political control of literature, with special reference to the period 1943–1956. *OXFORD MP 1986.*

2058. **KEARNS, C.** The theme of the Civil War in Soviet drama 1924–1934. *LEEDS D 1988.*

2059. **SCHULL, J.** Ideology and the politics of Soviet literature under NEP and perestroika. *OXFORD D 1990.*

2060. **COSGROVE, S.** *Nash sovremennik* 1981–1991: a case study in the politics of Soviet literature with special reference to Russian nationalism. *LONDON (SSEES) D 1998.*

19. MANAGEMENT, PLANNING, MARKETING

General and Comparative

2061. **KARRA, N.** An analysis of factors explaining accelerated internationalization processes in born-global firms [with special reference to fashion firms trading in Russia, FSU and E. Europe]. *CAMBRIDGE D 2005.*

Albania

2062. **SHEHAJ, E. F.** Ownership and performance in privatised firms in Albania. *STAFFORDSHIRE D 2006.*

Bosnia-Herzegovina

2063. **MUJAGIĆ, A.** The enterprise recovery process in Bosnian transitional conditions. *BRUNEL D 2006.*

Bulgaria

2064. **SIMEONOVA, A.** Managerial incentives for enterprise restructuring: evidence from Bulgaria. *OXFORD MP 1997.*

2065. **DRAGNEVA, R.** Corporate governance and privatisation funds: the case of Bulgaria. *SUSSEX D 1999.*

2066. **ZAHARIEVA, E.** Supply chain management and international marketing problems in transitional economies: evidence from the Bulgarian wine industry. *NEWCASTLE D 2002.*

Central and Eastern Europe (see also under individual countries)

2067. **KOERNER, R. E.** The development of marketing and the emergence of marketing research in the planned economies of Eastern Europe. *LANCASTER MP 1987.*

2068. **RATCHEVA, V. I.** Conceptual framework for market positioning of new products by East European companies (1989–1992). *LOUGHBOROUGH MP 1995.*

2069. **BLOOM, N.** How effective is corporate governance in the Czech Republic, Hungary, Poland and Russia? *OXFORD MP 1996.*

2070. **DUBEY-VILLINGER, N.** The management of alliances in East-Central Europe: Western dominance and the impact of culture and institutional background in the branded consumer goods industries. *CAMBRIDGE D 1996.*

2071. **VILLINGER, R.** Post-acquisition management and learning in East-Central Europe [Hungary, Poland, Czech Republic and Slovakia]. *CAMBRIDGE D 1997.*

2072. **BYGATE, S. C.** Inherited networks, economic indebtedness and developments in corporate governance: post-communist Czech and Slovak Republics with supporting evidence from Eastern Germany. *LOUGHBOROUGH D 1998.*

2073. **TAKLA, L.** Privatisation enterprise restructuring in transitional economies: an empirical investigation of the Visegrád countries, 1993. *LONDON (LBS) D 2005.*

Czech Republic

2074. **MEIN, V.** Cultural and environmental influences on the financial accounting system: a case study of the Czech Republic. *ABERDEEN D 1995.*

2075. **WILLIAMSON, D.** Perceptions of management control by mainland Chinese, Czech and British managers. *GLASGOW D 2001.*

2076. **VICKERSTAFF, A.** The development of marketing in a transforming economy: cases from the Czech Republic. *NOTTINGHAM TRENT D 2003.*

Estonia

2077. **LIUHTO, K. T.** The entrepreneurial and management cultural transformation in independent Estonia. *GLASGOW D 1996.*

2078. **MIAZHEVICH, G.** Business ethics in post-Soviet countries: the case of Estonia and Belarus. *MANCHESTER D 2006.*

Hungary

2079. **HARE, P. G.** Hungarian planning models based on input-output. *OXFORD D 1973.*

2080. **KAMALL, S. S.** Management of radical change: a case study of Hungarian telecommunications. *CITY D 1994.*

2081. **PIESSE, J.** Firm level approaches to the measurement of production efficiency, technical change and total factor productivity in the transition economies [with special reference to Hungary]. *LONDON (BIRKBECK) D 1997.*

2082. **LIEB-DÓCZY, E. E.** Transition to survival: enterprise restructuring in twenty East German and Hungarian companies. *WARWICK D 1999.*

Poland

2083. GALLAGHER, C. C.   Factory organisation in Poland. BIRMINGHAM D 1971.

2084. KEWELL, B.   Nation without a state, managers without management? A study of organisational change in post-socialist Poland, 1989–1994. BRUNEL D 1997.

2085. MUENT, H.   Inter-firm cooperation in a transitional economy: comparative experience in two Polish regions. LONDON (LSE) D 1998.

2086. ZALESKA, K. J.   Polish managers in subsidiaries of multinational corporations: international business as an agent of change. KENT D 1998.

2087. GAJEWSKA-DE MATTOS, H. M.   Mergers and acquisitions in Poland — a comparison of general management perceptions from Germany, the United Kingdom and Poland. LEEDS D 2001.

2088. PRZEPIÓRA, A.   Identification of marketing strategies in the Polish dairy sector. NEWCASTLE D 2001.

2089. FRYDRYCH, I.   Management and labour in transformation: an enterprise-level analysis of post-socialist Poland. WARWICK D 2002.

2090. HAENDLE, M. R. B.   The process of hypermarket retail internationalisation, from Germany to Poland. BRADFORD D 2002.

2091. HUNT, D.   The systemic transition in Poland and the social construction of organisational cultures. BRUNEL D 2002.

2092. SZYMAŃSKI, A.   An analysis of variation in the financial performance of enterprises in the Polish food processing industry. NEWCASTLE D 2006.

Romania

2093. NICOLESCU, L.   Privatization and organizational change in Romania: an analysis of two selected cases. KENT D 1997.

Russia (see also USSR)

2094. BARKHATOVA, N. M.   Enterprises in Russia: continuity and change.. MANCHESTER D 1995.

2095. WINTERS, S.   Cross-cultural values: interpersonal perceptions of Russian and Irish managers. NUI (DUBLIN) MPSYCHSC 1996.

2096. ZHUKOV, V. S.   Corporate governance, strategies and performance of privatised industrial firms in the FSU. NOTTINGHAM D 1999.

2097. GILBERT, K. M.   Problems of knowledge transfer to Russia: an exploratory study in the context of Western-sponsored management development programmes. UMIST D 2000.

2098. PAVLOVSKAYA, A. G.   An analysis of the transfer process of management development practices within multinationals: case studies of two British-based multinationals' operations in Russia. WARWICK D 2003.

2099. MASLOV, A. V.   Russian manufacturing industry — gaining competitiveness through organisational excellence: a study of quality practices, leadership and cultural differences. LOUGHBOROUGH D 2004.

2100. **MORRISON, C.** Soviet management and transition: the case of the Russian textile industry. *WARWICK D 2004.*

2101. **POLYAKOV, E.** Enterprise transformation in Russia: a corporate strategy perspective from the city of Bratsk. *BRUNEL D 2005.*

2102. **SAAKOV, K.** Corporate governance, employee welfare and firm performance in Russia. *DE MONTFORT D 2005.*

2103. **ZINCHENKO, O. L.** Role of Russian local and regional small business policies in transition: evidence from the regions of Novgorod and Pskov. *BRUNEL D 2005.*

2104. **DIXON, S. E. A.** Organisational transformation in the Russian oil industry. *BRUNEL D 2006.*

Slovakia *(see also Czechoslovakia)*

2105. **PEFFERS, J. A.** Policy transfer 'West' to 'East': the case of the Enterprise Education in Slovakia project. *WARWICK MP 1998.*

South Eastern Europe *(see also under individual countries)*

2106. **POPOVA, N. B.** MNEs and strategy making in transforming institutional contexts: global brewers in Bulgaria and Romania. *LONDON (R HOLLOWAY) D 2004.*

USSR *(see also Russia)*

2107. **INCH, P. J.** The evolutionary process of Soviet regional economic planning. *LONDON (LSE) MP 1970.*

2108. **ANDRLE, V.** Managerial power in the Soviet Union: the social position of industrial enterprise directors, 1963–1972. *BIRMINGHAM D 1975.*

2109. **CAVE, M.** The development of automated planning and management systems in the Soviet Union. *OXFORD D 1977.*

2110. **AHMAD, A. A. M.** Accounting for planning and control in the evolution of accounting in the UK, the USSR and Iraq, with special emphasis on the textile sector. *STRATHCLYDE D 1979.*

2111. **BAILEY, D. T.** Soviet industrial accounting. *BIRMINGHAM D 1989.*

2112. **RICHTER, R.** The transformation of the Soviet poll-taking regime: the emergence of a survey and market research industry in Russia. *OXFORD MP 1995.*

Yugoslavia *(see also under former republics)*

2113. **TAMADDON, M. H.** The political basis of central planning with special reference to Yugoslav and French economic policy and planning. *LONDON (LSE) D 1966.*

2114. **HASHI, I.** Yugoslavia's labour-managed firms and labour-managed economy in the post-War period. *KEELE D 1979.*

2115. **EAMES, A. H.** The Yugoslav system of self-management. *BRADFORD D 1980.*

2116. **ESTRIN, S.** Self-management: economic theory and Yugoslav practice. *SUSSEX D 1980.*

2117. **ZAPP, K. M.**   Income distribution in Yugoslav self-management.   *LANCASTER D 1982.*

20. MEDIA (BROADCASTING, CINEMA, PRESS, PUBLISHING)

Albania

2118. **MAI, N.**   Between losing and finding oneself: the role of Italian television in the Albanian migration to Italy.   *SUSSEX D 2002.*

Austria-Hungary

2119. **CORNWALL, J. M.**   The undermining of Austria-Hungary: the Allied propaganda campaign of 1918 against the Austro-Hungarian army on the Italian Front.   *LEEDS D 1987.*

Bosnia-Herzegovina

2120. **TOBLER, U. F.**   Portrayal of Bosnian Islam in the press and parliaments of Britain, Germany and France from 1983–1995.   *BIRMINGHAM D 1998.*

2121. **ROBINSON, P. G.**   The news media and intervention [with case studies of US intervention in Bosnia, Kosovo and Somalia].   *BRISTOL D 2000.*

2122. **ROBINSON, B. A.**   British military-media relations and the geopolitics of intervention in Bosnia-Herzegovina, 1992–95.   *LONDON (R HOLLOWAY) D 2001.*

2123. **CLEMSON, G.**   What they led us to believe: the television media and the Bosnian War, 1991–1995.   *BIRMINGHAM MP 2002.*

2124. **KENT, G.**   Media accuracy and the effects of framing in distant crises: British television news representation of the war in Bosnia.   *SUSSEX D 2002.*

2125. **DOWLING, J. P.**   British media, parliamentary and military accounts of the war in Bosnia, 1992–95.   *CAMBRIDGE D 2003.*

Bulgaria

2126. **BALABANOVA, E.**   Media-foreign policy interaction in the age of new military humanitarianisms: Britain and Bulgaria compared.   *MANCHESTER D 2005.*

Central and Eastern Europe *(see also under individual countries)*

2127. **McLAUGHLIN, G.**   Cold War news: a paradigm in crisis. [The role of the media in the East European revolutions of 1989].   *GLASGOW D 1994.*

Croatia

2128. YEOMANS, R. Ideology, propaganda and mass culture in the Independent State of Croatia, 1941–1945. *LONDON (UCL) D 2005.*

Czech Republic

2129. KOUDELOVA, R. Cross-cultural advertising in Europe: an empirical survey of television advertising in the UK and the Czech Republic. *SALFORD MP 1999.*

2130. SORFA, D. E. The fetishism of meaning: disavowal in Kafka, Švankmajer and the Quay brothers. *KENT D 2006.*

Czechoslovakia

2131. HAMES, P. J. B. Czechoslovak cinema in the sixties: an explanation and evaluation of the Czechoslovak new wave. *LONDON (UCL) D 1980.*

2132. BALLESTER, C. The establishing shot: film space and the Czechoslovak New Wave. *LONDON (UCL) D 2005.*

Hungary

2133. ELVY, P. Broadcasting evangelical Christianity: a critical comparison of Britain and Hungary, 1989–1993. *EDINBURGH D 1995.*

2134. MILOTAY, N. The social function of the women's periodical in late eighteenth-century Hungary and Germany: *Uránia*, 1794–5 and *Magazin für Frauenzimmer*, 1782–91. *CAMBRIDGE D 2001.*

2135. DRAGON, Z. The spectral body: the mapping of the cinematic oeuvre of István Szabó. *OPEN MP 2005.*

Kosovo

2136. MURPHY, A. C. Evaluation in English and Italian newspaper opinion articles on the Kosovo crisis. *BIRMINGHAM D 2004.*

2137. WILLCOX, D. R. Propaganda, the British press and contemporary war: a comparative study of the Gulf War 1990–1991 and Kosovo conflict 1999. *KENT D 2004.*

2138. LATHAM, M. L. British coverage of the Kosovo conflict. *LEEDS D 2005.*

Poland

2139. DISTELHEIM, L. B. Propaganda and illusion: the history, theory and practice of US broadcasting to Poland. *LONDON (LSE) MP 1988.*

2140. ZAJĄCZKOWSKI-GOTIN, A. Ideological control of Polish press and literature 1944–1982. *ESSEX MP 1991.*

Romania

2141. TRANDAFOIU, R. Nationhood and Europeanness: discursive constructions in the British and Romanian press. *WESTMINSTER D 2003.*

Russia (see also USSR)

2142. MALCOLM, N. Ideology and intrigue in Russian journalism under Nicholas I: *Moskovskii telegraf* and *Severnaya pchela*. OXFORD D 1974.

2143. O'FLAHERTY, D. M. Tsarism and the politics of publicity, 1865–1881. OXFORD D 1975.

2144. HABBERJAM, B. L. The socio-political and artistic significance of Russian satirical journalism, 1905–1907. OXFORD BP 1978.

2145. SMITH, J. T. A study of Russian pro- and anti-war propaganda from 1914 to February 1917, with particular emphasis on its effect on public opinion. LEEDS MP 1984.

2146. McGOVERN, F. The cinema of Andrei Tarkovsky in the Russian literary and philosophical traditions. OXFORD D 1992.

2147. WILLIAMS, H. S. Periodical publishing by Russian radical émigrés in the second half of the nineteenth century. LONDON (SSEES) MP 1998.

2148. FLANAGAN, M. J. Mikhail Bakhtin and Hollywood film. SHEFFIELD D 2001.

2149. BELIN, L. The fall and rise of state power over the Russian media, 1995–2001. OXFORD D 2002.

2150. BURKE, M. A search for evidence: the evolution of film editing in Russian and early Soviet fiction and non-fiction film. NUI (DUBLIN) D 2002.

2151. CHAPPLE, F. Shakespeare's women on the Russian and Soviet screen: Othello, Hamlet, King Lear, Macbeth. SHEFFIELD MP 2002.

2152. SANDERSON, B. The interrelation of religion and film in Soviet and post-Soviet Russia. EXETER D 2005.

Slovenia

2153. NOVAK, M. The change from a socialist to a market-led media system in Slovenia. WESTMINSTER D 1996.

United Kingdom

2154. FOSTER, A. J. The British press and the origins of the Cold War. OPEN D 1987.

2155. SCOTT, J. D. The British press and the Holocaust, 1942–1943. LEICESTER D 1994.

2156. MILLAND, G. Some faint hope and courage: the BBC and the Final Solution, 1942–45. LEICESTER D 1998.

2157. DEFTY, A. British anti-communist propaganda and cooperation with the United States. SALFORD D 2002.

USSR (see also Russia)

2158. KATONA, P. The Cominform: a study in propaganda. LONDON (LSE) D 1958.

2159. WALKER, G. P. M. Soviet book publishing policy. SHEFFIELD D 1976.

2160. GLEISNER, J. I. The agitation and propaganda work of the Communist Party of the Soviet Union, 1956–1974. BIRMINGHAM D 1978.

2161. OILLE, J. The art and politics of Soviet agitation, 1917–1925: film, poster, theatre. SUSSEX MP 1978.

2162. **DYNES, M. E.** The ether and the superpowers, 1945–1975. *OXFORD MP 1984.*

2163. **MURRAY, J.** Soviet journalism under perestroika. *TC DUBLIN D 1991.*

2164. **SOLOGUBENKO, A.** Regulation and deregulation of the media in the UK and the USSR, 1985–90. *MANCHESTER MP 1991.*

2165. **DÉTRAZ, M. -P.** The attrition of dogma in the legal press under Brezhnev: *Literaturnaya gazeta. BIRMINGHAM D 1992.*

2166. **BECKER, J. A.** Changing Soviet press coverage of the United States in the Gorbachev era: domestic and foreign considerations. *OXFORD D 1993.*

2167. **DAVIES, S. R.** Propaganda and popular opinion in Soviet Russia, 1934–1941. *OXFORD D 1994.*

2168. **HERZ, M.** The Soviet image of Latin America: sources and components. *LONDON (LSE) D 1994.*

2169. **STOLLERY, M.** Alternative empires: Soviet montage cinema, the British documentary movement and colonialism. *WARWICK D 1994.*

2170. **ROBERTS, G.** Stride Soviet! An investigation into the history of Soviet non-fiction film, 1917–1932. *SUSSEX D 1996.*

2171. **NANSON, S. J.** Fleet Street's dilemma: the British press and the Soviet Union, 1933–1941. *ST ANDREWS D 1997.*

2172. **SARGEANT, A.** Pudovkin and Pavlov's dog. *BRISTOL D 1997.*

2173. **LOVELL, S.** The Russian reading revolution: society and the printed word, 1986–1995. *LONDON (SSEES) D 1998.*

2174. **WIDDIS, E. K.** Projecting a Soviet space: exploration and mobility in Soviet film and culture, 1920–1935. *CAMBRIDGE D 1998.*

2175. **MICHALSKI, M. L.** Iurii Olesha, Abram Room and *Strogii Iunosha*: artistic form and political context. *LONDON (SSEES) D 1999.*

2176. **HAYNES, A. J.** Patriarchal disorder: men and masculinity in Stalinist Soviet cinema. *MANCHESTER D 2000.*

2177. **STEPHENSON, C.** Italian cinema and the Soviet model from the late 1920s to the early 1940s. *READING D 2004.*

2178. **EYNON, A. D.** Meyerhold and Eisenstein: the creation of a non-realist aesthetic in revolutionary art. *KEELE D 2005.*

2179. **TCHOUVAROVA, V.** An American Trojan horse, or how the Hollywood musical influenced Soviet musicals of Grigorii Aleksandrov in the 1930s [NCR]. *SUNDERLAND MP 2006.*

Yugoslavia (see also under former republics)

2180. **TOPHAM, S. W.** Economic propaganda in Yugoslav society. *BRADFORD D 1981.*

2181. **PEARSON, J. S.** British press reactions to the onset of war in ex-Yugoslavia. *CAMBRIDGE D 2001.*

2182. **SYMVOULIDIS, C.** British and Greek press reactions to the disintegration of Yugoslavia, 1991–1999. *LIVERPOOL D 2005.*

21. MILITARY, SECURITY, DISARMAMENT

Albania

2183. **BAILEY, R.** The Special Operations Executive (SOE) and British policy towards wartime resistance in Albania and Kosovo, 1940–44. *EDINBURGH D 2004.*

Austria-Hungary

2184. **ALAICA, N.** A mixing of identities: Orthodox and Catholic peasants in the First Banat Regiment [on the Austrian Military Frontier in Croatia]. *OXFORD D 2004.*

Baltic States *(see also under individual countries)*

2185. **ALDRIDGE, D. D.** Sir John Norris and the British naval expeditions in the Baltic Sea, 1715–1727. *LONDON (LSE) D 1972.*

2186. **BULLEN, J. R.** The Royal Navy in the Baltic, 1918–20. *LONDON (KCL) D 1983.*

Bosnia-Herzegovina

2187. **HAGMAN, H.-C.** UN–NATO operational cooperation in peacekeeping 1992–1995 [with special reference to Bosnia]. *LONDON (KCL) D 1997.*

2188. **MARTIN, R. C.** Understanding the role of combat air power in Bosnia. *ST ANDREWS MP 1997.*

2189. **BUCKNAM, M. A.** The influence of UN and NATO theater-level commanders on the use of airpower over Bosnia during Operation Deny Flight, 1993–1995. *LONDON (KCL) D 1999.*

2190. **MEYER, E.** The German debate over participation in peace support operations: the cases of Somalia and Bosnia-Herzegovina. *OXFORD MP 1999.*

2191. **SMITH, M.** The British Army, peace support operations doctrine and Bosnia 1992–1995: a tale of three commanders. *WALES (ABERYSTWYTH) D 2000.*

2192. **KOTOUC, E.** The causes of violent conflict in Bosnia and the contemporary effort to establish lasting peace. *OXFORD MP 2001.*

2193. **MACE, C.** The dual key in UN–NATO co-operation in Bosnia, 1993–95. *OXFORD MP 2001.*

2194. **McQUEEN, C.** Safety zones in the 1990s: Iraq, Bosnia and Rwanda. *OXFORD D 2002.*

2195. **MIKHOS, A.** United Nations conflict resolution with special reference to the Bosnian and Somali wars. *READING D 2002.*

2196. **ORSINI, D.** Democratisation, reintegration and the security sector: assessing the peacebuilding effort in Bosnia-Herzegovina, 1995–2000. *LONDON (LSE) D 2002.*

2197. **DONLEY, P. H.** Population protection in the 1990s: managing risk in the new security environment [with special reference to Bosnia-Herzegovina and Kosovo]. *LONDON (LSE) D 2003.*

2198. GORDON, D. S. Providing emergency assistance in war: [...] the relationship between and operations of [UNHCR], the humanitarian NGO community and [UNPROFOR] in Bosnia-Herzegovina 1992–1995. *LANCASTER D 2003.*

2199. MOE, M. The Contact Group in Bosnia-Herzegovina and Kosovo: the institution and its mediation role. *LONDON (UCL) MP 2003.*

2200. MIYAMOTO, K. Peace from below: developing inter-ethnic dialogue among citizens for bottom-up conflict transformation in Bosnia. *KENT D 2004.*

2201. COLLANTES CELADOR, G. Role of police reform in peacebuilding missions: lessons from post-Dayton Bosnia and Herzegovina. *WALES (ABERYSTWYTH) D 2005.*

2202. LAUZZANA, S. Does relief aid prolong wars? Explaining the interaction between humanitarian assistance and conflict during the war in Bosnia-Herzegovina. *CAMBRIDGE D 2006.*

Byzantium

2203. CARROLL, A. I. The role of the Varangian Guard in Byzantine rebellions and usurpations, 988–1204. *QUEENS BELFAST D 2005.*

Central and Eastern Europe *(see also under individual countries)*

2204. ALI, M. A. J. The negotiations on Mutual and Balanced Force Reductions in Central Europe. *KEELE D 1991.*

2205. COTTEY, A. East-Central European security after the Cold War: an examination of the security concerns and policies of Poland, Czechoslovakia and Hungary, 1989–92. *BRADFORD D 1993.*

2206. BLOOD, P. W. Bandenbekämpfung: Nazi occupation security in Eastern Europe and Soviet Russia 1942–45. *CRANFIELD D 2001.*

2207. STOJANOVITS, G. The changing nature of security in post-Cold War Central and Eastern Europe: predicaments, perceptions and policy-responses. *LOUGHBOROUGH D 2001.*

2208. BETZ, D. J. Politics of mimicry — politics of exclusion: comparing post-communist civil-military relations in Poland and Hungary, Russia and Ukraine, 1991–1999. *GLASGOW D 2002.*

2209. GOGOLEWSKA, A. A comparative study of civil-military relations in post-communist Central and Eastern Europe: Poland, the Czech Republic, Ukraine and Lithuania. *LONDON (KCL) D 2002.*

2210. KRIVOSHEEV, D. Visions of European security: Britain's post-Cold War security relations with Poland and the Czech Republic. *MANCHESTER D 2002.*

2211. ZILBERMAN, A. Perceptions of change in the European security environment [NCR]. *BIRMINGHAM D 2004.*

2212. HIGASHINO, A. The role of security discourses in the eastern enlargement of the European Union. *BIRMINGHAM D 2005.*

Central Asia *(see also under individual countries)*

2213. **HORSMAN, S.** Security issues of the newly independent states of Central Asia: the cases of Kazakstan and Uzbekistan. SHEFFIELD D 1999.

2214. **MARSHALL, A. G.** Dar Al-Harb. The Russian General Staff and the Asiatic frontier, 1860–1917. GLASGOW D 2001.

2215. **SHASHENKOV, M.** Stability and instability in Central Asia: security dimensions, 1991–1993. OXFORD D 2001.

Croatia

2216. **BECKETT, G. R.** Constructing peace in Croatia: complementarity and the transformation of conflict. BRADFORD D 1996.

Czechoslovakia

2217. **BROWN, A. C.** The Czechoslovak Air Force in Britain, 1940–1945. SOUTHAMPTON D 1998.

Finland

2218. **SCREEN, J. E. O.** The entry of Finnish officers into Russian military service, 1809–1917. LONDON (SSEES) D 1976.

2219. **PENTTILÄ, R. E. J.** Finland's search for security through defence: defence policy in the stabilisation of Finland's international position 1944–1967. OXFORD D 1988.

2220. **VAN DYKE, C.** The Soviet–Finnish war of 1939–1940. CAMBRIDGE D 1995.

Hungary

2221. **FINKEL, C.** The administration of warfare: the supply and provisioning of the Ottoman army in Hungary, 1593–1606. LONDON (SOAS) D 1986.

2222. **DÁKAI, Z.** NATO as an issue in Hungarian domestic politics from 1994 to 1997. OXFORD MP 1999.

2223. **BUTLER, E.** The European Union and Eastern enlargement: Hungary and the security lens. STRATHCLYDE D 2005.

Kosovo

2224. **OWENS, P.** The humanitarian condition: US public spheres and the 1999 war over Kosovo. WALES (ABERYSTWYTH) D 2003.

2225. **PEAKE, G. P.** Policing peace: the establishment of police forces in the Palestinian territories and Kosovo. OXFORD D 2003.

2226. **BAHADOR, B.** The impact of globalization on war: the CNN effect and Western policy before the Kosovo intervention. LONDON (LSE) D 2005.

2227. **HENRIKSEN, D.** Operation Allied Force: a product of military theory or political pragmatism? An examination of the role of air power in handling the Kosovo crisis. GLASGOW D 2005.

2228. **MOORE, C.** Reconceptualising the phenomenon of war: the NATO intervention in Kosovo. *NOTTINGHAM TRENT D 2005.*

2229. **NEOPHYTOU, M.** Gender and peacebuilding: the United Nations mission in Kosovo and beyond. *CAMBRIDGE D 2005.*

Macedonia

2230. **STAMNES, E.** United Nations preventive deployment in Macedonia: a critical security studies analysis. *WALES (ABERYSTWYTH) D 2002.*

Poland

2231. **HANSON, J. K. M.** The civilian population and the Warsaw uprising of 1944. *LONDON (SSEES) D 1978.*

2232. **WOHLFELD, M. J.** Security cooperation in Central Europe: Polish views. *LONDON (KCL) D 1995.*

2233. **McGILVRAY, E.** The military in Poland's transition from communism, 1989–1997: a transition from the Warsaw Pact to NATO. *BRADFORD MP 2000.*

2234. **TROMAN, W. M. J.** Anglo-Polish naval relations 1918–1947. *EXETER D 2001.*

2235. **HOPE, M.** The abandoned legion: a study of the background and process of the postwar dissolution of Polish forces in the West. *LEICESTER MP 2002.*

2236. **SZWED, R. S.** Germany in the reorientation of Polish defense and security policy, 1989–1999. *OXFORD MP 2002.*

2237. **PIÓRKO, I. D.** Enlarging the area of freedom, security and justice: Poland's accession to the European Union in the field of external border controls. *SUSSEX D 2006.*

Russia *(see also USSR)*

2238. **MAWDSLEY, E.** The Baltic Fleet in the Russian Revolution, 1917–1921. *LONDON (SSEES) D 1972.*

2239. **TOWLE, P. A.** The influence of the Russo-Japanese War on British military and naval thought, 1904–1914. *LONDON (KCL) D 1973.*

2240. **SIEGELBAUM, L. H.** The War Industries Committees and the politics of industrial mobilization in Russia, 1915–17. *OXFORD D 1975.*

2241. **GATRELL, P. W.** Russian heavy industry and state defence, 1908–1918: pre-War expansion and wartime mobilization. *CAMBRIDGE D 1979.*

2242. **LEE, C. D.** The political role of the peasant army in the formation of the Soviet state (March 1917–March 1918). *OXFORD ML 1980.*

2243. **PERRINS, M.** The Russian military, 1904–1917, and its role in Russian political affairs. *LONDON (LSE) D 1980.*

2244. **DALY, J. C. K.** The Russian Black Sea Fleet and the 'Eastern Question', 1827–1841. *LONDON (SSEES) D 1986.*

2245. **VAN DYKE, C.** Culture of soldiers: the role of the Nicholas Academy of the General Staff in the development of Russian Imperial military sciences, 1832–1912. *EDINBURGH MP 1989.*

2246. **BELLAMY, C. D.** The Russian and Soviet view of the military-technical character of future war, 1877–2017. *EDINBURGH D 1990.*

2247. **MORGAN, R. T.** Management of defense industry conversion in St Petersburg: the shipbuilding industry, 1988–1993. *OXFORD MP 1993.*

2248. **BOLI, F. C.** Transformation of the Russian military: the relationship between the transformation process and the concept of future war. *EDINBURGH D 1994.*

2249. **BRADSHAW, N. F.** The military implications of the post-October 1993 events in Moscow. *EXETER MP 1994.*

2250. **LYNCH, D.** Russian peacekeeping and Russian foreign and security policy towards the 'Near Abroad', 1992–1994: the cases of Moldova, Georgia and Tajikistan. *OXFORD MP 1995.*

2251. **ASTON, B. A.** The effect of the Russian Revolution and Civil War on the British forces in North Russia, Siberia and the Don during the Allied intervention. *ABERDEEN ML 1997.*

2252. **LYNCH, D.** Russian peacekeeping strategies in the CIS, 1992–1996: the cases of Moldova, Georgia and Tajikistan. *OXFORD D 1997.*

2253. **PAPAVLASSOPOULOS, K.** Diplomatic, ideological and military aspects of the Russo-Turkish War (1768–1774). *ABERDEEN D 1997.*

2254. **PERSSON, G. I.** The Russian army and foreign wars 1859–1871. *LONDON (LSE) D 1998.*

2255. **ROBINSON, P.** The White Russian army in exile, 1920–1941. *OXFORD D 1999.*

2256. **BITIS, A.** The Russian army and the Eastern Question 1831–34. *LONDON (LSE) D 2000.*

2257. **TSAI, M. -Y.** The limits of Chinese and Russian military cooperation after the end of the Cold War. *LONDON (KCL) D 2000.*

2258. **JAMISON, M. C.** Why Russia chose war: the Russo-Turkish War, 1877–8. *OXFORD MP 2002.*

2259. **GORYUNOV, V.** Russian national security and Central Europe: Russian perspectives and policies. *WOLVERHAMPTON D 2003.*

2260. **BABCOCK-LUMISH, B. C.** The tensions of profession: a critical analysis of the late Imperial Russian army and the implications for post-Cold War America. *OXFORD MP 2004.*

2261. **CHEN, J. L.** The failure of Russian military reform, 1991–2004. *OXFORD MP 2004.*

2262. **BOSWORTH, K. L.** The evolution of Russia's security relations with NATO and the European Union, 1994–2004: a critical analysis. *BATH D 2005.*

2263. **DOUGHERTY, T. S.** Russian arms transfers in the post-Cold War era: China, India and Iran (1992–2002). *OXFORD D 2005.*

2264. **MONAGHAN, A.** Evolving Russian perspectives of the European Union as a security institution, 1991–2004. *LONDON (KCL) D 2005.*

2265. **RENZ, B.** Civil-military relations in post-Soviet Russia: the case of 'military politicians'. *BIRMINGHAM D 2005.*

2266. **AHN, S. H.** Multi-dimensional security cooperation between Russia and South Korea: progress and obstacles. *LONDON (LSE) D 2006.*

2267. **GATICA, A. V.** Weapons of mass destruction and terrorism: the analysis of Chechnya. *BRADFORD MP 2006.*

2268. **PAPASTRATIGAKIS, N.** Russian naval strategy in the Far East, 1895–1904. *LONDON (LSE) D 2006.*

Serbia

2269. **RYAN, B. J.** Police reform in the Republic of Serbia: a participatory perspective. *LIMERICK D 2005.*

South Eastern Europe *(see also under individual countries)*

2270. **BONO, G.** NATO's 'out-of-area' tasks and the role of 'policy communities' (1990–1995) [with special reference to NATO's role in the Balkans]. *KENT D 2000.*

2271. **RICKLI, J. -M.** The coercive use of air power in the Balkans. *OXFORD MP 2002.*

2272. **TZIFAKIS, N.** Securitization and desecuritization dynamics in South-Eastern Europe. *LANCASTER D 2002.*

2273. **LANGAN, W. B.** Dyadic nexus of interstate and intrastate conflict prevention [with special reference to Kosovo and Macedonia]. *KENT D 2004.*

2274. **KAVALSKI, E.** Peace in the Balkans: the influence of Euro-Atlantic actors on the promotion of security-community relations in Southeastern Europe. *LOUGHBOROUGH D 2005.*

Soviet Bloc

2275. **FODOR, N.** The Warsaw Treaty Organisation: a political and organisational analysis. *GLASGOW D 1987.*

Ukraine

2276. **MALET, M. I. G.** Nestor Makhno in the Russian Civil War, 1917–21. *LONDON (LSE) D 1975.*

2277. **SANDERS, D. L.** Neoliberal institutionalism and neorealism: a case study of military-security cooperation between Russia and Ukraine 1991–1995. *WALES (ABERYSTWYTH) D 1997.*

2278. **OGILVIE-WHITE, T.** Theorising nuclear weapons proliferation: understanding the nuclear policies of India, South Africa, North Korea and Ukraine. *SOUTHAMPTON D 1998.*

United Kingdom

2279. **SWEETMAN, J.** The effect of the Crimean War upon the administration of the British Army, 1852–1856. *LONDON (KCL) D 1972.*

USSR *(see also Russia)*

2280. **KREBS, P.** The political institutions of the Soviet army with special reference to the role of the political commissars. OXFORD D *1958*.

2281. **SELLA, A.** Surprise attack: Soviet response to German threats, December 1940–June 1941. EDINBURGH D *1973*.

2282. **YERGIN, D. H.** The rise of the national security state: anti-communism and the origins of the Cold War. CAMBRIDGE D *1974*.

2283. **BEAUMONT, J. E.** Great Britain and the Soviet Union: the supply of munitions, 1941–1945. LONDON (KCL) D *1975*.

2284. **COLLINS, D. N.** The origins, structure and role of the Russian Red Guard. LEEDS D *1975*.

2285. **FREEDMAN, L. D.** The definition of the Soviet threat in strategic arms decisions of the United States, 1961–1974. OXFORD D *1975*.

2286. **SARGENT, R. E.** The Soviet-American strategic competition: the action-reaction process reconsidered. EDINBURGH D *1976*.

2287. **GERHARDT, P.** The development of military aid as a factor in Indo-Soviet relations. OXFORD D *1978*.

2288. **GERSON, M. B.** Problems of theory and practice: difficulties in formulating and achieving American strategic objectives in the US–Soviet Strategic Arms Limitation Talks. OXFORD ML *1979*.

2289. **HEMSLEY, J.** Soviet command and control *(upravlenie voiskami)*: an investigation of theory and practice. EDINBURGH MP *1980*.

2290. **LACOUTURE, J. E.** The confrontation at sea between the US and Soviet navies. CAMBRIDGE ML *1980*.

2291. **EFRAT, M.** The defence burden in Egypt during the deepening of the Soviet involvement, 1962–1973. LONDON (LSE) D *1981*.

2292. **WRITER, R. M.** The identification of developing Soviet strategic interests in the Indian Ocean, 1968–1974. LONDON (LSE) D *1981*.

2293. **ADELMAN, J. L.** A comparison of the current Western and Soviet use of naval forces for political purposes. LONDON (KCL) D *1982*.

2294. **COCKCROFT, J. A. E.** An exercise in contemporary strategy (1976–81): a study of military power, influence, science and technology in determining the plausibility of a new Soviet limited war strategy. MANCHESTER D *1982*.

2295. **EL HUSSINI, M. M.** Soviet-Egyptian relations, 1945–1970, with special reference to strategic and naval affairs. LONDON (KCL) D *1982*.

2296. **TUPPER, S. M.** The Red Army and Soviet defence industry, 1934–1941. BIRMINGHAM D *1982*.

2297. **BARTOV, O.** The barbarisation of warfare: German officers and soldiers in combat on the Eastern Front, 1941–1945. OXFORD D *1983*.

2298. **GOREN, R. C.** The Soviet attitude and policy on international terrorism since 1917. LONDON (LSE) D *1983*.

2299. **SPEED, S. E.** NATO defence and the potential Soviet threat: an analysis of possible future war in Northern Norway. MANCHESTER MP *1984*.

2300. VALE, L. J. The limits of civil defence: the evolution of policies since 1945 in the United States, Switzerland, Britain and the Soviet Union. OXFORD D 1985.

2301. LITHERLAND, J. P. Soviet views of the arms race and disarmament. BRADFORD D 1986.

2302. AULIN, V. L. The evolution of Soviet disarmament policy. OXFORD MP 1987.

2303. SCHULTE, T. J. The German army and National Socialist occupation policies in the occupied areas of the Soviet Union, 1941–1943. WARWICK D 1987.

2304. PEPPER, R. H. 'Two three headed serpents'. An investigation of Soviet contemporary and future warfighting within a nuclear threatened environment. EDINBURGH MP 1988.

2305. BLUTH, C. H. Soviet strategic arms policy under Khrushchev. LONDON (KCL) D 1989.

2306. MAIN, S. J. The creation, organisation and work of the Red Army's political apparatus during the Civil War (1918–1920). EDINBURGH D 1989.

2307. MATHERS, J. G. Political and military aspects of Soviet ballistic missile defence. OXFORD MP 1989.

2308. CALINGAERT, D. The Gorbachev leadership's policy of nuclear disarmament. OXFORD D 1990.

2309. SCHEAR, J. A. From SALT to START: compliance behavior and the evolution of bargaining methodology in Soviet–American strategic arms diplomacy, 1972–1989. LONDON (LSE) D 1990.

2310. SCHWEIZER, P. F. The three revolutions: new technologies and the Soviet armed forces. OXFORD MP 1990.

2311. HOLDEN, G. A. Soviet strategy and the Warsaw Pact: military policy in the history of an alliance. LONDON (LSE) D 1991.

2312. PENNIE, K. R. Analysis of superpower nuclear strategy: compellence as a competing paradigm to that of deterrence. LONDON (LSE) D 1991.

2313. RICHARD, D. O. The rise of Soviet military doctrine (1918–1925). OXFORD ML 1991.

2314. EISENBAUM, B. The withdrawal of Soviet troops from Afghanistan: a case study of policy-making. OXFORD MP 1992.

2315. HOLOBOFF, E. M. The Soviet concept of reasonable sufficiency and conventional arms reductions. LONDON (KCL) D 1992.

2316. LIM, I. S. The role of naval power in the North-West Pacific 1953–1991. WALES (ABERYSTWYTH) D 1992.

2317. MARKUS, U. L. A case study of Soviet counterinsurgence: the guerilla wars in Lithuania and Western Ukraine 1944–53. LONDON (LSE) D 1992.

2318. VANDENBERG, M. E. 'Who lost Eastern Europe?' Gorbachev and the politicisation of the Soviet military. OXFORD MP 1992.

2319. HARRISON, R. W. The development of Russian-Soviet operational art, 1904–1937, and the imperial legacy in Soviet military thought. LONDON (KCL) D 1994.

2320. MARSHALL-HASDELL, D. The Soviet military: responses to reform initiatives in the Gorbachev era. WALES (ABERYSTWYTH) D 1994.

2321. **MATHERS, J. G.**   Soviet perspectives and policies on ballistic missile defence from Khrushchev to Gorbachev. OXFORD D 1994.

2322. **CLEARY, L. R.**   Security systems in transition: Soviet and Russian attempts to disarm and convert the military industrial complex. GLASGOW D 1995.

2323. **COLLINS, A. R.**   The security dilemma and its mitigation: the case of the Cold War and the Gorbachev era. WALES (ABERYSTWYTH) D 1995.

2324. **HINES, J. G.**   Soviet strategic intentions 1965–1985: an analytical comparison of US Cold War interpretations with Soviet post-Cold War testimonial evidence. EDINBURGH D 1995.

2325. **CHARLES, V.**   A reappraisal of doctrine: the ideological relevance of Soviet military thinking during the Gorbachev era 1985–1991. LANCASTER D 1996.

2326. **KEER, M.**   The impact of the Afghan War on the collapse of the Soviet Union 1979–1991. OXFORD MP 1996.

2327. **RYAN, J. F.**   The Royal Navy and Soviet sea power, 1930–1950: intelligence, naval cooperation and antagonism. HULL D 1996.

2328. **CANT, J. F.**   The development of the SS-20: a case-study of Soviet defence decisionmaking during the Brezhnev era. GLASGOW D 1998.

2329. **CLARK, T.**   The evolution of Russian strategic nuclear doctrine and operations: problems and prospects. LANCASTER D 1998.

2330. **PARK, J.**   Civil-military relations and arms control under Brezhnev. OXFORD MP 1998.

2331. **ELLETSON, H.**   The changing face of the military in Russian and Soviet politics, 1968–1997: a study of the military service and political career of Lieutenant-General Alexander Ivanovich Lebed'. BRADFORD D 1999.

2332. **SHEPHERD, B.**   German Army security units in Russia, 1941–1943: a case study. BIRMINGHAM D 2000.

2333. **DURIC, M.**   The Strategic Defense Initiative and the end of the Cold War: US policy and the Soviet Union. KEELE D 2001.

2334. **EVANS, N. C.**   Soviet nuclear weapons policy during the Gorbachev era. OXFORD MP 2001.

2335. **FREIRE, M. R. DE S.**   Conflict and security in the former Soviet Union: the role of the OSCE [with Estonia and Moldova as case studies]. KENT D 2001.

2336. **HILL, A. A.**   German occupation policy and the effectiveness of the Soviet Partisan movement as a military force 1941–1944 — the case of North-West Russia. CAMBRIDGE D 2001.

2337. **CROLL, N. H.**   Mikhail Tukhachevsky in the Russian Civil War. GLASGOW D 2002.

2338. **DEYERMOND, R.**   The interrelationship between sovereignty and security in the former Soviet Union. ESSEX D 2003.

2339. **HEATON, C. D.**   Racism versus logic: German racial policy, international law and the effect upon counterinsurgency development in the USSR during World War II. STRATHCLYDE MP 2003.

2340. **TANAKA, R.**   Imperial dilemma: the Japanese intervention in Siberia, 1918–1922. CAMBRIDGE D 2004.

2341. EVANS, N. C.   Continuity and change in Soviet and Russian ballistic missile defence policies, 1969–2002. OXFORD D 2005.

2342. GOODMAN, M. S.   British intelligence estimates of the Soviet nuclear weapons programme and their impact on strategic planning. NOTTINGHAM D 2005.

2343. STERRETT, J. J.   Soviet Air Force operational theory, 1918–1945. LONDON (KCL) D 2006.

2344. TERRY, N. M.   The German Army Group Centre and the Soviet civilian population, 1942–1944: forced labour, hunger and population displacement on the Eastern Front. LONDON (KCL) D 2006.

2345. WALSH, D. M.   Perceptions of power: American perceptions of the US–Soviet military balance and the course of the Cold War, 1976–1985. LONDON (LSE) D 2006.

Yugoslavia (see also under former republics)

2346. VAN CREVELD, M.   Greece and Yugoslavia in Hitler's strategy, 1940–1941. LONDON (LSE) D 1971.

2347. TREW, S.   No pity distilled. Britain and the Chetniks, 1941–1942. KEELE D 1991.

2348. GOW, A. J. W.   Legitimacy and the military: a theoretical perspective on the expansion of the Yugoslav People's Army's political role in the 1980s. LONDON (SSEES) D 1992.

2349. MANGASARIAN, L.   Independence or dependence? The arms industries in Israel, South Africa and Yugoslavia during the Cold War. LONDON (LSE) D 1993.

2350. WILLIAMS, H.   The Special Operations Executive and Yugoslavia, 1941–1945. SOUTHAMPTON D 1994.

2351. BRASHAW, N. C.   Signals intelligence, the British and the war in Yugoslavia 1941–1944. SOUTHAMPTON D 2001.

2352. O'SHEA, P. B.   Perception and reality in the modern Yugoslav conflict. NUI (CORK) D 2002.

2353. WATKINS, A.   Development of the Yugoslav military industry 1918–1991. LONDON (KCL) D 2002.

2354. YORDÁN, C. L.   Strategic versus communicative approaches to peacemaking: a critical assessment of the Dayton peace initiative. LONDON (LSE) D 2004.

22. MINORITIES, MIGRATION, NATIONALISM

General and Comparative

2355. CALDER, K. J.   National self-determination in British government policy during the First World War, with special reference to Poland, Yugoslavia, and Czechoslovakia. LONDON (LSE) D 1971.

2356. STRICKLAND-SCOTT, S.   The emergence of national identities from trans-national empires: the cases of Mongolia, Bulgaria, Moldova and Armenia. LEEDS D 2002.

2357. POHL, J. O. Shallow roots: the exile experiences of the Russian-Germans, Crimean Tatars and Meskhetian Turks in comparative perspective. *LONDON (SOAS) D 2004.*

Armenia

2358. GORILOVSKAYA, N. Perestroika and the national question: the case of Armenia and the Karabakh movement [NCR]. *OXFORD MP 2002.*

2359. AGHANIAN, D. Analysis of ethnic identity: the Armenian diaspora in Manchester. *YORK D 2004.*

2360. GEUKJIAN, O. B. Examining the Nagorno-Karabakh conflict: ethno-territorial conflict in the South Caucasus. *BRADFORD D 2005.*

Baltic States *(see also under individual countries)*

2361. JURADO, E. Russian homeland nationalism and the Baltic States: explaining Russia's policy towards the diaspora, 1991–1997. *OXFORD MP 1998.*

2362. GILBERT, E. Latvian, Lithuanian and Estonian displaced persons in Great Britain. *SHEFFIELD D 2001.*

2363. GALBREATH, D. J. Nation-building and minority politics: a comparative case study of Estonia and Latvia. *LEEDS D 2004.*

Belarus

2364. JOCELYN, E. A nation of shadows: the national question in Belarusan politics 1985–95. *BRADFORD D 1997.*

2365. LESHCHENKO, N. The national foundations of postcommunist transitions [with special reference to Belarus]. *LONDON (LSE) D 2006.*

Bosnia-Herzegovina

2366. SIVELL-MULLER, M. The fall of Kozarac: an ethnographic account of wartime and refugee experiences in Bosnia and Hercegovina, 1992–1994. *OXFORD MP 1994.*

2367. HAMOURTZIADOU, D. National truths: justifications and self-justifications of three nationalisms in Bosnia-Herzegovina. *KEELE D 2000.*

2368. HOVERD, M. J. Humanitarian action in Bosnia; a study of the office of the United Nations High Commissioner for Refugees, 1991–1999. *OXFORD D 2001.*

2369. KELLY, L. C. Programme, policies, people: the interaction between Bosnian refugees and British society. *WARWICK D 2001.*

Bulgaria

2370. ASHLEY, S. Bulgarian nationalism (1830–1876): the ideals and careers of Ivan Bogorov, Georgi Rakovski and Petko Slaveikov. *OXFORD D 1984.*

2371. MAHON, M. The politics of nationalism under communism in Bulgaria: myths, memories and minorities. *LONDON (UCL) D 2001.*

2372. PLOUMIDIS, S. Symbiosis and friction in multiethnic Plovdiv/Philippoupolis: the case of the Greek Orthodox and the Bulgarians (1878–1906). *LONDON (KCL) D 2004.*

2373. **MIHAYLOVA, D.** Bulgarian, Turk, Pomak: discerning nation-state borders and identity frontiers. *OXFORD D 2005.*

2374. **RECHEL, B.** Minority rights in post-communist Bulgaria. *BIRMINGHAM D 2006.*

Caucasus *(see also under individual countries)*

2375. **GAMMER, M.** Shamil and the Muslim resistance to the Russian conquest of the North-Eastern Transcaucasus. *LONDON (LSE) D 1989.*

Central and Eastern Europe *(see also under individual countries)*

2376. **HANSON, J.** Sympathy, antipathy, hostility: British attitudes to non-repatriable Poles and Ukrainians after the Second World War and to the Hungarian refugees of 1956. *SHEFFIELD D 1996.*

2377. **ROE, P. R.** The inter-societal security dilemma: ethnic violence in Krajina and Transylvania. *WALES (ABERYSTWYTH) D 1998.*

2378. **HARRIS, E.** The role of nationalism in the democratisation process: Slovakia and Slovenia 1989–1998. *LEEDS D 2000.*

2379. **NG, A.** Nationalism and political liberty: Josef Redlich, Lewis Namier and the nationality conflict in Central and Eastern Europe. *OXFORD D 2001.*

2380. **KENGERLINSKY, M.** Eastward enlargment of the EU and restrictive immigration and asylum policies in the EU. *QUEENS BELFAST D 2006.*

Central Asia *(see also under individual countries)*

2381. **MEGORAN, N. W.** Borders of eternal friendship? The politics and pain of nationalism and identity along the Uzbekistan-Kyrgyzstan Ferghana Valley boundary, 1999–2000. *CAMBRIDGE D 2003.*

Croatia

2382. **CARTER, S. R.** The geo-politics of diaspora: Croatian community and identity in the United States. *BRISTOL D 2001.*

2383. **OH, S. E.** The Croatian Democratic Union and Croatian nationalism. *LONDON (KCL) D 2002.*

2384. **WHITE, A. -F.** Endgame in Croatia: the dilemma of UNHCR's exit strategy in the Balkans. *OXFORD MP 2003.*

Czech Republic *(see also Czechsolovakia)*

2385. **SKILLING, H. G.** The German-Czech national conflict in Bohemia, 1879–1893. *LONDON (SSEES) D 1940.*

2386. **BRADLEY, J.** An analysis of Czech nationalism, 1880–1914, with special reference to T. G. Masaryk. *CAMBRIDGE ML 1960.*

Czechoslovakia

2387. **CHINYAEVA, E.** The Russian emigration into Czechoslovakia in the interwar period. OXFORD D 1994.

Estonia

2388. **RAUSING, S. M.** Reforming habitus: identity and the restoration of Swedishness on a former collective farm in North West Estonia. LONDON (UCL) D 1997.

2389. **SMITH, D. J.** Legal continuity and post-Soviet reality. Ethnic relations in Estonia 1991–95. BRADFORD D 1997.

2390. **JURADO, E.** Complying with 'European' standards of minority protection: Estonia's relations with the European Union, OSCE and Council of Europe. OXFORD D 2002.

2391. **ZDANOWSKI, M. J.** Estonia's Russian-speaking population, 1987–2005: origins, identity transformation and the European Union. LEEDS D 2006.

Georgia

2392. **PARSONS, J. W. R.** The emergence and development of the national question in Georgia, 1801–1921. GLASGOW D 1987.

2393. **SABANADZE, N.** Globalisation and nationalism: the cases of Georgia and the Basque Country. OXFORD D 2005.

2394. **SIDERI, E.** The Greeks of the former Soviet republic of Georgia: memories and practices of diaspora. LONDON (SOAS) D 2006.

Greece

2395. **KERAMIDA, F.** Relocating: bureaucratic and migrant practices concerning the resettlement of Pontian Greeks from the former Soviet Union in Northern Greece. SUSSEX D 2001.

2396. **KONIDARIS, G.** Immigration in post-communist Europe: Greece and Albanian migratory movement. SHEFFIELD D 2002.

2397. **HATZIPROKOPIOU, P. A.** Globalisation, migration and socio-economic change in contemporary Greece: processes of social incorporation of Albanian and Bulgarian immigrants in Thessaloniki. SUSSEX D 2005.

Hungary

2398. **KURAT, Y. T.** The European powers and the question of the Hungarian refugees of 1849. LONDON (SSEES) D 1958.

2399. **COMPTON, P. A.** Some geographical aspects of the internal migration of population in Hungary since 1957. LONDON (EXTERNAL) D 1970.

2400. **ASZALÓS, Z.** Anti-asylum policies of Hungary. OPEN MP 2000.

2401. **O'REILLY, W.** To the East or to the West? Agents and the recruitment of migrants for British North America and Habsburg Hungary, 1717–1770. OXFORD D 2001.

2402. FÜZESI, J. Explaining irredentism: the case of Hungary and its transborder minorities in Romania and Slovakia [NCR]. *LONDON (LSE) D 2006.*

Jews

2403. LEW, M. S. The works of Rabbi Moses Isserls as a source of the history of the Jews in Poland in the sixteenth century. *LONDON (JEWS' COLLEGE) D 1941.*

2404. FRANKEL, J. Socialism and Jewish nationalism in Russia, 1892–1907. *CAMBRIDGE D 1962.*

2405. RIFF, M. A. The assimilation of the Jews of Bohemia and the rise of political anti-semitism, 1848–1918. *LONDON (SSEES) D 1974.*

2406. MARSDEN, N. C[haim] Aronson: the autobiography of a Russian Jew under the Tsars, 1825–1888 [translated and edited]. *OXFORD D 1977.*

2407. MARSDEN, R. M. Hungarian Jews and the Liberal party system, 1867–1914. *OXFORD D 1977.*

2408. GARAI, G. The policy towards the Jews, Zionism and Israel of the Hungarian Communist Party, 1945–1953. *LONDON (LSE) D 1979.*

2409. HEWKO, J. The Ukrainian-Jewish political relationship during the period of the Central Rada, March 1917 to January 1918. *OXFORD ML 1981.*

2410. BARTOSZEWSKI, W. T. Ethnocentrism: beliefs and stereotypes: a study of Polish-Jewish relations in the early twentieth century. *CAMBRIDGE D 1984.*

2411. KADISH, S. Bolsheviks and British Jews: the Anglo-Jewish community, Britain and the Russian Revolution. *OXFORD D 1986.*

2412. SALITAN, L. An analysis of Soviet Jewish emigration in the 1970s. *OXFORD D 1986.*

2413. SCHNEIDER, J. S. The Jewish problem in Romania prior to the First World War. *SOUTHAMPTON D 1986.*

2414. GASSENSCHMIDT, C. Jewish liberal politics in Tsarist Russia, 1900–1914: the modernization of Russian Jewry. *OXFORD D 1993.*

2415. JONES, C. A. Soviet Jewish aliyah 1989 to 1992: impact and implications for Israel and the Middle East. *WALES (ABERYSTWYTH) D 1994.*

2416. MIAN, N. L. Alexander III: a pogrom-maker? Culpability and capability in Russian society, 1881–1894. *LIVERPOOL D 1995.*

2417. SIEVERT BLOM, P. Martin Buber and the spiritual revolution of the Prague Bar Kochba: nationalist rhetoric and the politics of beauty. *OXFORD D 1996.*

2418. MICHLIC, J. B. Ethnic nationalism and the myth of the threatening other: the case of Poland and perceptions of its Jewish minority from the late nineteenth century to the modern period. *LONDON (UCL) D 2000.*

2419. PRIEST, A. The Haskalah: a cultural response to anti-Semitism in Eastern Europe 1840–1920. *KINGSTON D 2000.*

2420. GOLBERT, R. L. Constructing self: Ukrainian Jewish youth in the making. *OXFORD D 2001.*

2421. SHTERNSHIS, A. Soviet and kosher: Soviet Jewish cultural identity in the Soviet Union, 1917–41. *OXFORD D 2001.*

2422. **CHARLES, L.** Polish-Jewish relations during the Second Polish Republic, 1918–1939 [NCR]. *STIRLING MP 2003.*
2423. **McPHARLIN, M. C.** Hungarian Jewry: three aspects. *GLASGOW ML 2003.*
2424. **OCHMAN, E.** Remembering the Polish-Jewish past a decade after the collapse of communism. *SALFORD D 2003.*
2425. **COHEN, R. L.** Resilience and achievement: the case of Jewish Lithuanian child Holocaust survivors. *ANGLIA RUSKIN D 2005.*
2426. **WEBER, P.** Regime changes, public memory and the pursuit of justice: the case of German-speaking Jews in Bukovina, 1920–1960. *SUSSEX D 2006.*

Kazakhstan

2427. **LONG, S. K.** Ethnic boundaries and communities in transition: the Cossack revival in Kazakhstan. *LEEDS D 2002.*
2428. **JARVIS, C.** Competing ethno-historic claims to North Kazakhstan: the potential for future conflict. *LONDON (UCL) MP 2006.*
2429. **SHIN, J. F. -M.** Being a 'Soviet Korean' in Alma-Ata, Kazakhstan. *LONDON (LSE) D 2006.*

Kosovo

2430. **AMORE, K.** Refugees and return: a comparative study of Kosovar Albanians in Italy and the UK. *WARWICK D 2005.*

Latvia

2431. **AASLAND, A.** Russians in Latvia: ethnic identity and ethnopolitical change. *GLASGOW D 1994.*

Lithuania

2432. **POPOVSKI, V.** National minorities and citizenship rights: a case study of Lithuania from 1988 to 1993. *CAMBRIDGE D 1999.*
2433. **LENN, M.** Nationalism, democratization and inter-ethnic relations in the new Lithuanian state, 1988–1992. *LONDON (UCL) D 2000.*
2434. **ERIKSONAS, L.** National heroes and national identities: a comparative framework for smaller nations [with special reference to Scotland, Norway and Lithuania]. *ABERDEEN D 2002.*

Poland

2435. **WISELEY, W. C.** The German settlement of the 'incorporated territories' of the Wartheland and Danzig–West Prussia, 1939–45. *LONDON (SSEES) D 1955.*
2436. **SWORD, K. R.** Ethnic identity and association among Polish émigrés in a British town. *SUSSEX D 1983.*
2437. **ZEBROWSKA, A.** Integration or assimilation: a study of second-generation Poles in England. *SURREY D 1986.*

2438. **TAYLOR, W. M.** Aspects of cultural nationalism in the Congress Kingdom of Poland in the 1840s. *OXFORD ML 1987.*

2439. **KERNBERG, T.** The Polish community in Scotland. *GLASGOW D 1990.*

2440. **OSTROWSKI, M.** To return to Poland or not to return: the dilemma facing the Polish armed forces at the end of the Second World War. *LONDON (SSEES) D 1996.*

2441. **RAITZ VON FRENTZ, C.** The minority protection system of the League of Nations in relation to the German minority in Poland, 1920–1934. *OXFORD D 1998.*

2442. **RABAGLIATI, A.** Participation of the national minorities within the Polish political system 1989–99. *EXETER D 2000.*

2443. **FLEMING, M.** National minorities in post-communist Poland: constructing identity. *OXFORD D 2001.*

2444. **WINSLOW, M.** War, resettlement, rooting and ageing: an oral history study of Polish émigrés in Britain. *SHEFFIELD D 2001.*

2445. **GÓRNY, A.** The role of social, economic and political networks in settlement migration to Poland: the case of Ukrainian immigrants. *LONDON (UCL) D 2002.*

2446. **BURRELL, K.** Moving lives: everyday experiences of nation and migration within the Polish, Greek-Cypriot and Italian population of Leicester since 1945. *LEICESTER D 2003.*

2447. **CAMPBELL, L. McL.** The Polish community in Scotland after 1945: assimilation [NCR]. *STIRLING MP 2004.*

2448. **CURRIE, S. J.** Free movement and European Union enlargement: a socio-legal analysis of the citizenship status and experiences of Polish migrant workers in the UK. *LIVERPOOL D 2006.*

Roma

2449. **GUY, W.** The attempt of socialist Czechoslovakia to assimilate its gypsy population. *BRISTOL D 1977.*

2450. **STEWART, M. S.** Brothers in song: the persistence of (Vlach) gypsy identity and community in socialist Hungary. *LONDON (LSE) D 1988.*

2451. **KERTÉSZ-WILKINSON, I. M.** Diversity in unity. A study of individual creativity through the performance of songs among the Vlach Gypsies of south-eastern Hungary. *LONDON (GOLDSMITHS) D 1994.*

2452. **KOVATS, M.** The development of Roma politics in Hungary, 1989–95. *PORTSMOUTH D 1998.*

2453. **BANCROFT, A.** Dimensions of European modernity and social exclusion: Roma, Gypsies and Travellers in the Czech Republic and Britain. *WALES (CARDIFF) D 1999.*

2454. **PINNOCK, K.** 'Social exclusion' and resistance: a study of Gypsies and the non-governmental sector in Bulgaria 1989–1997. *WOLVERHAMPTON D 1999.*

2455. **CARR, H.** The re-construction and re-negotiation of Roma identity in the Republic of Hungary. *OXFORD MP 2000.*

2456. **CARR, H.** The reconstruction of Roma identity. *OXFORD D 2003.*

2457. **SOBOTKA, E.** Mobilising international norms: issue-actors, Roma and the state [with special reference to East-Central Europe]. *LANCASTER D 2003.*

2458. DEANS, F. M. M.   Culture, community and enterprise in a Hungarian Romany settlement. *LONDON (UCL) D 2004.*

Romania

2459. EYAL, J.   International protection of ethnic minorities: the case of Romania between the wars. *OXFORD D 1987.*

2460. GRÚBER, K.   From the beginning of reason until the end of history: the politics of postmodernism and ethnonationalist renaissances of pre-post-modern natures [with special reference to Transylvanian Hungarian nationalism]. *SUSSEX D 1999.*

2461. DOW, F.   Representations of Hungarian minority identity in Romania from the Treaty of Trianon to the fall of Ceauşescu. *LONDON (UCL) D 2004.*

2462. TILEAGA, C.   A discursive analysis of prejudice and moral exclusion: Romanian talk of nationhood, difference and 'others'. *LOUGHBOROUGH D 2004.*

2463. CINPOES, R. P.   Continuity and discontinuity in nationalist discourse: the Greater Romania Party in post-1989 Romania. *KINGSTON D 2006.*

2464. ZDRENGHEA, M. V.   Homeland, nation and literature: the idea of Romania in the works of Panait Istrati, Constantin Noica and Emile Cioran. *EXETER D 2006.*

Russia (see also USSR)

2465. BARTLETT, R. P.   Foreign settlement in Russia, 1762–1804: aspects of government policy and its implementation. *OXFORD D 1971.*

2466. KONDRASHOV, S.   Nationalism and the drive of sovereignty in Tatarstan 1988–1992: origins and development. *MANCHESTER D 1996.*

2467. INGRAM, A. R.   'A nation split into fragments': Russian nationalism and the Congress of Russian Communities. *CAMBRIDGE D 1998.*

2468. VALIULLIN, S. M.   Will the Russian Federation disintegrate? Politics of nationalism and separatism in Bashkortostan and Tatarstan. *OXFORD MP 1998.*

2469. FRYER, P. J. W.   Elites, language and education in the Komi ethnic revival. *CAMBRIDGE D 1999.*

2470. DROUGHT, B. L.   Resettlement in the Russian Federation: a case study of refugees and forced migrants from Tadzhikistan. *WALES (SWANSEA) D 2000.*

2471. GERMAN, T. C.   The Russian Federation in transition and the causes of the Chechen War (1994–1996). *ABERDEEN D 2000.*

2472. LANKINA, T.   Local self-government and ethnic mobilisation in the Russian Federation, 1990–1999. *OXFORD D 2000.*

2473. NOBL-ØVERLAND, I.   Politics and culture among the Russian Sami; leadership, representation and legitimacy. *CAMBRIDGE D 2000.*

2474. FLYNN, M.   Global frameworks, local realities: migrant resettlement in the Russian Federation. *BIRMINGHAM D 2001.*

2475. KOTIN, I. Y.   Ethnic groups in the post-Soviet city: a case study of the Azeri community in St Petersburg [NCR]. *OXFORD D 2001.*

2476. KHRYCHIKOV, S. V. Managing ethnic differences in the post-Soviet states: political accommodation of the Russophone minorities in Estonia and Ukraine. *LANCASTER D 2002*.

2477. KOPNINA, H. 'Invisible communities': Russian migration in the nineteen nineties in London and Amsterdam. *CAMBRIDGE D 2002*.

2478. TANRISEVER, O. F. The politics of Tatar nationalism and Russian federalism: 1992–1999. *LONDON (UCL) D 2002*.

2479. TOMLINSON, K. G. Coping as kin: responses to suffering amongst displaced Meskhetian Turks in post-Soviet Krasnodar, Russian Federation. *LONDON (UCL) D 2002*.

2480. VEINGUER, A. A. Representing identities in Tatarstan: a cartography of post-Soviet discourses, schooling and everyday life. *WALES (BANGOR) D 2002*.

2481. KARIMOVA, Z. Z. Literary and historical construction of Bashkir national identity. *MANCHESTER D 2004*.

2482. CASHABACK, D. P. Accommodating multinationalism in Russia and Canada: a comparative study of federal design and language policy in Tatarstan and Quebec. *LONDON (LSE) D 2005*.

2483. POPOV, A. Transnational locals: the cultural production of identity among Greeks in the Southern Russian Federation. *BIRMINGHAM D 2005*.

Serbia

2484. MACNAB, N. A. Turning points in relation to the Serb national question, 1980–1986. *KEELE MP 2003*.

2485. PETSINIS, V. The Serbs and Vojvodina: ethnic identity in a multiethnic region. *BIRMINGHAM D 2005*.

Slovakia (see also Czechoslovakia)

2486. HILDE, P. S. Slovak nationalism and the break-up of Czechoslovakia. *OXFORD MP 1997*.

2487. LILOVICS, M. The development of ethnic identity in children and adolescents: the Hungarian linguistic minority in Slovakia. *OXFORD D 2002*.

2488. HILDE, P. S. Nationalism in post-communist Slovakia and the Slovak nationalist diaspora (1989–1992). *OXFORD D 2003*.

South Eastern Europe (see also under individual countries)

2489. MACDONALD, D. B. Balkan Holocausts? Comparing genocide myths and historical revisionism in Serbian and Croatian nationalist writings, 1986–1999. *LONDON (LSE) D 2001*.

Ukraine

2490. MYKULA, W. Nationality policy and nationalism in Soviet Ukraine, 1920–1929. *OXFORD BL 1960*.

2491. BOJCUN, J. M.   Ukrainian nationalism and Soviet power in the Second World War. GLASGOW ML 1977.

2492. FEDOROWYCZ, I. O.   The policies of the Great Powers and the problem of Ukrainian national self-determination in East Galicia, 1918–1923. OXFORD MP 1981.

2493. KRAWCHENKO, B. A.   Social mobilisation and national consciousness in 20th century Ukraine. OXFORD D 1982.

2494. STEWART, A.   Nationalism in Ukraine. OXFORD MP 1992.

2495. WILSON, A. L.   Modern Ukrainian nationalism: nationalist political parties in Ukraine 1988–1992. LONDON (LSE) D 1994.

2496. DYCZOK, M.   Ukrainian refugees and displaced people at the end of World War II. OXFORD D 1995.

2497. SHIELDS, S. M.   A historical study of ethnicity in Ukraine. QUEENS BELFAST MP 1995.

2498. SLYSZ, G. M.   Soviet nationality policy and the politics of self-determination: intra and extra regime nationalism in Ukraine, 1963–1991. KENT D 1996.

2499. JACKSON, L. J.   The construction of national identity in Ukraine: a regional perspective. BIRMINGHAM D 1998.

2500. HORBOKON, V.   A conflict of values and political identity of the Ukrainian diasporic community in Great Britain. WALES (CARDIFF) D 2000.

USSR (see also Russia)

2501. MAHER, J. E.   Nationality and society: a study of trends in national stratification among the union republics of the USSR. ESSEX D 1980.

2502. SMITH, J. R. C.   The Bolsheviks and the national question, 1917–23. LONDON (SSEES) D 1996.

2503. KLEINKNECHT-STRÄHLE, U.   Three phases of post-World War II Russian German migration from the former Soviet Union to Germany. OXFORD D 1998.

2504. SPENCE, T. M.   The development of Russian nationalism under Gorbachev (1985–91). LONDON (SSEES) D 1998.

2505. BRENNAN, C.   The Buriats and the Far Eastern Republic: an aspect of revolutionary Russia 1920–22. ABERDEEN D 1999.

2506. MULTANEN, E. H.   British policy towards Russian refugees in the aftermath of the Russian Revolution. LONDON (UCL) D 2000.

Uzbekistan

2507. WEBB, A. J. K.   Will Uzbekistan become a focus for regional nationalism? SUSSEX MP 1991.

2508. PARK, J. -W.   The national identity of a diaspora: comparative study of the Korean identity in China, Japan and Uzbekistan. LONDON (LSE) D 2005.

Yugoslavia (see also under former republics)

2509. THORBURN, J.   Refugee protection in Europe: lessons of the Yugoslav crisis. KENT D 1996.

2510. O'SHEA, S. J.   Cyber-peace constituencies: challenging ethno-nationalist groups mobilised for war [in former Yugoslavia]. *BRADFORD MP 1997.*

2511. JOHNSON, T.   Nihilistic uncertainty: Freud, Kristeva, Keynes and the rise of ethno-nationalism in Yugoslavia 1980–1990. *LONDON (LSE) D 2000.*

2512. GALLIVAN, R. D.   Were 'ancient ethnic hatreds' a factor in the Yugoslav War of 1991–1995? Can the ideas of 'ancient ethnic hatreds' be traced in British policy? *STIRLING ML 2004.*

2513. EVANS, J. R.   The creation of Yugoslavia: British attitudes to questions of South Slav nationality, 1900–1921. *OXFORD D 2005.*

2514. CASPERSEN, N. F.   Intra-ethnic competition and inter-ethnic conflict: Serb elites in Croatia and Bosnia, 1990–1995. *LONDON (LSE) D 2006.*

23. MUSIC

General and Comparative

2515. MALLOCH, S. N.   Timbre and technology: an analytical partnership. The development of an analytical technique and its application to music by Lutosławski and Ligeti. *EDINBURGH D 1995.*

Albanian

2516. KOÇO, E.   The Albanian urban lyric song in the 1930s. *LEEDS D 1998.*

2517. PRITCHARD, E. M.   Lyrics and the construction of Albanian identity in post-war Kosovar songs. *LONDON (UCL) MP 2004.*

Armenian

2518. NERCESSIAN, A. H.   Marxism-Leninism, national identity and the perception of Armenian music. *CAMBRIDGE D 2003.*

Byzantine

2519. STEFANOVIĆ, D.   The *Stichera* for January: transcription and commentary. *OXFORD BL 1960.*

2520. STEFANOVIĆ, D. I.   The tradition of the *Sticheraria* manuscripts. *OXFORD D 1967.*

Croatian

2521. HUDOVSKY, Z. V.   Eastern and Western elements in medieval music of (northern) Croatia. *OXFORD BL 1968.*

Czech

2522. GROSS, E.   The string quartets of František Xaver Dušek: a critical edition. *ABERDEEN ML 1970.*

2523. **WINGFIELD, P.**   Source problems in Janáček's music: their significance and interpretation. *CAMBRIDGE D 1988.*

2524. **SMACZNY, J.**   A study of the first six operas of Antonín Dvořák: the foundations of an operatic style. *OXFORD D 1990.*

2525. **CARROLL, M.**   J. L. Dussek and his role in the development of the piano repertory. *OPEN MP 2002.*

2526. **RAWSON, R. G.**   From Olomouc to London: the early music of Gottfried Finger (c.1655–1730). *LONDON (R HOLLOWAY) D 2002.*

2527. **RIDDING, J.**   Cultural considerations of 'rubato' in Czech piano performance, with specific reference to Chopin's works. *KINGSTON D 2002.*

2528. **STAPLETON, K.**   Czech music culture in Prague 1858–1865: a catalogue of Prague concert life [...]. *BIRMINGHAM D 2002.*

Hungarian

2529. **GOODALL, C. J.**   Percussive effects in the music of Bartók. *WALES (BANGOR) D 1973.*

2530. **WILSON, A. G.**   Form and harmony in the orchestral works and string quartets of Bartók. *CAMBRIDGE ML 1975.*

2531. **EMMERSON, S. B.**   Two early orchestral works of Béla Bartók: a study of programmatic form and orchestral technique. *OXFORD MP 1983.*

2532. **MERRICK, P. W.**   The religious music of Franz Liszt. *SHEFFIELD D 1985.*

2533. **McLAY, M. P.**   The music of György Kurtág, 1959–1980. *LIVERPOOL D 1986.*

2534. **DAWSON, J. P.**   The programmatic principle in the symphonic poems of Franz Liszt. *LEEDS MP 1987.*

2535. **GILLIES, M. G. W.**   Notation and tonal structure in Bartók's later works. *LONDON (EXTERNAL) D 1987.*

2536. **EMMERSON, S. B.**   Programmatic and symbolic references in some early works of Bartók. *OXFORD D 1989.*

2537. **HAMILTON, K. L.**   The opera fantasias and transcriptions of Franz Liszt: a critical study. *OXFORD D 1989.*

2538. **BAYLEY, A.**   Bartók performance studies: aspects of articulative notation in the context of changing traditions of composition and performance in the twentieth century. *READING D 1996.*

2539. **BECKLES WILLSON, R.**   György Kurtág's *The Sayings of Péter Bornemisza*, Op.7: song in a cycle in 1960s Hungary. *LONDON (KCL) D 1999.*

2540. **YAMAMOTO, R.**   György Kurtág's *Játékok*: an analytical study of his musical language. *ROEHAMPTON D 2004.*

2541. **DULLEA, R.**   Nation, race and religion in Franz Liszt's *Des bohémiens et de leur musique en Hongrie*. *NUI (CORK) D 2005.*

2542. **KORY, A.**   Béla Bartók and ethnomusicology. *LONDON (KCL) MP 2005.*

2543. **PARSONS, J. L.**   Stylistic change in violin performance 1900–1960, with special reference to recordings of the Hungarian Violin School. *CARDIFF D 2005.*

Jewish

2544. GILBERT, S. Music in the Nazi ghettos and camps (1939–1945) [with special reference to Warsaw, Vilna, Sachsenhausen and Auschwitz]. OXFORD D 2002.

2545. SCHMIDT, E. From the ghetto to the conservatoire: the professionalisation of Jewish cantors in the Austro-Hungarian Empire (1826–1918). OXFORD D 2003.

Polish

2546. WIGHTMAN, A. R. The music of Karol Szymanowski. YORK D 1972.

2547. HUNT, R. E. Moniuszko's musical treatment of texts by Mickiewicz. LONDON (SSEES) D 1980.

2548. BROUGH, D. Polish seventeenth-century church music with reference to the influence of historical, political and social conditions. OXFORD D 1981.

2549. DOGGETT, J. C. The development of certain processes in Witold Lutosławski's compositions after 1960, with particular reference to the post-1978 works. CNAA (KINGSTON POLY) MP 1986.

2550. CZEPIEL, T. M. M. Music at the Royal Court and Chapel in Poland during the second half of the sixteenth century. OXFORD D 1991.

2551. DOWNES, S. C. Szymanowski as post-Wagnerian: the Love Songs of Hafiz, Op. 24. LONDON (GOLDSMITHS) D 1992.

2552. RUDNICK, P. P. A study of the music of Witold Lutosławski. WALES (BANGOR) MP 1992.

2553. ĆWIŻEWICZ, K. Musical rites of entertainment among Górale of the Polish Tatra Mountains. LONDON (GOLDSMITHS) D 2001.

2554. REYLAND, N. 'Akcja' and narrativity in the music of Witold Lutosławski. CARDIFF D 2005.

Roma

2555. THEODOSIOU, A. Authentic performances and ambiguous identities: gypsy musicians on the Greek-Albanian border. MANCHESTER D 2003.

Romanian

2556. NIXON, P. J. Transylvanian nexus: human interdependencies and music-making in the Gurghiu valley. QUEENS BELFAST D 1993.

Russian

2557. SEAMAN, G. R. The influence of folk-song on Russian opera up to and including the time of Glinka. OXFORD D 1961.

2558. GARDEN, E. J. C. Mily Alekseyevich Balakirev: a critical study of his life and music. EDINBURGH DM 1969.

2559. McALLISTER, M. N. The operas of Sergei Prokofiev. CAMBRIDGE D 1970.

2560. O'RIORDAN, C. L. Aspects of the inter-relationship between Russian folk and composed music. CAMBRIDGE D 1971.

2561. **BLACKWOOD, B. W.** The music of the Ballets Russes, 1909–1919. *CAMBRIDGE D 1972.*

2562. **HENDERSON, L.** The evolution of Prokofiev's style and treatment of structure in his instrumental music, with special reference to the piano and violin concertos. *SOUTHAMPTON MP 1976.*

2563. **NORRIS, J. P.** A survey of Russian piano music from its origins to the year 1917. *LANCASTER ML 1979.*

2564. **GRIFFITHS, S. A. K.** A critical study of the music of Rimsky-Korsakov up to 1890. *SHEFFIELD D 1982.*

2565. **TAYLOR, R. D.** Rhythmic and metrical structure in the music of Stravinsky. *OXFORD D 1982.*

2566. **POPLE, A. J. L.** Skryabin and Stravinsky 1908–1914: studies in analytical method. *OXFORD D 1984.*

2567. **CAMPBELL, S.** V. F. Odoyevsky and the formation of Russian musical taste in the nineteenth century. *GLASGOW D 1985.*

2568. **ZAJĄCZKOWSKI, H.** Tchaikovsky's musical style. *SHEFFIELD D 1985.*

2569. **ROBERTS, P. D.** Aspects of modernism in Russian piano music 1910–1929. *CNAA (KINGSTON POLY) D 1988.*

2570. **McCARTHY, A. J.** A consideration of three Russian piano concertos, with reference to the lives and careers of their composers [Rachmaninov, Prokofiev]. *ABERDEEN MM 1989.*

2571. **NORRIS, J. P.** The development of the Russian piano concerto in the nineteenth century. *SHEFFIELD D 1989.*

2572. **BARTLETT, R. A.** Wagner and Russia: the influence of the music and ideas of Richard Wagner on the artistic and cultural life of Russia and the Soviet Union, 1841–1941. *OXFORD D 1990.*

2573. **CHEONG, W. -L.** The late Scriabin: pitch organisation and form in the works of 1910–14. *CAMBRIDGE D 1991.*

2574. **TUCKER, S.** Stravinsky and his sketches: the composing of *Agon* and other serial works of the 1950s. *OXFORD D 1992.*

2575. **WHELAN, L. P.** Shostakovich's Second, Third and Fourth Symphonies. *SHEFFIELD MP 1992.*

2576. **RITCHIE, C. C.** The Russian Court Chapel Choir: 1796–1917. *GLASGOW D 1994.*

2577. **POWLES, J.** Continuity and discontinuity in the music of Stravinsky: analysis, theory and meta-theory. *OXFORD D 1995.*

2578. **YANDELL, N. J.** Keyboard music in Russia during the late eighteenth and early nineteenth centuries. *OXFORD D 1995.*

2579. **STYRKAS, T.** The twentieth-century Russian *romans*. *OXFORD ML 1998.*

2580. **KISZKO, M. E.** The origins and place of the balalaika in Russian culture, its migration to the USA, and the dissemination of balalaika orchestras in America [...]. *BRISTOL D 1999.*

2581. **POWELL, J. A.** After Scriabin: six composers and the development of Russian music. *CAMBRIDGE D 1999.*

2582. **Davies, B. J.** Debussy and Stravinsky: friendship and interaction, 1910–1918. *CAMBRIDGE D 2000.*

2583. **Muir, S. P. K.** The operas of N. A. Rimsky-Korsakov from 1897 to 1904. *BIRMINGHAM D 2000.*

2584. **Austen, P. T.** Chasing the Fox: on the trail of Stravinsky's neglected masterpiece. *MANCHESTER MP 2001.*

2585. **Caulfield, F. G.** Template morphology and serial invariants: compositional procedures in Stravinsky's late sketch collections, 1958–66. *TC DUBLIN D 2001.*

2586. **Askew, C. M.** Sources of inspiration in the music of Sofia Gubaidulina: compositional aesthetics and procedures. *HUDDERSFIELD D 2002.*

2587. **Smith, S. E.** Analysing and performing texture in Scriabin's piano music. *LONDON (R HOLLOWAY) D 2004.*

2588. **Reeve, B.** Nikolai Rimsky-Korsakov's use of the *byliny* (Russian oral epic narratives) in his opera *Sadko*. *NOTTINGHAM D 2005.*

2589. **Thomas, G. J.** The impact of Russian music in England, 1893–1929. *BIRMINGHAM D 2005.*

2590. **Lucas, D. J.** Neo-classicism: historical and modern perspectives. A comparative study of two piano concertos of 1924 by Igor Stravinsky and Paul Hindemith. Commentaries on the folio of compositions. *READING D 2006.*

2591. **Lupishko, M.** The 'Rejoicing Discovery' revisited: re-accentuation in Stravinsky's settings of Russian folk-verse. *CARDIFF D 2006.*

Serbia

2592. **Todorović, M.** The underground music scene in Belgrade, Serbia: a multidisciplinary study. *BRUNEL D 2003.*

Slovene

2593. **O'Loughlin, N.** Slovenian composition since the First World War. *LEICESTER D 1978.*

Tajikistan

2594. **Spinetti, F.** Music, politics and identity in post-Soviet Tajikistan. *LONDON (SOAS) D 2006.*

USSR (see also Russia)

2595. **Edmunds, N. E.** Music to the masses: the Soviet proletarian music movement 1917–1932. *SUSSEX D 1994.*

2596. **Brooke, C. M.** The development of Soviet music policy, 1932–41. *CAMBRIDGE D 1999.*

2597. **Fairclough, P.** Shostakovich's Fourth Symphony: context and analysis. *MANCHESTER D 2002.*

2598. FRANCESCHETTI, A. L.   Soviet musicals of the 1930s: an historical interpretation. LEEDS D 2002.

24. PHILOSOPHY

Hungary

2599. HALL, T. W.   The philosophy of praxis: a re-evaluation of Georg Lukács' *History and Class Consciousness*. ESSEX D 2002.

2600. BLACK, T.   The ideology of modernism [with special reference to György Lukács]. SUSSEX D 2006.

Poland

2601. MCNERNEY, J.   Footbridge towards the other: with special reference to the paradigm of the neighbour: a philosophical investigation into the notion of the human person in the writings of Karol Wojtyła. NUI (DUBLIN) ML 2001.

Russia (see also USSR)

2602. KELLY, A. M.   Attitudes to the individual in Russian thought and literature, with special reference to the *Vekhi* controversy. OXFORD D 1970.

2603. PHILLIPS, K. H.   The influence of German romanticism on Russian linguistic philosophy, with particular reference to the period 1844–1891. KEELE D 1976.

2604. CHANT, C.   Russian materialism: an investigation of the pre-Revolutionary materialist tradition. KEELE D 1977.

2605. CHAMBERLAIN, L. V.   The contribution of German aesthetic theory to Russian thought, 1820–1848. OXFORD ML 1981.

2606. SUTTON, J. F.   Vladimir Solovyov: his restatements of a traditional cosmology. DURHAM D 1983.

2607. GARDINER, M. E.   The dialogics of critique: M. M. Bakhtin and the theory of ideology. YORK D 1991.

2608. BOOBBYER, P. C.   A Russian philosopher: the life and work of Semen Liudvigovich Frank, 1877–1950. LONDON (LSE) D 1992.

2609. HILL, C.   F. M. Dostoevsky and V. S. Solovyov: a study in philosophical and ideological contrast. OXFORD ML 1992.

2610. TATE, A.   'All in language': Bakhtin, addressivity and the poetics of objectivity. STRATHCLYDE D 1992.

2611. TAYLOR, B.   Bakhtin, carnival and comic theory. NOTTINGHAM D 1995.

2612. DIMBLEBY, L. L.   Rozanov and the Word [i.e. V. V. Rozanov]. LONDON (SSEES) D 1997.

2613. FREDE, V. S.   P. L. Lavrov's thought as humanist thought. LONDON (SSEES) MP 1997.

2614. **BIDDLE, P. M.** Time and the polyphony of music: an investigation of the works of Freud, Klein and Winnicott using the cultural and aesthetic theories of Mikhail Bakhtin. SHEFFIELD D 1998.

2615. **NIKIFOROV, V.** The individual in Husserl, Rickert and Bakhtin: an investigation into phenomenology and moral philosophy for a world in ruins. LONDON (HEYTHROP) D 1999.

2616. **QUINSEY, J.** Lévinas and Bakhtin: alterity, textuality, ethics. SHEFFIELD MP 2000.

2617. **DOP, E.** Bakhtin and the Hegelian tradition. SHEFFIELD D 2003.

2618. **AL-ALI, M. R.** Mikhail Bakhtin, Jacques Derrida and the dialogics of answerability. ESSEX D 2005.

2619. **HERRICK, T.** From Kant to phenomenology: the philosophical affiliations of M. M. Bakhtin and Jacques Derrida. SHEFFIELD D 2005.

2620. **VAUGHAN-WILLIAMS, R. R.** The Bakhtin Circle and beyond: ideas and institutions of the Russian intelligentsia and Soviet scholarship in the 1920s. SHEFFIELD D 2005.

USSR *(see also Russia)*

2621. **BAKHURST, D.** E. V. Ilyenkov and contemporary Soviet philosophy. OXFORD D 1988.

Yugoslavia *(see also under former republics)*

2622. **HARRISON, J.** Marx, Yugoslavia and the limits of revolutionary philosophy: roots of the unperfect society. SOUTHAMPTON D 1993.

2623. **SHIGENO, R.** From the dialectics of the universal to the politics of exclusion: the philosophy, politics and nationalism of the *Praxis* group from the 1950s to the 1990s. ESSEX D 2004.

25. POLITICS, GOVERNMENT

General and Comparative

2624. **KOWALSKI, R. I.** The development of 'Left Communism' until 1921: Soviet Russia, Poland, Latvia and Lithuania. GLASGOW D 1978.

2625. **WHITE, A.** Cultural enlightenment in the USSR, Hungary and Poland, 1953–1987: ideology and leisure policy. LONDON (LSE) D 1989.

2626. **DRIVER, I. D.** A history of the Fourth International 1923–53. CNAA (THAMES POLY) MP 1990.

2627. **KONJHODŽIĆ, I.** The process of political development of small European nations at the point of their historical conjunction: the Finnish and the Slovene experiences in the comparative perspective. SUSSEX D 1999.

2628. **BOBROVA, M.** State participation in non-governmental organisations' activity in emerging democracies: the case of Armenia and Poland. LEEDS D 2002.

2629. **FREIZER, S.** What civil society after civil war? A study of civil society organisations' effect on peace consolidation in Bosnia-Hercegovina and Tajikistan. *LONDON (LSE) D 2004.*

Armenia

2630. **NAHAPETYAN, A.** Legal, political and social environments of the non-governmental sector of Armenia. *OPEN MP 2000.*

2631. **AGHUMIAN, A. A.** The role of elites in political and economic transition: a case study of post-Soviet Armenia. *LONDON (LSE) D 2005.*

2632. **BABAJANIAN, B. V.** Promoting community participation and capacity building in post Soviet transition: the Armenia Social Investment Fund. *LONDON (LSE) D 2006.*

Belarus

2633. **KOROSTELEVA-POLGLASE, E. A.** Explaining party system development in post-communist Belarus. *BATH D 2001.*

Bosnia-Herzegovina

2634. **ROSENBLUM, K. R.** The communal system in Yugoslavia; participation, coordination and development: the experience of Mostar commune, 1965–1969. *LONDON (LSE) D 1974.*

2635. **ANDJELIĆ, N.** Bosnia-Herzegovina: politics and society at the end of Yugoslavia. *SUSSEX D 2000.*

2636. **KEANE, R.** Creating space in which to live. Deconstructing binary opposition: the case of Bosnia and Herzegovina. *LIMERICK D 2000.*

2637. **HUSANOVIĆ, J.** Recasting political community and emancipatory politics: reflections on Bosnia. *WALES (ABERYSTWYTH) D 2003.*

2638. **MITCHELL, I. R.** Democracy in Bosnia and Herzegovina: by protectorate or popular will. *WALES (ABERYSTWYTH) D 2005.*

2639. **SIRCAR, I.** Transnational consociation in Northern Ireland and in Bosnia-Herzegovina: the role of reference states in post-settlement power-sharing. *LONDON (LSE) D 2006.*

Bulgaria

2640. **ROTHSCHILD, J. A.** A history of the Communist Party of Bulgaria to 1935. *OXFORD D 1954.*

2641. **MILLER, M. L.** Bulgaria during the Second World War: a political and diplomatic study. *OXFORD BL 1972.*

2642. **GIATZIDIS, A.** Civil society in post-communist Bulgaria. *SHEFFIELD D 2000.*

Caucasus *(see also under individual countries)*

2643. POTIER, T. The constitutional development of three post-Soviet Transcaucasian autonomies [Nagorno-Karabakh, Abkhazia, South Ossetia]: a comparative analysis. *KEELE D 2000.*

2644. EDWARDS, C. Small state strategies in the South Caucasus, 1994–2001: the impact of identity. *OXFORD MP 2003.*

Central and Eastern Europe *(see also under individual countries)*

2645. SCHLESINGER, R. A. J. Federalism in Central and Eastern Europe. *LONDON (UCL) D 1945.*

2646. WEITZ, R. The rise of communist power in Central Europe: Poland, Czechoslovakia and East Germany. *OXFORD MP 1986.*

2647. ARIKAN, E. B. The extreme right-wing parties in Eastern and Western Europe: a comparison of the common ideological agenda. *EXETER D 1995.*

2648. SACKER, R. A. The French Communist Party and Eastern Europe (1944–1956). *SOUTHAMPTON D 1995.*

2649. BUTCHER, B. J. Germany and its Eastern neighbours: a comparative perspective on perceptions of civil society. *BIRMINGHAM MP 1997.*

2650. KEMP, W. A. Nationalism and communism in Eastern Europe and the Soviet Union: a basic contradiction? *LONDON (LSE) D 1997.*

2651. JUDSON, T. Civil society, second society and the breakdown of communist regimes in Central and Eastern Europe: Poland, Czechoslovakia and Romania. *LOUGHBOROUGH D 1999.*

2652. SITTER, N. The East Central European party systems: the development of competitive politics in a comparative politics perspective. *LONDON (LSE) D 1999.*

2653. RODDA, R. The 1989 revolutions in East-Central Europe: a comparative analysis [of Poland, Hungary, Bulgaria and Romania]. *PLYMOUTH D 2000.*

2654. VOGT, H. The utopia of post-communism: the Czech Republic, Eastern Germany and Estonia after 1989. *OXFORD D 2000.*

2655. RODITI, O. Assessment of civil society's role in promoting democracy and preventing nationalism: a comparative study of NGOs in the Czech Republic, Slovakia, Hungary and Romania. *SUSSEX D 2001.*

2656. McGINTY, S. P. Democratic consolidation in Central and Eastern Europe: civil society in the Czech Republic, Romania and Ukraine. *MANCHESTER D 2002.*

2657. RENWICK, A. Complex causal modelling: institutional choice in Hungary, Czechoslovakia and Poland, 1989–1990. *OXFORD D 2003.*

2658. MYKHNENKO, V. The political economy of post-communism: a comparison of Upper Silesia (Poland) and the Donbas (Ukraine). *CAMBRIDGE D 2005.*

Central Asia *(see also under individual countries)*

2659. KIRMSE, S. B. Islamic radicalism in Central Asia: the implications of different institutional settings in Uzbekistan and Kyrgyzstan. *OXFORD MP 2003.*

Czech Republic *(see also Czechoslovakia)*

2660. **PRAVDA, A.** The Czech reform movement (January to 21 August 1968), with special reference to the role of the workers. OXFORD D 1972.

2661. **HARTMANN, E.** Thomas G. Masaryk's realism: the development of a Czech political concept, 1882–1914. LONDON (LSE) D 1981.

2662. **MEADE, C. W.** How did Stalinism come to Prague? Socialist internationalism and the Czech working class, 1848–1929. LONDON (LSE) D 1984.

2663. **FAGIN, A.** The transition to democracy in the Czech Republic: an alternative perspective and assessment. MANCHESTER D 1996.

2664. **REED, Q.** Political corruption, privatisation and control in the Czech Republic: a case study of problems in multiple transition. OXFORD D 1996.

2665. **TOLSTOY, M. M.** The political theology of Václav Havel. CAMBRIDGE D 1997.

2666. **HANLEY, S. L.** Normative concepts of party in post-communist party system formation: the case of the Czech Republic 1989–98. BIRMINGHAM D 1999.

2667. **SCHENDLER, R.** Remembering state socialism in the Czech Republic. ESSEX D 2000.

2668. **HIDALGO-REDONDO, O.** Problems of post-communist transition: a decade of democratic transformation in the Czech Republic. KENT MP 2003.

2669. **LAWSON, G.** Negotiated revolutions: the Czech Republic, South Africa and Chile. LONDON (LSE) D 2003.

2670. **NOVOTNÝ, V.** The creation of regional government in Czechia in the 1990s. STRATHCLYDE D 2003.

Czechoslovakia *(see also Czech Republic and Slovakia)*

2671. **MABEY, M. P.** The origin and development of the Communist Party of Czechoslovakia (until 1938). OXFORD D 1955.

2672. **SZPORLUK, R.** The political ideas of Thomas Masaryk. OXFORD BL 1960.

2673. **PORKET, J. L.** Authority in communist Czechoslovakia prior to 1968. LONDON (LSE) D 1973.

2674. **RYBÁŘ, J.** The influence of Soviet ideology on left-wing Czech intellectuals in the period 1918–1939. LANCASTER ML 1973.

2675. **BLOOMFIELD, J.** The passive revolution: politics and the Czechoslovak labour movement, 1945–1948. CAMBRIDGE D 1975.

2676. **MYANT, M. R.** The Czechoslovak road to socialism: the strategy and role of the Communist Party of Czechoslovakia in the development of a socialist society in the 1945–1948 period [...]. GLASGOW D 1978.

2677. **WHEATON, B.** The origins of the Communist Party of Czechoslovakia [NCR]. SUSSEX D 1984.

2678. **McDERMOTT, K. F.** Debates and schisms in the Czech Social Democratic and Red trade unions and their relations with the Communist Party of Czechoslovakia [1918–1929]. LEEDS D 1985.

2679. **STEPHENS, C. J.** One nation or two: the politics of Slovak autonomy in the Czechoslovak Republic 1918–1939. OXFORD MP 1991.

2680. **DIMOND, M. J.**   Nation or nation-state: the politics of Slovak independence in the Czech and Slovak Federal Republic, 1989–1992. *OXFORD MP 1993.*

2681. **WILLIAMS, K. D.**   The 'normalization' of Czechoslovakia, 1968–1971. *OXFORD D 1993.*

2682. **WILLIAMS, R. C.**   The politics of opposition in a one-party state: the case of Czechoslovakia 1977–1988. *LONDON (LSE) D 1993.*

2683. **MALÝ, R.**   Patterns of party competition in post-communist Czechoslovakia: a road to separation. *OXFORD MP 1995.*

2684. **INNES, A. J.**   The partition of Czechoslovakia. *LONDON (LSE) D 1997.*

2685. **LEASK, M. F.**   Political parties and social cleavages in the former Czechoslovakia and the Czech Republic. *SHEFFIELD MP 2000.*

Estonia

2686. **KASEKAMP, A.**   The politics of popular initiative: the radical right in inter-war Estonia. *LONDON (SSEES) D 1996.*

2687. **RANDMA, T.**   Civil service careers in small and large states: the cases of Estonia and the United Kingdom. *LOUGHBOROUGH D 1999.*

GDR

2688. **DEXTER, H. A.**   A study of Erich Honecker with particular reference to the reformist movement emanating from the Soviet Union. *EXETER MP 1997.*

Georgia

2689. **OGDEN, D. J.**   National communism in Georgia, 1921–1923. *LONDON (SSEES) D 1977.*

2690. **JONES, S. F.**   Georgian social democracy, 1892–1921: in opposition and in power. *LONDON (LSE) D 1984.*

2691. **HAMILTON, K.**   The development of 'civil society' in post-Soviet Georgia. *SUSSEX MP 1999.*

2692. **HAMILTON, K.**   Producing civil society: development intervention and its consequences in post-Soviet Georgia. *SUSSEX D 2004.*

Hungary

2693. **LOMAX, W. A.**   The politics of revolution: opposition and revolution in the Hungarian Uprising of 1956. *SUSSEX D 1974.*

2694. **PARNELL, R. H.**   Ferenc Deák and Hungarian politics 1848–1876. *LONDON (SSEES) MP 1988.*

2695. **FOWLER, B.**   Shaping a post-communist party system: Liberal Party strategies before the 1994 Hungarian parliamentary election. *OXFORD MP 1996.*

2696. **BERÉNYI, Z.**   Constitutional democracy and civil society in post-communist Hungary. *QUEENS BELFAST D 1999.*

2697. **Renwick, A.** Combining rational choice and political culture: the case of institutional choice in Hungary, 1989–1990. OXFORD MP 2000.

2698. **Benedek, M.** The conflict over land ownership in postsocialist Hungary. OXFORD MP 2001.

2699. **Lorman, T.** The domestic politics of the Bethlen government, 1921–1925. LONDON (UCL) D 2001.

2700. **Bátory, Á.** Attitudes to Europe: a comparative politics approach to the issue of European Union membership in Hungarian party politics. CAMBRIDGE D 2002.

2701. **Mevius, M.** Agents of Moscow: the Hungarian Communist Party and the origins of socialist patriotism, 1941–1953. OXFORD D 2002.

2702. **Tóth, A.** The political and economic characteristics of East European transformation: the case of Hungary. DE MONTFORT D 2002.

2703. **Czaga, P.** The development of interest representation in Hungary: a case of uneven Europeanisation. SUSSEX D 2003.

2704. **Jodah, U.** The Hungarian Social Democrats and the British Labour Party, 1944–8. WEST OF ENGLAND D 2003.

2705. **Meyer-Sahling, J. -H.** Governance by discretion: civil service reform in post-communist Hungary. LONDON (LSE) D 2003.

2706. **Karadeli, S. C.** Legitimacy and the post-communist Hungarian political Change. GLASGOW D 2004.

2707. **Palonen, M. E. E.** Reading Budapest: political polarisation in contemporary Hungary. ESSEX D 2006.

Kazakhstan

2708. **Cummings, S. N.** The political elite in Kazakhstan since independence (1991–1998): origins, structure and policies. LONDON (LSE) D 2000.

Kyrgyzstan

2709. **Amos-Wilson, P.** Leadership approaches among appointed public sector leaders of the Kyrgyz Republic: an investigation into the perception by leaders of transformational and transactional leadership. BRADFORD D 2001.

Latvia

2710. **Auers, D.** Potemkin democracy? Political parties and democratic consolidation in Latvia. LONDON (UCL) D 2006.

Lithuania

2711. **Pogorelis, R.** Votes and parties in the mixed electoral system in Lithuania. ESSEX D 2004.

Macedonia

2712. **TERRY, G. M.** The origins and development of the Macedonian revolutionary movement, with particular reference to the Tayna Makedonsko-Odrinska Revolutsionerna Organizatsiya [1893–1903]. *NOTTINGHAM MP 1974.*

2713. **COUTARELLI, M. -L.** Nationalism and democracy: a case study of the former Yugoslav Republic of Macedonia. *OXFORD MP 1999.*

2714. **SAPOUNTZIS, A.** The dilemma of patriotism vs. nationalism: Greek political party members talk about the Macedonian issue. *LANCASTER D 2003.*

Moldova

2715. **KING, C.** The politics of language in Moldova, 1924–1994. *OXFORD D 1995.*

Poland

2716. **SAKWA, G.** The role of parliament in a Communist political system: the Polish Sejm, 1952–1972. *LONDON (EXTERNAL) D 1974.*

2717. **DANZIGER, G. H.** The development of workers' attitudes toward the government in postwar Poland. *OXFORD BP 1978.*

2718. **REYNOLDS, J. C. J.** The Polish Workers' Party and the opposition to Communist power in Poland, 1944–47. *LONDON (LSE) D 1984.*

2719. **MALINOWSKI, T. P.** Liberty, equity, solidarity: egalitarianism and the Polish revolution. *OXFORD MP 1991.*

2720. **CHAN, K. K.-L.** On the road to Solidarity: the Polish intelligentsia and workers 1970–1980. *OXFORD MP 1992.*

2721. **GŁUCHOWSKI, L. W.** The collapse of Stalinist rule in Poland: the Polish United Workers' Party from the XX CPSU Congress to the VIII KC PZPR Plenum, February-October 1956. *CAMBRIDGE D 1992.*

2722. **MASTNAK, L.** The process of engagement in non-violent collective action: case studies from the 1980s [including Wolność i Pokój in Poland]. *BATH D 1995.*

2723. **MIZRAHI, S.** Theory of constitutional change: game theoretical analysis of socio-political processes in Poland, 1976–1981. *LONDON (LSE) D 1995.*

2724. **ROZUMIŁOWICZ, B.** Spatial theories of party competition and the development of the political party system in Poland, 1989–1994. *OXFORD MP 1995.*

2725. **SNYDER, T. D.** Kazimierz Kelles-Krauz (1872–1905): a political and intellectual biography. *OXFORD D 1995.*

2726. **BRZEZINSKI, M. F.** The development of constitutionalism in Poland. *OXFORD D 1996.*

2727. **WYLIE, G.** Creating alternative visions: the role of national and transnational social movements in the demise of Polish state socialism. *ABERDEEN D 1996.*

2728. **CIERLIK, B.** A comparative analysis of some aspects of political life in Ireland and Poland 1918–1939. *NUI (CORK) D 1997.*

2729. **KEARNS, I. P.** Political risk analysis: a conceptual re-evaluation [with a case study of Poland]. *STAFFORDSHIRE D 1997.*

2730. **BELL, J.** The effects of economic transition on voting patterns in Poland: 1990–1995. *LONDON (SSEES) D 1998*.

2731. **CHAN, K. K.-L.** Explaining political parties and party system formation in post-communist Poland. *OXFORD D 1998*.

2732. **DAY, S. R.** The process of social-democratization: from Leninist to social-democratic parties in Central and Eastern Europe. A comparative based approach focusing specifically upon the Social Democracy of the Republic of Poland (SdRP). *WARWICK D 1998*.

2733. **FERRY, M. H.** The 'intelligentsia in power' and the development of civil society: Mazowiecki's Poland. *GLASGOW D 1998*.

2734. **HARPER, J. B.** Continuity within chaos: the role of political discourse in the rebuilding of Communist Party legitimation in Poland, 1988–90. *LONDON (LSE) D 1999*.

2735. **ROZUMIŁOWICZ, B.** Organizational structures and programmatic stances: the development of the political party system in Poland, 1989–1997. *OXFORD D 1999*.

2736. **SZCZERBIAK, A. A.** The emergence and development of political parties in post-communist Poland. *LONDON (SSEES) D 1999*.

2737. **MAJCHERKIEWICZ, T.** An elite in transition: an analysis of the higher administration of the region of Upper Silesia, Poland, 1990–1997. *LONDON (LSE) D 2001*.

2738. **BARDELL, G.** The role of pre-1945 national and Catholic myths in transforming an illiberal Polish political culture of opposition under communism. *BRUNEL D 2002*.

2739. **HAYDEN, J. P.** Exploring the collapse of communism in Poland: how the strategic misperception of Round Table negotiators produced an unanticipated outcome. *TC DUBLIN D 2002*.

2740. **SAMUELS, R. I.** Evaluating the support for democracy in post-communist Europe: the case of Poland. *SOUTHAMPTON D 2002*.

2741. **STABROWSKI, F.** The dilemma of the non-communist left in post-communist Poland [NCR]. *OXFORD MP 2002*.

2742. **RAE, G. J.** Social democracy in a transition state: a Polish third way? *SOUTH BANK D 2003*.

2743. **TERRANOVA, F.** Regional structures in Poland: reshaping governance in a global and European context. *EXETER D 2003*.

2744. **TRHULJ, A.** The non-consolidation of the Polish political right, 1989–2001. *OXFORD MP 2003*.

2745. **WALECKI, M. P.** Money and politics in Poland: a new democracy in comparative perspective. *OXFORD D 2003*.

2746. **RUNDELL, B.** Republican political theory in the eighteenth-century University of Kraków. *OXFORD MP 2004*.

2747. **McMENAMIN, K. I.** The 'soft state': business-government relations in post-communist Poland. *LONDON (LSE) D 2005*.

2748. **PONTES MEYER RESENDE, M.** A party family theory of party positions on European integration: a Polish case study. *LONDON (LSE) D 2005*.

2749. **DAVIS, M.** Freedom in the English-language writings of Zygmunt Bauman. *LEEDS D 2006*.

Romania

2750. **CAVALCANTI, M. DE B. DE A. U.**   Urban reconstruction and autocratic regimes: a case study of Bucharest. *OXFORD BROOKES D 1994.*

2751. **SIANI-DAVIES, P. J.**   The Romanian revolution of December 1989: myth and reality — myth or reality? *LONDON (SSEES) D 1995.*

2752. **HASEGANU, C.**   Transition to democracy in Romania: political developments, 1990–1997. *LONDON (SSEES) MP 1999.*

2753. **POP, L.**   The political economy of transformation in Romania, 1989–2001. *WARWICK D 2001.*

2754. **TANASOIU, I. -C.**   Intellectuals and politics. From communism to post-communism: the case of Romanian intellectuals. *WEST OF ENGLAND D 2003.*

2755. **ADAMSON, K. D.**   Socialism, revolution and transition: the ideological construction of the Romanian post-communist order. *ESSEX D 2004.*

2756. **PARAU, C. E.**   The interplay between domestic politics and Europe: how Romanian civil society and government contested Europe before EU accession. *LONDON (LSE) D 2006.*

Russia *(see also USSR)*

2757. **BRANFOOT, A. I. S.**   A critical survey of the Narodnik movement, 1861–1881. *LONDON (SSEES) D 1926.*

2758. **FADNER, F. L.**   Development of Panslavist thought in Russia from Karamzin to Danilevski, 1800–1870. *LONDON (SSEES) D 1949.*

2759. **RIASANOVSKY, N. V.**   Russia and the West in the teaching of the Slavophiles: a study of Romantic ideology. *OXFORD D 1949.*

2760. **TREADGOLD, D. W.**   The growth and interrelations of political groups and parties in Russia, 1898–1906. *OXFORD D 1949.*

2761. **GROSSHANS, H. P.**   The European revolutionaries in London, 1848–70   [NCR]. *OXFORD BL 1951.*

2762. **BILLINGTON, J. H.**   N. K. Mikhailovsky and Russian radical thought in the final third of the nineteenth century. *OXFORD D 1953.*

2763. **KEEP, J. L. H.**   The development of Social-Democracy in Russia, 1898–1907. *LONDON (SSEES) D 1954.*

2764. **TIDMARSH, K. R.**   A study of the Russian reactionary writers in the second half of the nineteenth century. *OXFORD D 1956.*

2765. **KINDERSLEY, R. K.**   'Legal Marxism' in Russia. *CAMBRIDGE D 1957.*

2766. **SQUIRE, P. S.**   The Third Department: an examination of the establishment and practices of the political police in the Russia of Nicholas I. *CAMBRIDGE D 1958.*

2767. **SHUKMAN, H.**   The relations between the Jewish Bund and the RSDRP, 1897–1903. *OXFORD D 1961.*

2768. **PIOTROW, F. J.**   Paul Milyukov and the Constitutional-Democratic Party. *OXFORD D 1962.*

2769. **GETZLER, I.**   Julius Martov: his role and place in Russian Social Democracy. *LONDON (LSE) D 1965.*

2770. **PAPMEHL, K. A.** Freedom of expression in Russia, 1750–1800: the history of the idea and its practical expression. *LONDON (SSEES) D 1965.*

2771. **HOLLINGSWORTH, B.** Nicholas Turgenev: his life and works. *CAMBRIDGE D 1966.*

2772. **HUTCHINSON, J. F.** The Octobrists in Russian politics, 1905–17. *LONDON (SSEES) D 1966.*

2773. **LANE, D. S.** The social composition, structure, and activity of Russian Social-Democratic groups, 1898–1907. *OXFORD D 1966.*

2774. **GALAI, S.** The Liberation Movement and its role in the first Russian Revolution. *LONDON (LSE) D 1967.*

2775. **ENTICOTT, P. W.** The rise of the Constitutional-Democratic Party in Russia, 1904–06. *LONDON (SSEES) MP 1968.*

2776. **ZIMMERMANN, E. R.** The Right Radical movement in Russia, 1905–1917. *LONDON (SSEES) D 1968.*

2777. **LENTIN, A.** M. M. Shcherbatov, with special reference to his memoir *On the Corruption of Morals in Russia. CAMBRIDGE D 1969.*

2778. **HOSKING, G. A.** Government and Duma in Russia (1907–1914). *CAMBRIDGE D 1970.*

2779. **CHAPMAN, M. C.** Ivan V. Kireyevsky (1806–56): life and thought. *LIVERPOOL D 1971.*

2780. **JONES, M. I.** A critical assessment of the non-fictional work of Konstantin N. Leont'ev. *LEEDS MP 1971.*

2781. **PEARSON, R.** The Russian moderate parties in the Fourth State Duma, 1912–February 1917. *DURHAM D 1972.*

2782. **DOWLER, E. W.** The native soil (*pochvennichestvo*) movement in Russian social and political thought, 1850–1870. *LONDON (LSE) D 1973.*

2783. **CHRISTIAN, D.** The reform of the Russian Senate, 1801–1803. *OXFORD D 1974.*

2784. **OFFORD, D. C.** Revolutionary populist groups in Russia in the 1880s. *LONDON (BIRKBECK) D 1974.*

2785. **OWEN, R. C.** The revolutionary career of M.A. Natanson, 1868–1906. *LONDON (LSE) D 1975.*

2786. **ACTON, E. D. J. L. -D.** Alexander Herzen and the role of the intellectual revolutionary, 1847–1863. *CAMBRIDGE D 1976.*

2787. **LONGLEY, D. A.** Factional strife and policy making in the Bolshevik Party, 1912–April 1917, with special reference to the Baltic Fleet organisations, 1903–17. *BIRMINGHAM D 1978.*

2788. **O'MEARA, P. J.** K. F. Ryleev (1795–1826): a political biography, with special reference to his political and cultural activities in the Decembrists' Northern Society. *OXFORD D 1978.*

2789. **RAVINDRANATHAN, T. R.** Bakunin and the Italians. *OXFORD D 1978.*

2790. **VASUDEVAN, H. S.** Russian provincial politics: central government and the Tver' provincial zemstvo, 1897–1900. *CAMBRIDGE D 1978.*

2791. **SWAIN, G. R.** Political developments within the organised working class: St Petersburg, 1906–14. *LONDON (LSE) D 1980.*

2792. CALDER, L. D. The political thought of Yu. F. Samarin, 1840–1864. *LONDON (SSEES) MP 1981.*

2793. GOODERHAM, P. The anarchist movement in Russia, 1905–1917. *BRISTOL D 1981.*

2794. NAJENSON, J. L. Borochovism: an early Marxist theory of the national question. *CAMBRIDGE D 1981.*

2795. SEDDON, J. H. The Petrashevtsy and the influence of French socialism in Russia. *OXFORD D 1981.*

2796. TEMPEST, R. Pyotr Chaadaev: his impact on Russian society and thought between 1812 and 1856. *OXFORD D 1981.*

2797. ATKIN, M. G. The social thought of Vissarion Belinskii (1840–1848) [NCR]. *OXFORD ML 1982.*

2798. LOIZOU, M. The development of the agrarian programme of the Russian Social-Democratic Labour Party, 1900–1907. *BIRMINGHAM MP 1982.*

2799. HAY, D. W. The development of the revolutionary movement in the south of the Russian Empire, 1873–1883. *GLASGOW D 1983.*

2800. CAHM, J. C. Peter Kropotkin and revolutionary action: a study of the development of his approach in the context of the development of the anarchist movement in Western Europe, 1873–1886. *LONDON (UCL) D 1984.*

2801. RICE, C. The Socialist-Revolutionary Party and the urban working class in Russia, 1902–1914. *BIRMINGHAM D 1984.*

2802. DONALD, M. Karl Kautsky and Russian Social Democracy, 1900–1914. *LEEDS D 1986.*

2803. GEORGE, M. The All-Russian Zemstvo Union and the All-Russian Union of Towns, 1914–1917: a political study. *LONDON (SSEES) D 1986.*

2804. SUTTON, K. A. Class and revolution in Russia: the Soviet movement of 1905. *BIRMINGHAM D 1987.*

2805. KINNA, R. Anarchist organization: Kropotkin's scientific theory. *OXFORD D 1991.*

2806. THATCHER, I. D. Leon Trotsky and World War One: August 1914–March 1917. *GLASGOW D 1993.*

2807. BRANDIST, C. S. Dialectics and dialogue: the politics of ideological struggle in the works of the Bakhtin school. *SUSSEX D 1994.*

2808. SCHLEITER, P. The peculiarities of the Soviet / Russian transition: political agency and constraint. *OXFORD MP 1994.*

2809. UMLAND, A. Vladimir Zhirinovskii in Russian politics: emergence and rise of the Liberal-Democratic Party of Russia. *OXFORD MP 1994.*

2810. BROWN, R. The development of political parties in three Russian oblasts 1988 to October 1993. *LONDON (SSEES) D 1995.*

2811. CHAISTY, P. E. The organisation and powers of the Russian Supreme Soviet 1990–1993. *LEEDS D 1995.*

2812. CHRYSSIS, A. A. Intellectuals, political power and emancipation from Marx to the October Revolution. *LEICESTER D 1995.*

2813. CRAIG, M. G. The regular state: post-revolutionary state development in Nicaragua, Iran and Russia. *KEELE D 1995.*

2814. **Ferretti, P.** Vasilii Fedorovich Malinovskii (1765–1814): a study of his life and thought. CAMBRIDGE D 1995.

2815. **Kirkow, P.** Russia's provinces: transformation versus autonomy? BIRMINGHAM D 1995.

2816. **Morgan-Jones, E.** The failure of Russian constitutionalism: 1991–93. OXFORD MP 1995.

2817. **Morland, D.** Human nature and politics in nineteenth-century social anarchism: an examination of the writings of Proudhon, Bakunin and Kropotkin. YORK D 1995.

2818. **Lentini, P.** Electoral reform in the former USSR and Russian Federation 1989–1993: continuity, contradiction and departure. GLASGOW D 1996.

2819. **Stenning, A. C.** The changing politics of local economic development in the Russian Federation. BIRMINGHAM D 1997.

2820. **Gray, E. F.** Signposts to the past: re-inventing political symbols, Moscow 1985 to 1996. CAMBRIDGE D 1998.

2821. **Michalis, C.** Regional responses to federal decision making in the Russian Federation: assymetry and elite power. OXFORD MP 1998.

2822. **Slater, W. N.** Imagining Russia: the ideology of Russia's patriotic opposition, 1985–1995. CAMBRIDGE D 1998.

2823. **Gallo, C.** Russian Duma elections in the territorial districts: explaining patterns of proliferation of independent candidates, 1993–1999. LONDON (LSE) D 1999.

2824. **Hackett, A. N.** Russian revolutionaries in America 1915–1919. SUSSEX D 1999.

2825. **Kahn, J.** A federal façade: problems in the development of Russian federalism. OXFORD D 1999.

2826. **March, L. G. F.** Communism in transition? The Communist Party of the Russian Federation in the post-Soviet era. BIRMINGHAM D 1999.

2827. **Moran, D.** Russia's emerging margins: the 'transition' in the north of Perm´ Oblast. OXFORD D 1999.

2828. **Schleiter, P.** Legislative politics, institutional choice and democratic stability: the dynamics of executive control in Russia, 1991–1993. OXFORD D 1999.

2829. **Skach, C.** Semi-presidentialism and democracy: Weimar Germany, the French Fifth Republic and postcommunist Russia in comparative perspective. OXFORD D 1999.

2830. **Troxel, T. A.** Parliamentary power and the policy process in Russia, 1994 to 1998. OXFORD D 1999.

2831. **Badcock, S.** Support for the Socialist Revolutionary Party during 1917, with a case study of events in Nizhegorodskaia guberniia. DURHAM D 2000.

2832. **Gamblin, G. J.** Russian populism and its relations with anarchism 1870–1881. BIRMINGHAM D 2000.

2833. **Kim, S.** Regionalism in the Congresses of People's Deputies of the USSR and Russia: a case study of Siberia and the Far East. GLASGOW D 2000.

2834. **Nelson, T. D.** The August 1998 crisis: politics of economic developments in Russia. OXFORD MP 2000.

2835. **Argounova, T.** Scapegoats of *natsionalizm*: ethnic tensions in Sakha (Yakutia), northeastern Russia. CAMBRIDGE D 2001.

2836. HUTCHESON, D. S. The development of party activism in Russia: a local perspective. GLASGOW D 2001.

2837. STROHBACH, A. B. The trophy art problem in Russian political decision making and the evolution of a national consensus on the controversial 'Federal Law of cultural values removed to the USSR as a result of World War II [...]' [NCR]. OXFORD MP 2001.

2838. YUN, Y. Setting the political agenda in the Russian Far East in the post-Soviet era. GLASGOW D 2001.

2839. BEDIRHANOĞLU, P. Predicaments of transnationalised passive revolutions: transformation of the Russian Nomenklatura in the neoliberal era. SUSSEX D 2002.

2840. KAEHNE, A. Russian political liberalism and Western political theory. WALES (SWANSEA) D 2002.

2841. YORKE, A. Business and politics in Russia's regions: the case of Krasnoyarsk kray [NCR]. OXFORD MP 2002.

2842. HORE, E. Centre-periphery relations in Russia: the case of Siberia. ESSEX D 2003.

2843. MUNRO, N. Contrasting legacies: determinants of support for incomplete democracies in the Republic of Korea and the Russian Federation. STRATHCLYDE D 2003.

2844. MORGAN-JONES, E. Insitutions and uncertainty: constitutional bargaining in Russia, 1990–1993. OXFORD D 2004.

2845. GOLOLOBOV, I. V. Regional ideologies in contemporary Russia: in search of a post-Soviet identity. ESSEX D 2005.

2846. PODPLATNIK, T. Big business and the state in Putin's Russia, 2000–2004: towards a new state corporatism. OXFORD D 2005.

2847. WHITE, D. J. The Yabloko party in Russia, 1993–2003. BIRMINGHAM D 2005.

2848. WHITE, E. The Russian Socialist Revolutionary Party in emigration, 1921–1939. BIRMINGHAM D 2005.

2849. WITZENRATH, C. Institutional culture and the Government of Siberia. LONDON (KCL) D 2005.

2850. PLEKHANOV, A. Essays on the political economics of fiscal federalism in Russia. CAMBRIDGE D 2006.

Serbia

2851. KILIBARDA, D. Serbia between the past and the future [democracy, constitutionalism, civil society]. OXFORD D 1998.

2852. VLADISAVLJEVIĆ, N. Serbia in turmoil: the collapse of communism, mobilization and nationalism. LONDON (LSE) D 2004.

2853. HARTWELL, M. B. Perceptions of justice, identity and political processes of forgivenes and revenge in early post-conflict transitions. Case studies: Northern Ireland, Serbia, South Africa. OXFORD D 2005.

Slovakia *(see also Czechoslovakia)*

2854. SKOLKAY, A. Political communication in transition: a study of Slovakia 1989–1996. LIVERPOOL MP 1997.

2855. SOLK, H. J. Slovakia: politics and economy 1993–1995. LEEDS MP 1998.

2856. HAUGHTON, T. J. Explaining the Slovak 'Sonderweg': Slovakia's path of political transformation during her first five years of independence (1993–8). LONDON (UCL) D 2002.

2857. MENZIES, C. Mečiarism and the HZDS (Movement for a Democratic Slovakia), 1992–1998: the ideology of a post-communist political party. LONDON (UCL) D 2004.

South Eastern Europe *(see also under individual countries)*

2858. ENGSTRÖM, J. M. Democratisation and the prevention of violent conflict in South Eastern Europe: the cases of Bulgaria and Republic of Macedonia. LONDON (LSE) D 2004.

2859. HATZOPOULOS, P. Non-nationalist ideologies in the Balkans: the interwar years. LONDON (LSE) D 2006.

Turkmenistan

2860. DENISON, M. J. Why do sultanistic regimes arise and persist? A study of government in the Republic of Turkmenistan, 1992–2006. LEEDS D 2006.

Ukraine

2861. BOSHYK, G. Y. The rise of Ukrainian political parties in Russia, 1900–1907, with special reference to social democracy. OXFORD D 1981.

2862. DIUK, N. M. M. P. Drahomanov and the evolution of Ukrainian cultural and political theory. OXFORD D 1986.

2863. GRODELAND, A. B. The 'Greening' of Ukraine: an assessment of the political significance of the Ukrainian Green Movement. GLASGOW D 1996.

2864. SIMON, R. E. Workers, state and democracy in Russia and Ukraine. BIRMINGHAM D 1997.

2865. BIRCH, S. The social determinants of electoral behaviour in Ukraine, 1989–1994. ESSEX D 1998.

2866. SASSE, G. Bringing the regions back in: the Crimean issue in post-Soviet Ukraine. LONDON (LSE) D 1999.

2867. WOLCZUK, K. Politics of state-building: the constitutional process in Ukraine, 1990–1996. BIRMINGHAM D 2000.

2868. WHITMORE, S. V. Building institutions in Ukraine: the case of Parliament 1990–2000. BIRMINGHAM D 2002.

United Kingdom

2869. BOLTE, C. G. The Soviet question in British politics [NCR]. OXFORD BL 1949.

2870. HUDSON, K. J. The double blow: 1956 and the Communist Party of Great Britain. LONDON (SSEES) D 1992.

2871. REID, A. The death of revolutionary socialism? The reception of the systemic collapse of East European and Soviet communism by the Marxist left in Britain. BRISTOL MP 1993.

2872. LILLEKER, D. G. Against the Cold War: the nature and traditions of pro-Soviet sentiment in the British Labour Party, 1945–89. SHEFFIELD D 2002.

USA

2873. BUBIS, M. D. The Soviet Union and Stalinism in the ideological debates of American Trotskyism 1937–51. LONDON (LSE) D 1986.

2874. ZUMOFF, J. The Communist Party of the United States and the Communist International, 1919–1929. LONDON (UCL) D 2003.

USSR (see also Russia)

2875. RIGBY, T. H. The selection of leading personnel in the Soviet state and Communist Party. LONDON (LSE) D 1954.

2876. UTECHIN, S. V. The origin of the ruling class in Soviet society. OXFORD BL 1954.

2877. ACHMINOW, H. The Party apparatus of the CPSU and its relationship to the various groups of the Soviet population in the transition stage from Socialism to Communism. OXFORD BL 1958.

2878. BERSON, A. C. Changes in structure and personnel in the Soviet state and Communist Party from 1953 to 1959: a study of party-state relations. LONDON (LSE) D 1963.

2879. BIGGART, J. The career of B. M. V'yunov: a case-study in the sovietization of Lithuania and in Soviet agricultural administration, 1945–1960. GLASGOW BL 1969.

2880. CARVER, T. F. Revolutionary goals, soviets and counter-revolution: Russia and Germany, 1917–1919. OXFORD BP 1970.

2881. ALI, J. D. The development, structure and functions of the Russian Communist Party's central apparatus, October 1917 to May 1924. LEEDS D 1972.

2882. HILL, R. J. Tiraspol: a study of a Soviet town's political elite. ESSEX D 1973.

2883. KNAPHEIS, B. The social and political thought of Leon Trotsky. OXFORD D 1973.

2884. SELCHEN, D. H. Trotsky and the Communist International, 1919–1924: from the formation of the Comintern to the end of the first phase of Bolshevization. OXFORD BP 1973.

2885. CARLSNAES, W. The concept of ideology and political analysis: a critical examination of its usage by Marx, Lenin, and Mannheim. OXFORD D 1976.

2886. SERVICE, R The Bolshevik Party in revolution, 1917–1923: a study of organisational change. ESSEX D 1977.

2887. DONNELLY, J. R. C. Politics and deviance: the social control of dissidents in the Soviet Union, 1965–78. ESSEX D 1980.

2888. PADGETT, S. A study of Marx's method in the work of V. I. Lenin and Rosa Luxemburg. KENT D 1980.

2889. **SMITH, S. A.** The Russian Revolution and the factories of Petrograd, February 1917 to June 1918. *BIRMINGHAM D 1980.*

2890. **SPENCER, S. S.** A political biography of Alexandr Shlyapnikov. *OXFORD ML 1980.*

2891. **POLAN, A. J.** The end of politics: democracy, bureaucracy and utopia in Lenin. *DURHAM MP 1982.*

2892. **REES, E. A.** Rabkrin and the Soviet system of state control, 1920–1930. *BIRMINGHAM D 1982.*

2893. **SHANDRO, A. M.** Orthodox Marxism and the emergence of Lenin's conception of revolutionary hegemony: on the relation of theory and practice. *MANCHESTER D 1982.*

2894. **EVANS, A. T. B.** The Soviet Union, Comintern and the British Labour movement, 1929–35. *BIRMINGHAM MP 1983.*

2895. **HYDE-PRICE, A. G. V.** Lenin, the state and democracy: from parlamentarism to Soviet power. *KENT D 1983.*

2896. **THORNILEY, D.** The impact of collectivization on the Soviet rural Communist Party, 1927–1937. *BIRMINGHAM D 1983.*

2897. **ANDREYEV, C. C. L.** The nature and development of opposition to Stalin as expressed by Soviet citizens in German hands during the Second World War. *CAMBRIDGE D 1984.*

2898. **FERDINAND, C. I. P.** The Bukharin group of political theoreticians: their ideas and their importance in the Soviet Union in the 1920s. *OXFORD D 1984.*

2899. **MARSHALL, W. J.** Ideology and literary expression in the works of Victor Serge. *OXFORD D 1984.*

2900. **POLAN, A. J.** The end of politics: democracy, bureaucracy and utopia after Lenin. *DURHAM D 1984.*

2901. **SAKWA, R.** The Communist Party and War Communism in Moscow, 1918–1921. *BIRMINGHAM D 1984.*

2902. **STOKES, H. R.** The Soviet ministerial system, 1965–1983. *OXFORD MP 1984.*

2903. **FOX, P. L.** Culture, society and the Communist Party, 1917–1928. *OXFORD MP 1985.*

2904. **CHUNG, H.-K.** Interest representation in Soviet policy-making: a case study of a Siberian energy coalition, 1969–1981. *LONDON (LSE) D 1986.*

2905. **GEARING, M. L.** Neo-Slavophilism and Russian nationalism in the Soviet Union since 1960. *OXFORD ML 1986.*

2906. **HAZAREESINGH, S. K.** Relations between the French Communist Party and the Soviet Union under Waldeck Rochet: the limit of evolution. *OXFORD MP 1986.*

2907. **ROSS, C.** City and *oblast'* soviets under Brezhnev: problems of implementation and control. *CAMBRIDGE D 1986.*

2908. **TEAGUE, E.** The impact of the Polish events of 1980 on Soviet internal policies. *BIRMINGHAM D 1986.*

2909. **LAW, D. S.** Trotsky in opposition: 1923–1940. *KEELE D 1987.*

2910. **MAHONEY, S. O.** Political theory in context: the significance of *State and Revolution* in Lenin's political thought and policy. *OXFORD ML 1987.*

2911. MERRIDALE, C. A. The Communist Party in Moscow, 1925–1932. BIRMINGHAM D 1987.

2912. ROSE, M. T. Philips Price and the Russian Revolution. HULL D 1988.

2913. VICARY, S. C. Soviet regional development and the nationalist challenge: the case of Armenia and Kazakhstan. OXFORD MP 1988.

2914. WALKER, R. Soviet Marxism-Leninism and the question of ideology: a critical analysis. ESSEX D 1988.

2915. BERRY, D. G. The response of the French anarchist movement to the Russian revolution (1917–24) and to the Spanish revolution and civil war (1936–39). SUSSEX D 1989.

2916. BIGGART, J. Alexander Bogdanov, Left-Bolshevism and the Proletkult 1904–1932. EAST ANGLIA D 1989.

2917. FOWLER, A. The Soviet conception of the leading role of the Communist Party. SOUTHAMPTON D 1989.

2918. MEEROVICH, A. The problem of civil society in the USSR: sociopolitical change in late totalitarianism. OXFORD MP 1989.

2919. SHARPE, P. J. Bukharin's contribution to Marxist political economy. SHEFFIELD MP 1989.

2920. CURRIE, J. R. Soviet perceptions of social justice in transition: the issue of inequality 1985–89. OXFORD ML 1990.

2921. FARMAN-FARMA, A. A. A comparative study of counter-revolutionary mass movements during the French, Mexican and Russian revolutions with contemporary application. OXFORD D 1990.

2922. FEDARKO, K. From village prose to Pamyat´: a study of Russian nationalist ideas. OXFORD MP 1990.

2923. JANG, C. W. The Kronstadt uprising 1921: the end of the revolutionary political culture. OXFORD MP 1990.

2924. LIPSCHITZ, A. The lessons of cooperatives: prospects for property reform under perestroika. OXFORD MP 1990.

2925. THATCHER, I. D. Leon Trotsky: three aspects. GLASGOW ML 1990.

2926. HOWARD, S. The new thinking and the politics of empowerment [in the Soviet Union 1985–90]. BRADFORD D 1991.

2927. PRIESTLAND, D. R. Ideological conflict within the Bolshevik Party, 1917–1939: the question of 'bureaucracy' and 'democracy'. OXFORD D 1991.

2928. STEIN, H. W. Presidential power in the USSR on paper and in practice. OXFORD MP 1991.

2929. STUART, J. M. The Soviet experiment in English revolutionary thought and politics, 1928–1941. CAMBRIDGE D 1991.

2930. TOMPSON, W. J. Nikita Khrushchev and the territorial apparatus, 1953–1964. OXFORD D 1991.

2931. WHITEFIELD, S. Soviet industrial ministries as political institutions, 1965–90. OXFORD D 1991.

2932. GALEOTTI, M. The impact of the Afghan War on Soviet and Russian politics and society, 1979–1991. LONDON (LSE) D 1992.

2933. **GUEDES DE OLIVEIRA, M. A.**　Stalinism and the Brazilian Communist Party. ESSEX D 1992.

2934. **HARRISON, F. M. E.**　The leadership of N. S. Khrushchev: a reassessment, triumphs and limitations, 1961–2. GLASGOW ML 1992.

2935. **MAJUMDAR, M. A.**　Louis Althusser and Leninism. LONDON (KCL) D 1992.

2936. **MERRITT, M.**　Accountability in Soviet politics. OXFORD D 1992.

2937. **PRAST, J. M.**　A history of the Russian proletarian cultural revolution (Proletkult). OXFORD ML 1992.

2938. **SANDLE, M. A.**　Gorbachev's ideological platform: a case study of ideology in the USSR. BIRMINGHAM D 1992.

2939. **MacINNIS, D. M.**　A matter of doctrine: the decline of Soviet civil-military relations in the Gorbachev era. OXFORD MP 1993.

2940. **SEO, C.**　Reform debate between the High Command and various civilian authorities and its contribution to the collapse of the Soviet Union, 1985–1991. GLASGOW D 1993.

2941. **SIDERIS, E. S.**　A change of paradigm: the last years of Soviet — Greek Communist Party relations (1985–1991). KENT D 1993.

2942. **TOLZ-ZILITINKEVICH, V.**　Russian academicians under Soviet rule. BIRMINGHAM D 1993.

2943. **CUNNINGHAM, E. M.**　The Soviet state administration: rationality and authority. TC DUBLIN ML 1994.

2944. **ROBINSON, N.**　Understanding perestroika: the Party and the Soviet model of politics. ESSEX D 1994.

2945. **LIPSCHITZ, A.**　The politics of property reform in the Soviet Union, 1985–1991: with special reference to the Perm′ region. OXFORD D 1995.

2946. **SRIVASTAVA, V. N.**　The Central Committee of the Communist Party of the Soviet Union during perestroika — 1985–1991. CAMBRIDGE ML 1995.

2947. **HATCH, W.**　The 1987 Law on the State Enterprise (Association): a case study of policy-making in the Soviet Union. OXFORD D 1996.

2948. **PATRIKEEFF, F.**　Continuity and change in Russian politics in Northern Manchuria, 1924–1931. OXFORD D 1996.

2949. **GORDON, C. E.**　The politics of central economic policy-making in the USSR, 1988–1991. OXFORD D 1997.

2950. **LUKIN, A. V.**　'Democratic' groups in Soviet Russia (1985–1991): a study in political culture. OXFORD D 1997.

2951. **CAPPELLI, O.**　Democracy without representation? A study in political rhetoric, institutional design and democratic failure in the USSR. BIRMINGHAM D 1998.

2952. **ZINCONE, C. L.**　First attempts to reform the Soviet system: the Malenkov era (1953–1955). CAMBRIDGE D 1999.

2953. **KANG, Y.**　The Leningrad Party organisation during the first Five Year Plan. GLASGOW D 2000.

2954. **LIU, J.**　The origins of the Chinese Communist Party and the part played by Soviet Russia and the Comintern. YORK D 2000.

2955. **LIN, Y. -F.** The development of civil society in the former Soviet Union and Russia, 1985–1999. *OXFORD D 2001.*

2956. **ARMBRUSTER, L. C.** Explaining 1989? A reconstruction of historical research programmes on Soviet world power status [...] and a comparative appraisal of their explanatory reliability and reach. *LANCASTER D 2002.*

2957. **DAVIS, J. S.** Altered images: the Labour Party and the Soviet Union in the 1930s. *DE MONTFORT D 2002.*

2958. **JONES, P.** Strategies of de-mythologisation in post-Stalinism and post-communism: a comparison of de-Stalinisation and de-Leninisation. *OXFORD D 2002.*

2959. **DOBSON, M. J.** Refashioning the enemy: popular beliefs and the rhetoric of de-Stalinisation, 1953–1964. *LONDON (UCL) D 2003.*

2960. **WARREN, J. C.** Evolution and regression: changing power structures in Soviet and post-Soviet Russia and their relationship with the mass media. *READING D 2004.*

2961. **McGREGOR, A. R.** The shaping of popular consent: a comparative study of the Soviet Union and the United States 1929–1941. *EAST ANGLIA D 2005.*

2962. **OGUSHI, A.** The disintegration of the Communist Party of the Soviet Union. *GLASGOW D 2005.*

2963. **McGRATH, M.** Stalinism and modernity [NCR]. *OXFORD D 2006.*

2964. **PIRANI, S.** The changing political relationship between Moscow workers and the Bolsheviks, 1920–24. *ESSEX D 2006.*

2965. **RITTS, M.** Believing is seeing: Fabianism and Soviet communism. *SUSSEX D 2006.*

Uzbekistan

2966. **KHAN, S.** The development of Muslim reformist (Jadid) political thought in the Emirate of Bukhara (1870–1924), with particular reference to the writings of Ahmad Donish and Abdal Rauf Fitrat. *LONDON (SOAS) D 1998.*

2967. **RASANAYAGAM, M. J.** The moral construction of the state in Uzbekistan: its construction within concepts of community and interaction at the local level. *CAMBRIDGE D 2002.*

2968. **STEVENS, D. J.** Conceptual travels along the Silk Road: on civil society aid in Uzbekistan. *LONDON (SOAS) D 2004.*

2969. **MORRISON, A.** Russian rule in Samarkand, 1868–1910: a comparison with British India. *OXFORD D 2005.*

Yugoslavia (see also under former republics)

2970. **AVAKUMOVIĆ, I.** History of the Communist Party of Yugoslavia: an interim study. *OXFORD D 1957.*

2971. **CARTER, A. F.** Democratic reform in Yugoslavia: the changing role of the Party 1964–1972. *OXFORD D 1982.*

2972. **POTTS, G. A.** The development of the system of representation in Yugoslavia with special reference to the period since 1974. *MANCHESTER D 1992.*

2973. **WAINWRIGHT, E.** Law, politics and security in the post-Cold War world: the conflict in the former Yugoslavia. *OXFORD MP 1996.*

2974. **MALEŠEVIĆ, S.** The form and content of ideology, political legitimacy and the new state: Yugoslavia, Serbia and Croatia. *NUI (CORK) D 1998.*

2975. **JOVIĆ, D.** The breakdown of the elite ideological consensus: the prelude to the disintegration of Yugoslavia (1974–1990). *LONDON (LSE) D 1999.*

2976. **PUPAVAC, V.** From statehood to childhood: a study of self-determination and conflict resolution in Yugoslavia and post-Yugoslav states. *NOTTINGHAM D 2000.*

2977. **MULAJ, K.** The political dynamics of ethnic cleansing in the Balkans with particular reference to the former Yugoslavia in the 1990s. *LONDON (LSE) D 2004.*

2978. **FISHER, O.** The dynamics of violent collapse: centre-periphery elite interaction in Yugoslavia. *STRATHCLYDE D 2006.*

26. PSYCHOLOGY, PSYCHIATRY

General and Comparative

2979. **BARBU, Z.** The psychology of democracy, Nazism and Communism. *GLASGOW D 1954.*

Bosnia-Herzegovina

2980. **SMITH, P. A.** Psychological effects of war on children in Bosnia. *LONDON (KCL) D 1998.*

Croatia

2981. **MITCHELS, B. M.** Trauma, therapy and conflict: posttraumatic stress and the process of peacemaking following the 1991–1995 war in Croatia, explored through the works of Adam Curle. *BRADFORD D 2003.*

Czech Republic

2982. **HOUDKOVÁ, P.** A cross-linguistic and cross-cultural investigation of Irish and Czech children's accounts of socially-constructed emotions. *TC DUBLIN D 2003.*

Russia (see also USSR)

2983. **SIMSOVA, S.** An evaluation of Nicholas Rubakin's concept of bibliopsychology in the light of current psychological research. *LONDON (UCL) MP 1975.*

2984. **WILLIAMS, R. J. C.** The psychological impact of westernization within the context of contemporary global trends [with special reference to Russia]. *BRISTOL D 2000.*

2985. **SIROTKINA, I.** The psychiatrist and the writer: the social and cultural roots of psychiatry and psychotherapy in Russia. *MANCHESTER D 2001.*

2986. SHAITELMAN, K. Mental illness in Russia: a neglected component of the health crisis in the transition period [NCR]. OXFORD MP 2002.

2987. DERRY, J. Vygotsky and his critics: philosophy and rationality. LONDON (INST EDUC) D 2003.

2988. POLLARD, R. Dialogue and desire: a critical evaluation of the use of Mikhail Bakhtin in psychotherapy, with particular reference to cognitive analytic therapy. MANCHESTER D 2006.

USSR (see also Russia)

2989. SPENCER, I. H. An investigation of the relationship of Soviet psychiatry to the state. GLASGOW D 1997.

2990. THOMAS, A. Psychological therapies in the context of the Soviet psychiatric service and in post-Soviet Russia. PORTSMOUTH D 2000.

27. RELIGION

Albania

2991. GIAKOUMIS, K. The monasteries of Jorgucat and Vanishte in Dropull and of Spelaio in Lunxheri as monuments and institutions during the Ottoman period in Albania (16th-19th centuries). BIRMINGHAM D 2002.

Baltic States (see also under individual countries)

2992. SCHMIDT, I. M. F. The popes and the Baltic Crusades 1147–1254. CAMBRIDGE D 2004.

Bosnia-Herzegovina

2993. SORABJI, C. K. Muslim identity and Islamic faith in Sarajevo. CAMBRIDGE D 1989.

2994. AŠČERIĆ, I. Dervishes: the real founders of Ottoman Bosnia. The role of dervishes in the formation of Ottoman Bosnian society in the 15th and 16th centuries. OXFORD MP 2000.

2995. STOYANOV, Y. Apocryphal themes and apocalyptic elements in Bogomil dualist theology and their implications for the study of Catharism. LONDON (WARBURG) D 2000.

2996. AŠČERIĆ, I. Dervishes and Islam in Bosnia: the role of dervish orders in the Islamisation process in Bosnia and the formation of Bosnian Muslim society in the 15th and 16th centuries. OXFORD D 2004.

2997. GOODWIN, S. R. Fractured land, healing nations: a contextual analysis of the role of religious faith sodalities towards peace-building in Bosnia-Herzegovina. EDINBURGH D 2005.

Bulgaria

2998. **OBOLENSKY, D. D.**   A history of Bogomilism in Bulgaria. CAMBRIDGE D 1943.

2999. **PETKOFF, P.**   The legal framework of religion and the state in Bulgaria: church–state relations (1892–2002). LEEDS D 2003.

3000. **HOPKINS, J. L.**   The Bulgarian Orthodox Church: a socio-historical analysis of the evolving relationship between church, nation and state in Bulgaria. EDINBURGH D 2006.

Byzantium

3001. **ALFEYEV, H.**   St Symeon the New Theologian and Orthodox tradition. OXFORD D 1995.

Caucasus (see also under individual countries)

3002. **ZELKINA, A.**   The history of the Naqshbandi Sufi brotherhood in the North Caucasus: its impact on the religious, social and political life of the area in the first half of the nineteenth century. OXFORD D 1996.

3003. **O'FLYNN, T. S. R.**   The Western Christian presence in the Caucasus and Qajar Persia, 1802–70. OXFORD D 2003.

Central and Eastern Europe (see also under individual countries)

3004. **THEMELIS, T. P.**   The relation of the Eastern Church to the Western Churches from the sixteenth to the eighteenth century [NCR]. OXFORD BL 1907.

3005. **BASDEKAS, H.**   The teaching of the Eastern Church with regard to the Holy Eucharist in the sixteenth and seventeenth centuries [NCR]. OXFORD BL 1914.

3006. **YANOSHEVITCH, M.**   The problem of the second marriage of priests in the Orthodox Church of the East [NCR]. OXFORD BL 1921.

3007. **SHAW, P. E. S.**   The early Tractarians and the Eastern Church [NCR]. OXFORD BL 1924.

Czech Republic

3008. **BURLEIGH, J. H. S.**   The teaching of John Hus concerning the Church [NCR]. OXFORD BL 1922.

3009. **SEDLO, J.**   The influence of John Hus on Europe to the time of the Reformation, with special reference to Central and Eastern Europe. EDINBURGH D 1943.

3010. **BROCK, P.**   The political and social doctrines of the Unity of Czech Brethren in the fifteenth century. OXFORD D 1954.

3011. **CREWS, C. D.**   The theology of John Hus, with special reference to his concepts of salvation. MANCHESTER D 1975.

3012. **FUDGE, T. A.**   Myth, heresy and propaganda in the radical Hussite movement, 1409–1437. CAMBRIDGE D 1992.

3013. **ELSE, S. G.**   In the absence of the Supreme Judge: Kundera, ambiguity and the philosophy of religion. BIRMINGHAM D 1999.

3014. O'MAHONY, J. The emergence of civil society in Eastern Europe: church and state in the Czech Republic 1992–1998. *LONDON (LSE) D 2003.*

Czechoslovakia

3015. HAWORTH, J. M. The contextuality of theology: Jan Milič Lochman, theologian between Czechoslovakia and Switzerland. *BIRMINGHAM D 1982.*

3016. KUNG, L. Y. Christian witness in a Communist context: a study of the theological writings of Josef L. Hromádka and Jan M. Lochman from 1948 to 1969 and their relevance to the churches in Hong Kong facing 1997. *ST ANDREWS MP 1991.*

Georgia

3017. GVOSDEV, N. K. The Russian Empire and social groups in Transcaucasia: the case of the Georgian Orthodox Church. *OXFORD MP 1994.*

Hungary

3018. MURDOCK, G. International Calvinism and the Reformed Church of Hungary and Transylvania, 1613–1658. *OXFORD D 1996.*

3019. KOVÁCS, Á. The history of the Free Church of Scotland's mission to the Jews in Budapest, and its impact on the Hungarian Reformed Church: 1841–1914. *EDINBURGH D 2003.*

Jews

3020. MACIEJKO, P. The Frankist movement in Poland, the Czech Lands and Germany (1755–1816). *OXFORD D 2003.*

Lithuania

3021. ROWELL, S. C. The role of Christianity in the last pagan state in Europe: Lithuania, 1315–1342. *CAMBRIDGE D 1991.*

Macedonia

3022. KUSSEFF, M. St Clement of Ochrida. *LONDON (SSEES) D 1954.*

Montenegro

3023. PRVULOVICH, Z. R. The theology of Petar Petrovitch Nyegoš, Prince-Bishop of Montenegro (1813–51). *OXFORD D 1956.*

Poland

3024. ŚWIDERSKA, H. Stanisław Orzechowski (1513–66). *OXFORD D 1960.*

3025. PRONIEWICZ-ZALOMAY, J. The influence of the teaching of Luther and Calvin on the literary works of Mikołaj Rej. *LONDON (SSEES) D 1965.*

3026. HAROŃSKI, B.   Reform in the Polish church in the thirteenth century. OXFORD D 1972.

3027. POMIAN-SRZEDNICKI, M. J. I.   The sociology of religion in Poland: an enquiry into the approach to secularization in a communist state. LONDON (LSE) D 1979.

3028. SZAJKOWSKI, B.   Roman Catholic Church-state relations in Poland 1944–1983. WALES (CARDIFF) D 1987.

3029. SOROKOWSKI, A. D.   The Greek-Catholic parish clergy in Galicia 1900–1939. LONDON (SSEES) D 1991.

3030. GULA, J. Z.   The Roman Catholic Church in the history of the Polish exiled community in Britain (1939–1950). LONDON (SSEES) D 1992.

3031. HOLMGREN, S. C.   The Christian sexual ethics of Paul Ramsey and Karol Wojtyła: a critical study of some theoretical assumptions. OXFORD D 1995.

3032. GREGG, S.   Challenging the modern world: Karol Wojtyła / John Paul II and the development of Catholic social teaching. OXFORD D 1998.

3033. MANIURA, R. J.   Image and pilgrimage: the cult of the Virgin of Częstochowa in the late Middle Ages. LONDON (COURTAULD) D 1998.

3034. NOWAKOWSKA, N.   Papacy and piety in the career of Cardinal Fryderyk Jagiellon, Prince of Poland, 1468–1503. OXFORD D 2003.

3035. KOWALEWSKI, W. K.   A theology of mission for post-communist Poland: towards an integrative approach. CARDIFF D 2004.

3036. SPRINGER, M. S.   Church building and the Forma ac ratio: the influence of John a Lasco's ordinance in sixteenth-century Europe. ST ANDREWS D 2004.

3037. BURNELL, J. L.   Poetry, providence and patriotism: a study in Polish Messianism in dialogue with Dietrich Bonhoeffer. OPEN D 2005.

3038. WILSON, K. A.   The politics of toleration: dissenters in Great Poland (1587–1648). LONDON (UCL) D 2005.

Romania

3039. NEGRUT, P.   The development of the concept of authority within the Romanian Orthodox Church during the twentieth century. BRUNEL D 1994.

3040. VERZEA, G. I.   Personal and corporate salvation in the Eastern Orthodox theology of Dumitru Staniloae. QUEENS BELFAST MP 1996.

3041. STEBBING, M. N. L.   Spiritual eldership in the Romanian Orthodox Church. LEEDS D 2000.

3042. POPESCU, A. D.   The life and work of the Romanian Christian thinker Petre Tutea (1902–1991): an exposition and analysis. OXFORD D 2001.

3043. NADABAN, A.   A historical analysis of the origin and early development of the Greek-Catholic Church in Transylvania (1697–1761). BRUNEL D 2003.

3044. BALAJ, I.   Towards a missionary theology for churches in a post-dictatorial situation: Romanian Baptist Church and Church of Central Africa [...] and democratic consolidation. BIRMINGHAM DTh 2004.

3045. FORBESS, A. I.   Miraculous democracy: political and religious power in a convent and village of South Central Romania. LONDON (LSE) D 2005.

3046. CONSTANTINEANU, C. The social significance of reconciliation in Paul's theology, with particular reference to the Romanian context. LEEDS D 2006.

3047. KOVÁCS, J. The reception in Transylvania of Karl Barth's theology of the Word of God. OPEN D 2006.

Russia (see also USSR)

3048. STOYANOVIĆ, J. Vladimir Solovieff's religious philosophy [NCR]. OXFORD BL 1919.

3049. STOYANOVIĆ, J. The religious philosophy in Russia in the nineteenth century. LONDON (UCL) D 1926.

3050. GORODETZKY, N. The humiliated Christ in modern Russian thought [NCR]. OXFORD BL 1938.

3051. BOLSHAKOFF, S. The doctrine of the unity of the Church, with special reference to the works of Khomyakov and Moehler. OXFORD D 1943.

3052. GORODETZKY, N. St Tikhon of Voronezh. OXFORD D 1944.

3053. GRAVES, C. L. The Patriarch Nikon and the Russian Church. OXFORD BL 1966.

3054. PAIN, J. H. Sobornost: a study in modern Russian Orthodox theology. OXFORD D 1967.

3055. CRACRAFT, J. R. The church reform of Peter the Great, with special reference to the Ecclesiastical Regulation of 1721. OXFORD D 1968.

3056. FORTOUNATTO, M. St Vladimir of Kiev in the Russian medieval tradition. OXFORD BL 1970.

3057. READ, C. J. Religion and revolution in the thought of the Russian intelligentsia from 1900 to 1912: the Vekhi debate and its intellectual background. LONDON (LSE) D 1975.

3058. WILLIAMS, R. D. The theology of Vladimir Nikolaievich Lossky: an exposition and critique. OXFORD D 1975.

3059. GEEKIE, J. H. M. The Church and politics in Russia, 1905–1917: a study of the political behaviour of the Russian Orthodox clergy in the reign of Nicholas II. EAST ANGLIA D 1976.

3060. HOWLETT, J. R. The heresy of the Judaisers and the problem of the Russian Reformation. OXFORD D 1976.

3061. PALAN, J. R. The theory of religious knowledge of Vladimir Soloviev. OXFORD D 1976.

3062. CADDICK, L. R. The reality of spirit: the response to reductivist critiques of theism in the later work of Berdyaev. LONDON (KCL) D 1978.

3063. URRY, J. The closed and the open: social and religious change amongst the Mennonites in Russia (1789–1889). OXFORD D 1978.

3064. WALTERS, P. M. The development of the political and religious philosophy of Sergei Bulgakov, 1895–1922: a struggle for transcendence. LONDON (LSE) D 1978.

3065. McDONALD, A. Conflicting trends in the religious life of Novgorod and Pskov during the fourteenth and fifteenth centuries and the heresy of the Strigol'niki. LEEDS MP 1981.

3066. **OWEN, A. R.** The significance of 'the personal' in the writings of Nicolas Berdyaev, Martin Buber and John MacMurray. BRISTOL ML 1985.

3067. **NICHOLS, A.** The ecclesiology of N. N. Afanasev. Patristic ressourcement and ecumenical prospect in the Russian tradition. EDINBURGH D 1986.

3068. **PERA, P. G.** Theoretical and practical aspects of the debate on marriage among the priestless Old Believers [late 17th to mid-19th centuries]. LONDON (SSEES) D 1986.

3069. **KYRKE-SMITH, C. J.** Aspects of the theological and philosophical background of Sergei Bulgakov's sophiology. OXFORD ML 1987.

3070. **DUNCAN, P. J. S.** Russian messianism: a historical and political analysis. GLASGOW D 1989.

3071. **ROONEY, V.** Shestov's religious existentialism: a critique. OXFORD D 1991.

3072. **MOUSALIMAS, S. A.** The transition from shamanism to Russian Orthodoxy in Alaska. OXFORD D 1992.

3073. **DIXON, S. M.** Church, state and society in late Imperial Russia: the diocese of St Petersburg, 1880–1914. LONDON (SSEES) D 1993.

3074. **LANDOR, B. W.** The religious individual in the thought of Vladimir Solovyov, Lev Shestov, Semyon Frank and Nikolai Berdyaev. GLASGOW ML 1993.

3075. **COATES, R.** Falling into silence: Christian motifs as organising discourse in the work of M. M. Bakhtin. OXFORD D 1994.

3076. **GORDON, K. L.** A study of Russian Orthodox missions in the Russian Far East 1700–1917. LEEDS MP 1994.

3077. **BROWN, S. P.** The role of the Russian Orthodox Church and Orthodox missionary work in nineteenth-century Siberia and Russian America. OXFORD D 1995.

3078. **DE PRÉNEUF, F. M.** The historical and political significance of the reconstruction of the Cathedral of Christ the Saviour in Moscow. OXFORD MP 1997.

3079. **FENNELL, N.** The Russians on Athos, with special reference to the Prophet Elijah Skete. SOUTHAMPTON D 1997.

3080. **COULTER, D. A.** The Russian Orthodox White Clergy in the seventeenth century. LONDON (SSEES) D 1999.

3081. **McKENZIE, R. Y.** Secularizing tendencies in medieval Russian hagiography of the sixteenth and seventeenth centuries. LONDON (SSEES) D 1999.

3082. **SAKHAROV, N. V.** The theology of Archimandrite Sophrony. OXFORD D 1999.

3083. **SURER, J. M.** Colonel V. A. Pashkov and the late nineteenth-century Protestant movement in Russia. OXFORD MP 1999.

3084. **ASTRAKHARCHIK-FARRIMOND, C. M.** Tradition and originality in early Russian monasticism: the application of the Stoudite Rule at the Kievan Caves Monastery. CAMBRIDGE D 2000.

3085. **DOWLING, C.** The fabric of Old Belief: *staroobriadtsy* — traditions of clothmaking, dress and ritual from the 17th to the 20th century. TC DUBLIN D 2000.

3086. **KULAKOV, M.** 'The infinite diversity of persons': individual personality in the ascetical theology of St Feofan the Recluse (1815–1894). OXFORD D 2000.

3087. **ROCK, S.** Russian 'double-belief': text, context, concept. SUSSEX D 2000.

3088. **EVANS, A.** The role of the Russian Orthodox Church in Russia's external relations, 1994–2000 [NCR]. OXFORD MP 2001.

3089. HALEMBA, A. E.   Unity and diversity: contemporary spiritual life of the Telengits of Ere Chui (Republic of Altai, Russian Federation). *CAMBRIDGE D 2002.*

3090. WHITE, M. M.   Military saints in Byzantium and Rus, 900–1200. *CAMBRIDGE D 2004.*

3091. BRAZIER, P. H.   The influence of Dostoevsky on Karl Barth, 1915 to 1922. *LONDON (KCL) D 2005.*

3092. JÓNSSON-HRAUNDAL, T.   The Islamization of the Volga Bulghars. *CAMBRIDGE ML 2005.*

3093. MANNHERZ, J. C.   Popular occultism in late Imperial Russia. *CAMBRIDGE D 2005.*

3094. PETRENKO, V. I.   The development of the concept of authority within the Russian Orthodox Church. *DURHAM D 2005.*

3095. SINCLAIR, T. A.   Changing Buddhism in Russia: a study in the effects of truth. *CAMBRIDGE D 2005.*

3096. DYCK, J. H. A.   The language of community: an analysis of the concept and practice of *Wehrlosigkeit* amongst the Russian-Canadian Mennonites, 1870–1930. *OXFORD D 2006.*

Serbia

3097. ANDRITCH, Y. S.   The history of the Serbian Church from the foundation of its independence to the fall of the Serbian Patriarchate in the 15th century [NCR]. *OXFORD BL 1919.*

3098. YEVTIĆ, P.   The history of the Serbian Church under Turkish rule [NCR]. *OXFORD BL 1919.*

3099. MYLONAS, C.   Serbian Orthodox fundamentals: the quest for an eternal identity. *LONDON (UCL) D 2001.*

Slavs

3100. BURNS, Y. E.   A comparative study of the weekday lection systems found in some Greek and early Slavonic Gospel lectionaries. *LONDON (SSEES) D 1975.*

3101. BACHE, J. H.   The emerging perceptions of nationhood and spirituality in the prayers of the early Slavs and of Kievan Rus' in their literary context. *LONDON (SSEES) D 1997.*

Slovenia

3102. KUHAR, A. L.   The conversion of the Slovenes and the German-Slav ethnic boundary in the Eastern Alps. *CAMBRIDGE D 1949.*

3103. LAPAJNE, B. M.   Primus Trubar and the Slovene Protestant Reformation. *LONDON (INST HIST RES) D 1980.*

Ukraine

3104. HEPPELL, M.   The 'Paterikon of the Kievan Monastery of the Caves' as a source for monastic life in pre-Mongolian Russia. *LONDON (WESTFIELD) D 1954.*

3105. **DOLINA, O.** An examination of Ukrainian Protestant / Baptist Church history, with particular reference to its origin and development until 1939. *WALES (LAMPETER) MP 1996.*

3106. **BOWERS, S.** Finding the spirituality of Ukrainian students in a post Soviet world: a visual ethnography. *LONDON (KCL) D 2005.*

USSR *(see also Russia)*

3107. **LANE, C. O.** The impact of communist ideology and the Soviet order on Christian religion in the contemporary USSR, 1954–1974. *LONDON (LSE) D 1976.*

3108. **THROWER, J. A.** Marxist-Leninist 'scientific atheism' and the study of religion and atheism in the USSR today. *ABERDEEN D 1980.*

3109. **ANDERSON, J. P.** Soviet religious policy after Khrushchev. *LONDON (LSE) D 1987.*

3110. **PERIS, D.** Communism and the Cross: Soviet anti-religious propaganda in the 1920s. *OXFORD MP 1988.*

3111. **GOTTLIEB, C. V. G.** The Christian response to the Revolution in the works of Nikolaj Berdyaev, 1917–1924. *CAMBRIDGE ML 1994.*

3112. **DICKINSON, A.** The Council for the Affairs of the Russian Orthodox Church and the organisation of religious life in wartime Soviet Russia. *BIRMINGHAM D 1999.*

Yugoslavia *(see also under former republics)*

3113. **PALMER, P.** The Communists and the Roman Catholic Church in Yugoslavia, 1941–1946. *OXFORD D 2000.*

28. SCIENCE, TECHNOLOGY

Central and Eastern Europe *(see also under individual countries)*

3114. **McKENZIE, M. S.** The macroeconomic impact on Eastern Europe of technology transfer from the West in the postwar period. *LONDON (BIRKBECK) D 1996.*

Hungary

3115. **CONSTANTELOU, A.** Transformation dynamics in Southern and Eastern Europe: the emergence of advanced communication networks and services [with case studies of Hungary and Greece]. *SUSSEX D 1999.*

3116. **WORMALD, T. L. D.** Visions of the future: the promise of new technology for the new civil society in Hungary. *MANCHESTER D 2005.*

Poland

3117. **FAVRAT, E.** Joint-implementation and the diffusion of technology: the case of cleaner coal technologies in Poland. *SUSSEX D 1996.*

3118. NIZIOL, S. M. M.   British technologies and Polish economic development, 1815–1863. LONDON (LSE) D 1996.

Russia (see also USSR)

3119. WHITE, S. S.   The reception in Russia of Darwinian doctrines concerning evolution. LONDON (IMPERIAL) D 1968.

3120. SZANSER, A. J. M.   The work of the astronomers of Pulkovo, 1839–1918. LONDON (EXTERNAL) D 1969.

3121. SMITH, J. R.   Persistence and periodicity: a study of Mendeleev's contribution to the foundations of chemistry. LONDON (CHELSEA) D 1976.

3122. GOODE, J. P.   Informatizatsiya: computer networks and the consolidation of civil society in Russia. OXFORD MP 1997.

3123. ELLIS, J. C.   The scientific revolutions of Copernicus and Darwin and their repercussions on Russian political and sociological writing. BRISTOL D 1999.

3124. RUSANOVSCHI, S.   Russian space policy: managing post-Cold War challenges. OXFORD ML 1999.

3125. VAN NIEROP, F.   Russian science policy in transition, 1992–2000 [NCR]. OXFORD MP 2001.

USSR (see also Russia)

3126. AMANN, R.   The Soviet research and development system: its operation and performance. BIRMINGHAM D 1976.

3127. LAMPERT, N.   The technical intelligentsia in the USSR, 1928–1935. BIRMINGHAM D 1976.

3128. KNEEN, P. H.   Natural scientists and political authority in the Soviet Union. BIRMINGHAM D 1979.

3129. RIMMINGTON, A.   Biotechnology in the USSR. BIRMINGHAM D 1988.

3130. SNELL, P.   Soviet microprocessors, microcomputers and personal computers. BIRMINGHAM D 1989.

3131. HAN, P. -S.   Western technology transfer to the Soviet Union and Soviet successor states: technology absorption and institutional change. BIRMINGHAM D 1993.

3132. BARRY, W. P.   The Missile Design Bureaux and Soviet manned space policy 1953–1970. OXFORD D 1996.

3133. MADDRELL, J. P.   Britain's exploitation of occupied Germany for scientific and technical intelligence on the Soviet Union. CAMBRIDGE D 1999.

3134. FROGGATT, M.   Science in propaganda and popular culture in the USSR under Khruschëv (1953–1964). OXFORD D 2005.

29. SOCIETY

General and Comparative

3135. **Hoy, M.**   An appraisal of aspects of popular culture in relation to the application of some theories of Bakhtin, Barthes and Lacan. OXFORD D 1993.

3136. **Strezhneva, M. V.**   Institutions, culture and (dis)integration: a comparison of the European Union and post-Soviet experiences. MANCHESTER D 1998.

3137. **Hanhinen, S.**   Social problems in transition: perceptions of influential groups in Estonia, Russia and Finland. LONDON (UCL) D 2000.

Albania

3138. **Saltmarshe, D.**   Identity in a post-communist Balkan state: a study in North Albania. BATH D 1999.

3139. **Hough, K. L.**   The Albanian caseload: journeys through Britain, Italy and the Balkans. OXFORD D 2004.

Azerbaijan

3140. **Martin, R. J.**   Changes in the economic and social structure of Soviet Azerbaijan, 1970–1990. WALES (SWANSEA) D 1994.

Baltic States (see also under individual countries)

3141. **Timm, A.**   The production of ambition: the making of a Baltic business elite. LONDON (LSE) D 2003.

Bosnia-Herzegovina

3142. **Bringa, T. R.**   Gender, religion and the person: the 'negotiation' of Muslim identity in rural Bosnia. LONDON (LSE) D 1991.

3143. **Gillard, S. G.**   Identity and conflict: the transition from war to peace in Bosnia and Hercegovina 1995–1996. BRADFORD D 1999.

3144. **Coward, M.**   Urbicide and the question of community in Bosnia-Herzegovina. NEWCASTLE D 2001.

Bulgaria

3145. **Necheva, S. N.**   Food purchasing behaviour in Bulgaria: an empirical study of yoghurt and ice-cream. LONDON (IMPERIAL) D 2002.

3146. **Gaydarska, B. I.**   Landscape, material culture and society in south east Bulgaria. DURHAM D 2004.

3147. **Baloutzova, S.**   State legislation on family and social policy in Bulgaria, 1918–1944. CAMBRIDGE D 2005.

Central and Eastern Europe *(see also under individual countries)*

3148. **LETKI, N. M.** Social capital in East-Central Europe. *OXFORD D 2002.*

3149. **FISHER, S. L.** From nationalist to Europeanist: changing discourse in Slovakia and Croatia and its influence on national identity. *LONDON (UCL) D 2003.*

Central Asia *(see also under individual countries)*

3150. **GLENN, J.** Identities in transition: the Soviet legacy in Central Asia. *SOUTHAMPTON D 1996.*

Croatia

3151. **SMOLJAN, J.** Socio-economic aspects of peacebuilding: employment policy within the process of peaceful reintegration in Eastern Slavonia. *OXFORD MP 2002.*

3152. **UZELAC, G.** Perceptions of the nation: a sociological perspective on the case of Croatia. *LONDON (LSE) D 2002.*

3153. **DOMIĆ, D.** The historically situated Croat: a critical ethnographic investigation of postwar consumer behaviour [...]. *WOLVERHAMPTON D 2004.*

3154. **SMOLJAN, J.** Socio-economic aspects of peacebuilding: UNTAES and the reintegration of Eastern Slavonia, 1996–2000. *OXFORD D 2004.*

Czech Republic

3155. **QUESNELL, M. D.** An analysis of selected beliefs and values among Czech 14- and 15-year-old public school students [NCR]. *WALES D 2000.*

Czechoslovakia

3156. **HAJEK, H. J.** The sociology of T. G. Masaryk. *LONDON (LSE) D 1950.*

3157. **WOLLMAN, H. S.** Social stratification and political change in postwar Czechoslovakia. *OXFORD BP 1973.*

3158. **SMALES, M. B.** Class, estate and status in Czechoslovakia, 1918–1938. *OPEN D 1983.*

3159. **CASTLE, M.** Czechoslovak sociology in the 1960s: an examination of its historical background and contribution to the reform movement of 1968. *GLASGOW ML 1985.*

3160. **SMITH, S.** Beneath, behind and between normality: independent cultural spaces in Czechoslovakia during the 1970s and 1980s. *BRADFORD D 1998.*

Estonia

3161. **WULF, M.** Historical cultures, conflicting memories and identities in post-Soviet Estonia. *LONDON (LSE) D 2006.*

Georgia

3162. **DRAGADZE, T.** The domestic unit in a rural area of Soviet Georgia. *OXFORD D 1987.*

3163. **NANAVA, N.** Conceptualising the Georgian nation: the modern intellectual discourse of Georgian identity. LONDON (LSE) D 2005.

3164. **BREMNER, D. L.** Human needs and problem solving approaches to creating social structures: action on conflict resolution in Georgia, 2000–2002. LONDON (LSE) D 2006.

Germany

3165. **STRUCK-SOBOLEVA, J.** Communicative aspects of the integration process of Russian Germans in Germany. BIRMINGHAM D 2003.

3166. **THIEME, U.** Social implications of reparations in the Soviet Occupied Zone of Germany between 1945 and 1949. STIRLING ML 2003.

Hungary

3167. **VASARY, I. J.** Social change in a Hungarian village: from peasant farm to agricultural collective. LONDON (UCL) D 1983.

3168. **SZENT-GYORGYI, K. A.** Views of status differentiation in two villages of northeastern Hungary. LONDON (UCL) D 1991.

3169. **CZEGLÉDY, A. P.** Privatization from an anthropological perspective: the case of an international joint venture community in Hungary. CAMBRIDGE D 1996.

3170. **LELKES, O.** Well-being and inequality in transition: the case of Hungary. LONDON (LSE) D 2003.

Kazakhstan

3171. **RIGI, J.** Coping with the chaos (*bardak*): networking, sexualised strategies and ethnic tensions in Almaty, Kazakhstan. LONDON (SOAS) D 1999.

Kosovo

3172. **KËLLEZI, B.** Trauma and social identity: the case of Kosovo Albanians. ST ANDREWS D 2006.

Kyrgyzstan

3173. **BUNN, S. J.** The House of Meaning: tents and tent dwelling among the Kyrgyz of Central Asia. MANCHESTER D 2000.

3174. **AMSLER, S. S.** 'From truth to strength in truth': sociology, knowledge and power in Kyrgyzstan, 1966–2003. LONDON (LSE) D 2005.

3175. **GULLETTE, D. C.** Kinship, state and 'tribalism': the genealogical construction of the Kyrgyz Republic. CAMBRIDGE D 2006.

Latvia

3176. **KILIS, R.** Social organisation and knowledge of the past in a Latvian Siberian village. CAMBRIDGE D 1999.

3177. LUSE, A.   Changing discourses of distress and powerlessness in post-Soviet Latvia. BRISTOL D 2005.

Poland

3178. RAWIN, S. J.   Changes in social structure in Poland under conditions of industrialization, 1945–1963. LONDON (LSE) D 1965.

3179. CHAWLUK, A. L.   Social forces and economic reform: the case of Poland, 1956–1973. LONDON (LSE) D 1975.

3180. SOCHACKI, J.   Znaniecki's theory of action. LANCASTER ML 1976.

3181. PINE, F. T.   Kinship, marriage and social change in a Polish highland village. LONDON (EXTERNAL) D 1988.

3182. LOFMAN, B.   Constructing consumer identity in cultural context: perspectives from Polish and American consumers. BRADFORD D 1996.

3183. SIDORENKO, E. J.   Neo-liberalism after communism: constructing a sociological account of the political space of post-1989 Poland. LONDON (GOLDSMITHS) D 1998.

3184. EDGINTON, E.   Nation-ness, subjectivity, ethnography: a Polish-British case study. STRATHCLYDE D 2000.

3185. CONSTANTINE, S.   Social relations in the estate villages of Mecklenburg, c.1890–1924 [with special reference to Polish seasonal workers]. NOTTINGHAM D 2001.

3186. FRANKLIN, S.   Białowieża Forest, Poland: social function and social power. OXFORD D 2001.

Romania

3187. DRAZIN, A. M.   Care, cleanliness and consumption in urban Romania. LONDON (UCL) D 2001.

3188. HEINTZ, M   Changes in work ethic in post-socialist Romania. CAMBRIDGE D 2002.

3189. VANHAELEMEERSCH, P.   A generation without beliefs, and the idea of experience in Romania (1927–1934). OXFORD D 2004.

Russia (see also USSR)

3190. PINNICK, K. G. M.   The return of the *Afgantsy*: the social readaptation and political activism of the former USSR's veterans of the Afghan War. BRADFORD D 1994.

3191. WYMAN, M.   Continuity and change in Russian public opinion, 1988–93. BIRMINGHAM D 1994.

3192. ANDERSON, D. G.   National identity and belonging in Arctic Siberia: an ethnography of Evenkis and Dolgans at Khantaiskoe Ozero in the Taimyr Autonomous District. CAMBRIDGE D 1996.

3193. BADGER, M. O.   Visual ethnography and representation: two case studies in the Arctic. [One in Alaska, one among Khanty (Ob' Ostyaks) of W. Siberia]. CAMBRIDGE D 1996.

3194. LEDENEVA, A. V.   Formal institutions and informal networks in Russia: a study of 'blat'. CAMBRIDGE D 1996.

3195. **Oushakine, S.** The post-Soviet imaginary: constructing new Russian fantasies. *OPEN MP 1998.*

3196. **Ter-Sakaryan, D.** Political culture and social networks in Russia since 1991: an empirical survey. *LONDON (SSEES) D 1999.*

3197. **Solovyov, A.** Professional socialisation for social work in Russia. *ANGLIA POLY UNIV D 2000.*

3198. **Glatter, P. R. D.** Russian regional elites: continuity and change. *WOLVERHAMPTON D 2001.*

3199. **Jordan, P. D.** Material culture and the Forest Khanty: Siberian hunter fisher gatherers in time, space and contact. *SHEFFIELD D 2001.*

3200. **Anderson, S. M.** Loss and change: a social history of wild plant use in indigenous communities of the Russian Far East. *LONDON (UCL) D 2002.*

3201. **Hürelbaatar, A.** 'Tradition' as differently practised by the Buryat-Mongols of Russia and China. *CAMBRIDGE D 2002.*

3202. **Pickup, F.** Local level responses to rapid social change in a city in the Russian industrial Urals. *LONDON (LSE) D 2002.*

3203. **Round, J. P.** The social costs of transition in post-Soviet Russia: a case study of Magadan Oblast. *BIRMINGHAM D 2002.*

3204. **Shterin, M.** 'Cult controversies' in contemporary England and Russia: a sociological comparison. *LONDON (LSE) D 2002.*

3205. **Wynn, A.** Theorising transformation: the role of international financial institutions in forming a new mode of social regulation in Russia. *LEICESTER D 2002.*

3206. **Morley, K.** Is *blat* good for post-Soviet Russia? *KEELE MP 2003.*

3207. **Shubin, S. V.** (Net)working out poverty and social exclusion in rural Ireland and Russia. *BRISTOL D 2003.*

3208. **Willerslev, R.** In-between self and other: hunting, personhood and perception among the Upper Kolyma Yukaghirs of North-Eastern Siberia. *CAMBRIDGE D 2003.*

3209. **Thompson, N. S.** The nativeness of settlers: constructions of belonging in Soviet and contemporary Chukotka. *CAMBRIDGE D 2005.*

3210. **Yates, S. J.** Living with poverty in post-Soviet Russia: social perspectives on urban poverty. *LONDON (LSE) D 2005.*

Serbia

3211. **Byford, J. T.** Conspiracy theory in Serbian culture at the time of the NATO bombing of Yugoslavia. *LOUGHBOROUGH D 2002.*

3212. **Petrović, M.** The ways of dead bodies: dealing with human remains in postconflict Serbia and Tasmania. *CAMBRIDGE D 2006.*

Slavs

3213. **Obrebski, J.** Family organization among the Slavs, as reflected in the custom of *couvade*. *LONDON (LSE) D 1934.*

Slovenia

3214. BERCE-BRATKO, B. Culturological analysis in urban rehabilitation: cases in Slovenia and Scotland. STRATHCLYDE D 1993.

3215. POTRATA, B. The work of the self: spiritual economy of the New Age practitioners in post-socialist Slovenia. CAMBRIDGE D 2002.

Tajikistan

3216. TETT, G. Ambiguous alliances: marriage and identity in a Muslim village in Soviet Tajikistan. CAMBRIDGE D 1996.

Ukraine

3217. PETRYSHYN, W. R. Britain's Ukrainian community: a study of the political dimension in ethnic community development. BRISTOL D 1981.

3218. STEPANENKO, V. The social construction of identity in a post-communist society: school socialisation in Ukraine. MANCHESTER D 1998.

3219. GOSAL, V. Common-sense knowledge of social changes in Ukraine: social representations of freedom and responsibility in the public and private spheres. CAMBRIDGE D 2004.

3220. RODGERS, P. W. A study of identity change in the eastern borderlands of Ukraine. BIRMINGHAM D 2005.

USSR (see also Russia)

3221. WEINBERG, E. A. The development of sociological studies in Communist states: the case of the USSR. LONDON (LSE) D 1970.

3222. LITTLEJOHN, G. M. Class structure and production relations in the USSR. GLASGOW D 1981.

3223. COX, T. M. The development of empirical sociology in the Soviet Union: the rural research of Kritsman and his school. GLASGOW D 1983.

3224. SHENFIELD, S. D. The mathematical-statistical methodology of the contemporary Soviet family budget survey. BIRMINGHAM D 1984.

3225. BRINE, J. Adult readers in the Soviet Union. BIRMINGHAM D 1985.

3226. SAUNDERS, R. G. The sociological significance of British and Soviet poetry, 1945–1985. CITY D 1985.

3227. WATERS, E. From the old family to the new: work, marriage and motherhood in urban Soviet Russia, 1917–31. BIRMINGHAM D 1985.

3228. MEASOR, L. Bolshevik attempts at cultural transformation: a cultural October [NCR]. SUSSEX D 1987.

3229. FERNANDEZ, N. C. A critical contribution to an understanding of the nature of Soviet society: with special reference to working class self-assertion. GLASGOW D 1995.

3230. MASON, E. J. A social analysis of the Soviet prison camps of the 1930s. BIRMINGHAM D 2000.

3231. **Morcom, S.** The everyday social workings of late Stalinism: Soviet identities 1941–53 [NCR]. OXFORD MP 2001.

3232. **Trowel, K.** Politics and imagination: Soviet children's culture and the space age 1957–1964. OXFORD MP 2003.

3233. **Franco, R.** Social order and social policies towards displaced children: the Soviet case (1917–1953). MANCHESTER D 2006.

Yugoslavia (see also under former republics)

3234. **Barić, L. F.** Kinship and community in Yugoslavia. LONDON (LSE) D 1966.

3235. **Vodanovich, I. M.** The structure of roles and their ritual in a Yugoslav community. LONDON (LSE) D 1978.

30. THEATRE, BALLET

Central and Eastern Europe (see also under individual countries)

3236. **Willcocks, G.** Staging Europe in transition, conflict and trauma: images of the new Europe in recent British theatre and performance.. READING D 2005.

3237. **Pritchard, C.** Performative practices in process: transitional tactics in Central and Eastern European actions [with examples from Russia and Croatia]. LONDON (GOLDSMITHS) D 2006.

Croatia

3238. **Juričič, Ž. B.** Russian repertory in the Croatian National Theatre, 1874–1914. NOTTINGHAM D 1972.

Czechoslovakia

3239. **Day, B.** The Theatre on the Balustrade of Prague and the small stage tradition in Czechoslovakia. BRISTOL D 1985.

Kosovo

3240. **Dunkley, C.** Theatre and human rights: approaches to playwriting the Kosovo conflict. EXETER D 2003.

Poland

3241. **Allain, P. A. C.** Theatre practice in search of theory: the Gardzienice Theatre Association of Poland. LONDON (GOLDSMITHS) D 1993.

3242. **Misopolinou, A.** Grotowski: ecstasy and initiation in performance. LONDON (GOLDSMITHS) D 2004.

Russia (see also USSR)

3243. **MALNICK, B.** The origin and early history of the theatre in Russia. LONDON (SSEES) D 1936.

3244. **BURGESS, M. A. S.** A survey of the stage in Russia from 1741 to 1783 with special reference to the development of the Russian theatre. CAMBRIDGE D 1953.

3245. **BRAUN, E.** The dramatic theory and practice of Vsevolod Meierkhol´d. CAMBRIDGE D 1970.

3246. **WARNER, E. A.** The Russian folk-theatre. EDINBURGH D 1970.

3247. **COUSIN, G. A.** Stanislavsky and Brecht: the relationship between the actor and stage objects. EXETER D 1982.

3248. **BEUMERS, B.** Yury Lyubimov at the 'Taganka' Theatre and in exile (1964–1989). OXFORD D 1991.

3249. **BOWDEN, S.** *Petrouchka* in performance, 1911: tensions and illusions. SURREY D 1993.

3250. **HENRY, B. J.** Theatrical parody at the Krivoe Zerkalo. Russian 'Teatr Miniatyur', 1908–1931. OXFORD D 1996.

3251. **NOTT, A. C.** The Russian school of acting: the development and implementation of a psycho-physical acting technique. BIRMINGHAM D 1997.

3252. **FRAME, M. M.** The St Petersburg Imperial Theatres 1900–1920: culture and power during the Russian revolution. CAMBRIDGE D 1998.

3253. **DIXON, R. S.** Efros and Molière: a study of Anatoly Efros's productions of Bulgakov's *Molière* and of Molière's *Don Juan, Tartuffe* and *The Misanthrope*. TC DUBLIN D 1999.

3254. **OSTROVSKY, A. M.** Stanislavsky meets England: Shakespeare, Byron and Dickens at the Moscow Art Theatre and its First Studio, 1898–1920. CAMBRIDGE D 1999.

3255. **SAYERS, L. -A.** *Le Pas d'Acier* (1927): a study in the historiography and reconstruction of George Jakulov's set design for Diaghilev's 'Soviet' ballet. BRISTOL D 1999.

3256. **McCAW, R. N.** Bakhtin's other theatre. LONDON (R HOLLOWAY) D 2003.

3257. **WHYMAN, R.** The actor — an emotional and spiritual machine: towards an examination of Stanislavski's methods of actor training. MANCHESTER D 2003.

3258. **DADSWELL, S. J.** The spectacle of Russian Futurism: the emergence and development of Russian Futurist performance, 1910–1914. SHEFFIELD D 2005.

3259. **DRAGAŠEVIĆ, D.** Meyerhold, director of opera: cultural change and artistic genres. LONDON (GOLDSMITHS) D 2005.

3260. **SIMPSON, A.** Fragments of times and spaces: collage in the theatre of Vs. E. Meyerhold, 1906–1926. HULL D 2005.

Serbia

3261. **WALKER, M. H.** Russian repertory in the Serbian National Theatre in Belgrade, 1870–1929. NOTTINGHAM D 1974.

USSR *(see also Russia)*

3262. STOURAC, R.   Workers' theatre as a means of agitation and propaganda: its history, theory and practice since 1918, with particular reference to Russia, Germany and England. BRISTOL ML 1977.

3263. FRAME, M.   The politics of the Soviet theatre 1917–1927. ABERDEEN ML 1993.

Yugoslavia *(see also under former republics)*

3264. RADOSAVLJEVIĆ HEANEY, D.   Metatheatre as a political tool in Yugoslav drama in the 1980s and 1990s. HULL D 2003.

31. TRADE

General and Comparative

3265. ROBINSON, D.   Aspects of foreign trade practice in Poland and Hungary as exemplified in the pharmaceutical industry. OXFORD MP 1981.

Belarus

3266. LISOVSKAYA, N. S.   Implications of World Trade Organisation membership for countries in transition: a case study of the Republic of Belarus. MANCHESTER D 2004.

Bulgaria

3267. MILUSHEV, N.   Trade relations and the level of integration between Bulgaria and the European Union. LONDON (UCL) D 2002.

Central and Eastern Europe *(see also under individual countries)*

3268. PALIWODA, S. J.   Industrial cooperation as a corporate international trade and investment strategy in Eastern Europe. CRANFIELD D 1980.

3269. FRANKLIN, D. E.   Exporting to Eastern Europe: principles and practice, including a case study of the market for fire fighting equipment. ASTON D 1981.

3270. ZALEWSKA-MITURA, A.   Emerging markets from Central and Eastern Europe: evolving market efficiency, problems of thin trading and price limits. LONDON (LBS) D 1998.

3271. NAGY, A. M.   Export performance and potential of the Central and Eastern European countries. BIRMINGHAM D 1999.

3272. MALISZEWSKA, M. A.   Four essays on international trade and location of production in transition countries. SUSSEX D 2004.

Czech Republic

3273. **DOLARA, G.** The impact of prospective membership of the European Union on Czech domestic policy: the case of trade and minority policy. *OXFORD MP 1998.*

Czechoslovakia

3274. **DRABEK, Z.** Natural resource content of foreign trade and structural bias: an inter-country comparison of Czechoslovakia and Austria by means of input-output technique. *OXFORD D 1982.*

Poland

3275. **FLORECKI, S.** Foreign trade of Poland between 1918–1939, with special reference to the trade with Britain. *EDINBURGH D 1943.*

3276. **CLOWES, D. C.** Developments in Polish trade with the European Union and Germany since transition. *GLASGOW D 2002.*

3277. **LE NGUYEN, T.** Export orientation of Polish small and medium sized enterprises in Gdańsk: an empirical analysis. *KINGSTON D 2006.*

Romania

3278. **GHEORGHIU, P. R.** The foreign trade of Rumania. *LONDON (LSE) D 1932.*

Russia

3279. **FAIRLIE, S. E.** The Anglo-Russian grain trade, 1815–1861. *LONDON (LSE) D 1959.*

3280. **CLENDENNING, P. H.** The Anglo-Russian Trade Treaty of 1766. *CAMBRIDGE D 1976.*

3281. **NEWMAN, J.** Russian foreign trade, 1680–1780: the British contribution. *EDINBURGH D 1985.*

3282. **THOMPSTONE, S. R.** The organisation and financing of Russian foreign trade before 1914. *LONDON (EXTERNAL) D 1992.*

Soviet Bloc

3283. **BIRAY, G.** A medium-term dynamic simulation model for the inter-regional multi-commodity analysis of CMEA foreign trade flows. *BIRMINGHAM D 1974.*

3284. **SCHMICKLE, W. E.** The Soviet bloc and the pursuit of international trade cooperation through the United Nations, 1953–1964. *GLASGOW ML 1975.*

3285. **LAWSON, C. W.** The stability, structure and direction of communist foreign trade, 1960–1972. *LONDON (EXTERNAL) D 1980.*

3286. **COLOMBATTO, E.** The essential normality of East–West trade. *LONDON (LSE) D 1983.*

3287. **DANGERFIELD, M. V.** Changes in socialist states' policies on trade with OECD countries, 1976–1985. *CNAA (WOLVERHAMPTON POLY) D 1989.*

3288. **Watkins-Mathys, L.** The role of joint ventures in East–West trade up to 1990. *LOUGHBOROUGH D 1992.*

USSR *(see also Russia)*

3289. **Segal, L.** The foreign trade of Soviet Russia: a study of the economic development of the USSR, 1917–1935. *LONDON (LSE) D 1936.*

3290. **Chossudowsky, E. M.** Soviet trade and distribution, 1917–1937: the growth of planned consumption. *EDINBURGH D 1940.*

3291. **Davis, K. C.** Soviet-Japanese trade and economic relations, 1956–1973: a study in Soviet commercial policy. *BIRMINGHAM D 1976.*

3292. **Ó Corcora, M. G.** Irish-Soviet trade relations and policy. *TC DUBLIN ML 1980.*

3293. **Salter, J. B.** Soviet trade with the developed capitalist countries, with special reference to the expansion of Soviet imports between 1960 and 1980. *LONDON (QUEEN MARY) D 1981.*

3294. **Mehrotra, S. K.** Economic relations between a centrally planned and a developing market economy: Indo-Soviet trade (1970–1982) and technology transfer (post-1955). *CAMBRIDGE D 1986.*

3295. **Schafer, T. D.** The Soviet foreign trade system: institutions, policies and relations with the US 1970–85. *OXFORD MP 1986.*

3296. **Maltby, M. R.** The foreign trade reform of January 1st 1987 [in the USSR]. *OXFORD MP 1987.*

3297. **Martinsen, K. D.** Current reforms in Soviet foreign trade with special reference to Western Europe. *GLASGOW ML 1988.*

3298. **Seppain, H.** Politics by economic means: contrasting attitudes to Soviet trade (USA and Germany), 1917–1962. *CAMBRIDGE D 1988.*

3299. **White, C. A.** Prelude to trade: a re-assessment of Anglo-American trade and commercial relations with Soviet Russia, 1918–1924. *CAMBRIDGE D 1988.*

3300. **Venkataraman, R.** Trade and foreign policy: trade in the US–Soviet relationship, 1945–54. *OXFORD MP 1989.*

3301. **Heywood, A. J.** Reviving Soviet-Western trade in the early 1920s: a study of Soviet imports of railway equipment and related contracts. *LEEDS D 1991.*

3302. **Prime, R. H.** Soviet foreign trade policy: a case study of chemical exports to the European Community. *DUNDEE D 1992.*

3303. **Lee, C.** The geopolitics of South Korean trade relations with the former Soviet Union (1988–1993). *BIRMINGHAM D 1995.*

32. TRANSPORT, LOGISTICS

Baltic States

3304. **Liliopoulou, A.** An analysis of the role of the Baltic States ports in the Trans Siberian Railway market. *PLYMOUTH D 2003.*

Central and Eastern Europe *(see also under individual countries)*

3305. **LEDGER, G. D.** Analysis of the impact of East European change upon European Community and East European liner shipping. *PLYMOUTH D 1995.*

3306. **PRICE, P.** A model for logistics management in a post-Soviet transitional economy. *LONDON METROPOLITAN D 2002.*

Central Asia

3307. **BAVARSAD-AHMADI, P.** Iran's potential as a landbridge for former USSR republics: a scenario approach. *PLYMOUTH D 1997.*

Poland

3308. **PIECZEK, A. U.** Analysis of marketing strategies in Polish ports. *PLYMOUTH D 2000.*

Russia *(see also USSR)*

3309. **ARMSTRONG, T. E.** The development of the Northern Sea Route. *CAMBRIDGE D 1951.*

3310. **GULLEY, H. E.** Railways and the seaborne grain export trade in Tsarist Russia, 1861–1914. *LONDON (UCL) D 1987.*

3311. **BRIGHAM, L. W.** Sea ice variability in Russian Arctic coastal seas: influences on the Northern Sea Route. *CAMBRIDGE D 2000.*

3312. **MOUDRYCH, V.** Russian compulsory insurance: transport. *OXFORD D 2001.*

3313. **CAVE, P. S. E.** Freight transportation between the United Kingdom and western Russia? Modal choice [NCR]. *CARDIFF D 2006.*

USSR *(see also Russia)*

3314. **HAMBLY, M. V.** Road transport in the USSR. *GLASGOW ML 1970.*

3315. **FISHER, N. A.** The inter-relationships between urban passenger transport and urban morphology in Moscow, USSR. *LONDON (SSEES) MP 1982.*

3316. **LONG, D. M.** A study of the development and impact of the Soviet Baltic Steamship Company. *CNAA (PLYMOUTH POLY) MP 1985.*

3317. **TRAUTMAN, L.** Stalin's last frontier: Soviet Arctic in the 1930s, Glavsevmorput´ and the Northern Sea Route. *LONDON (LSE) D 2005.*

AUTHOR INDEX

The Author Index lists the names of all thesis authors in the form recorded in the bibliography entry. For conventions applied to spelling and diacritics, see 'Author's Name' in the Introduction. Cross-references are given from any other form of name under which the author has been found to be catalogued or published.

Arrangement is alphabetical word-by-word. Names beginning 'Mc...' are alphabetised as 'Mac...'.

SUBJECT INDEX

The Subject Index contains entries for:

- Personal and institutional names appearing in titles, subtitles and title notes.
- Subject headings used in the bibliography.
- Countries, places and nations, broken down where necessary by the same set of subject headings.
- Specific topics appearing in titles, subtitles and title notes.

Transliteration from Cyrillic is by the Library of Congress system.

www.ingramcontent.com/pod-product-compliance
Lightning Source LLC
Chambersburg PA
CBHW051726260326
41914CB00031B/1753/J